The Philosophy of War and Peace

The Philosophy of War and Peace

Jenny Teichman

ia

imprint-academic.com

Copyright © Jenny Teichman, 2006

The moral rights of the author have been asserted.
No part of any contribution may be reproduced in any form
without permission, except for the quotation of brief passages
in criticism and discussion.

Published in the UK by
Imprint Academic, PO Box 200, Exeter EX5 5YX, UK

Published in the USA by
Imprint Academic, Philosophy Documentation Center
PO Box 7147, Charlottesville, VA 22906-7147, USA

ISBN-10   1 84540 050 X
ISBN-13   9781845400507

A CIP catalogue record for this book is available from the
British Library and US Library of Congress

Contents

Preface   1

PART I: ON WAR AND JUSTICE

Chapter 1: The Causes and Aims of War   5

Causes and aims – Aims in history – von Clausewitz on war – Lenin on war – Speculation: George Orwell and Aldous Huxley – Speculation: Sigmund Freud

Chapter 2: Rules of War in the Ancient World   17

Customary law and the laws of war – Israel and Greece – Plato and Aristotle – Rome

Chapter 3: The Just War I:
   Philosophers and Jurists in the Middle Ages   23

The thoughts of St. Augustine – War and the religious orders – Developing the account of a just war – The conditions needed for a war to be just – War and punishment – Aggression, defence and uncertainty

Chapter 4: The Just War II:
   Philosophers and Clergy in the Twentieth Century   31

Elizabeth Anscombe's papers on war – The meaning of innocence – Anthony Kenny and others on war and deterrence – Vatican II and pacem in terris – Some difficulties.

Chapter 5: The Laws of War and the Red Cross   41

International law and the law of war – The Red Cross – International declarations – The resort to war and the methods employed – Savagery – The Nuremberg judgement – The Red Cross fundamental rules

PART II: THE LAWS OF WAR IGNORED

Chapter 6: All-out Aerial Warfare — 53

'Gott straf England' – Bomber Harris – Bishop Bell – Hiroshima and Nagasaki

Chapter 7: All-out War and the Ordinary Soldier — 61

Soviet soldiers in Afghanistan – American soldiers in S.E. Asia and Iraq

Chapter 8: War and Science — 67

Scientists and war – Aeroplanes – Chemical warfare – A scientific experiment – Engineers and physicists – Physicians and psychiatrists – Science and truth – Science and politics

Chapter 9: Deterrent Threats in the Cold War — 77

The Cold War and deterrence – The uselessness of nuclear weapons: George F. Kennan – The ethics of deterrence: John Finnis and colleagues – Stalin not immortal – On choosing between evils

PART III: TERRORISM, TORTURE, HOSTAGES

Chapter 10: Terrorism — 91

Politics and terrorism – Types of terror – On definitions – How to define the word terrorism – A multi-faceted account

Chapter 11: Torture — 99

Torture and the Inquisition – Dershowitz on torture – Official and unofficial torture – Reasons, good and bad, against advocating torture – Dershowitz and Bentham – Some opinions of clergy, scholars, physicians – Explaining torture and torturers

Chapter 12: Hostages and Ransoms — 111

Hostages in Entebbe 1976 – Hostages in Iran 1979-1981 – Hostages in London 1980 – Hostages in the Lebanon – Negotiating with hostage takers – The life and times of Terry Waite

PART IV: THE PEOPLE IN ARMS

Chapter 13: Guerillas and Partisans — 121

The just war revisited – Guerillas, partisans, rebels – Morality and resistance

Chapter 14: The SOE versus the Axis Powers — 125

The SOE and the resistance movements in occupied Europe – The inspiration of leaders in exile – The fates of Petain and Laval of Vichy France

Chapter 15: Resistance in Norway — 131

The German invasion and Quisling – The resistance movement – Nazi terrorism – the attack on the heavy water plant – the end of the war – the fate of traitors – the moral power of resistance

Chapter 16: Guerillas in Cuba — 139

The character and aims of Castro and Guevara – A very short history of Cuba – Guerilla war in Cuba – When and why did Castro embrace Marxism? – Von Clausewitz on guerilla war

PART V: AGAINST WAR

Chapter 17: Pacifism in the East — 153

The Jains – the Buddha and Buddhism – the Emperor Asoka – Mahatma Gandhi – Ghosananda – Buddhist violence and its excuses

Chapter 18: Pacifism in the West — 163

Pacifism and Christianity – Pacifist sects – The Society of Friends – Papal teachings during and after the Cold War – Pacifism not a unitary thesis – Possible classifications

Chapter 19: Conscription and Conscience — 173

Conscription – Quakers during the Boer war and WWI – The Vietnam war – 'Heck no, we won't go'

Chapter 20: Campaigns (Law-abiding) — 181

The Campaign for Nuclear Disarmament — Canon John Collins — Bertrand Russell's tergiversations

Chapter 21: Campaigns (Non-law-abiding) — 191

The Committee of 100 — The Greenham Common women

Chapter 22: Pugwash and the Test Ban Treaty — 199

The Pugwash conferences — John F. Kennedy and Nikita Khrushchev — Averell Harriman on the Test Ban Treaty — The Test Ban negotiations — The Cuban missile crisis — The Treaty is signed — Detente and SALT

PART VI: PATRIOTISM, PHILOSOPHY, RELIGION

Chapter 23: Patriotism and Solidarity — 211

Patriotism and treason — Patriotic veterans — Patriotic journalists — Solidarity

Chapter 24: Catholics and Quakers — 219

Quakers and the Cold War — Quakers and terrorism — the Catholic Worker movement — two priests

Chapter 25: Utility, Positivism, Error, Amoralism — 227

Consequentialist nonsense — War and utility — 'Anything goes' — Logical positivism — The error theory and quasi-realism — Amoralism

Chapter 26: The Resources of Philosophy and Religion — 237

On 'is' and 'ought' — Realism versus anti-realism — Rational animals and natural goodness — The common morality — War and delusion — Religion and philosophy

Appendices — 249

Sources — 251

Index — 257

Preface

Jonathan Glover in his excellent book *Humanity* advises philosophers to take more note of empirical facts (Glover, 1999). Perhaps he agrees with Wittgenstein's remark: 'generality leads the philosopher into complete darkness'.

Glover suggests that by concentrating on pure theory philosophical authors push themselves into making empty choices between a decreasing range of options. He advises his philosopher colleagues to direct their attention away from two methods of reasoning which he regards as barren and which appear even in books and papers in the relatively new branch of the subject called Applied Philosophy ('*Applied* Philosophy' *sounds* empirical!). He argues that the first such method, consequentialism, engages in naive tottings-up of the future imaginary consequences of future imaginary actions while the other too-popular method, a feeble descendant of Kantianism, makes banal lists of self-evident principles and their antitheses — as it might be justice versus injustice, honesty versus dishonesty — and then places future imaginary states of affairs under one or other of the resulting headings.

In *Humanity* Glover himself draws philosophical conclusions from considerations relating to empirical facts. As it happens other philosophers have independently decided that their work requires factual input. Peter Singer is a good example; in his early book, *Animal Liberation* (Singer, 1976) he writes about abattoirs, he describes the lives and deaths of chickens in battery farms and he recommends, and produces, a number of vegetarian recipes. More recently Alasdair MacIntyre, in *Dependent Rational Animals* (MacIntyre, 1999) informs his readers about the lives and habits of wolves and dolphins.

Glover's advice is clearly relevant to the topics of war and peace. The prevalence of warfare, the occasional outbreaks of peace, the nature of modern weapons and the many occurrences of torture and hostage-taking are facts the moral significance of which cannot be understood by the stripped down philosophical methods which he describes and rejects.

This book expounds the things philosophers, jurists, clergymen, soldiers and politicians have had to say about war and wars. It also describes certain real military practices and some real anti-war campaigns. It takes the concept of war to cover international conflicts, revolution, insurgency, terrorism when it has political aims, and the wars which dictators wage against their own people—as in Soviet Russia, Iraq before 2002, and parts of Latin America.

The historical, philosophical and literary sources are listed at the end of the book. In the case of recent events the sources have perforce included newspaper reports and entries in the World Wide Web.

PART I
ON WAR AND JUSTICE

Chapter 1

The Causes and Aims of War

It has not been given to mankind to live in perpetual peace
(B.J. Feist, cited by Coleman Phillipson)

Causes and aims

It seems that men can be motivated by a straightforward love of fighting and killing; we might call this the mark of Cain.

The prophet Isaiah, who proclaimed that peace is a wonderful state in which swords are beaten into ploughshares and prosperity envelops the people, also decided that war is inevitable if the chosen race behaves in ways that offend Almighty God. War is evil and also a punishment for evil. Isaiah says Jehovah forsook Judah and Jerusalem, leaving only a remnant, the cause being evil deeds that offended the Lord (Isaiah, 34-2). On the other hand it seems that in the long run their enemies, Babylon, Moab, Damascus and Egypt, were not to escape.

After the conflicts of the 20th and 21st centuries the idea of admiring war for its own sake can strike one as obscure or even downright horrible. But of course that was not always so. Shakespeare gives Henry V a speech in which he proclaims that those who miss the forthcoming battle of St. Crispian's Day will later bemoan their sad fate. Napoleon, viewing the French dead on the field after one of his victories said: '… a noble way to die.'

Hundreds of pages have been published in attempts to explain the forward-looking aims and backward looking causes of the first world war. School children were once told that the conflict was brought about by the assassination of the Archduke of Austria but nowadays a reference to that event is not thought of as a genuine explanation. The assassination was either a trigger setting off a pre-existing cause or an excuse for an unacknowledged aim—not the supposed political aim ('a war to end war') later ascribed to Britain,

France and America — an outcome which of course was not achieved.

What were the real causes and the real aims? Fear was possibly one cause, though, as argued later in this book, the fear that other countries are plotting against 'us' is sometimes delusional.

In 1939–40 revenge, punishment and lasting power were Nazi Germany's stated war aims. German citizens supported or silently agreed to Hitler's attacks on Belgium, Holland, Poland and Norway because they believed or perhaps half-believed his promise of a thousand-year Reich. They supported the attacks on France and England because he had persuaded them that it would be right to avenge the humiliating terms of the 1918 Armistice and the suffering caused by the allies' vengeful post-war blockade.

Aims in history

The aims of war in the ancient world generally included plunder and booty (cattle, gold, women). The Vikings fought first for booty and subsequently for land. In colonial times in Africa Masai warriors used to attack Kikuyu villages, stealing women as well as food because many of their own women had become sterile as a result of venereal diseases imported from Europe (Blixen, 1989).

Aggressive wars have often been waged for religious reasons and still are today. In the 7th century the followers of Mahomet were urged to make war against infidels. The aim of their aggression can be inferred from teachings concerning the treatment of prisoners: conquered or captured males were to be offered an immediate choice between conversion and death and captured women a delayed choice. In the 11th, 12th and thirteenth centuries crusaders from all over Europe traveled thousands of miles on horseback or on foot because they wanted to capture Jerusalem from non-Christian rulers.

In more recent times European nations have waged war in South America, India, Asia and Africa in order to acquire Empires from which to extract wealth. It could be argued that a desire to export some particular political or economic system has taken the place of religion as a motive for aggressive war.

Clausewitz on war

Carl von Clausewitz (1780–1831), a son of a retired Lieutenant, joined the Prussian army at the age of 12. In 1793–5 he was promoted to lance corporal then to subaltern during the Rhine campaign against revolutionary France. Between 1801 and 1803 he studied military history at the Prussian War College and in 1805 began publishing papers in military journals. After Napoleon won the battle of Jena von Clausewitz was captured by the French and spent two years as a prisoner of war. Between 1807 and 1812 he held a variety of posts including a job as tutor to the Crown Prince of Prussia. In 1812 he resigned his Prussian commission and joined the Russian army on the eve of Napoleon's invasion, rejoining the Prussian service in 1814. At the battle of Waterloo he was chief of staff of one of the Prussian corps. In 1819, after promotion to Major General in 1818, he began working on his celebrated book *Vom Kriege (On War)*. It was published posthumously in 1832.

Clausewitz began the book by defining war as a duel on a larger scale and went on to say that it also resembles wrestling. In a wrestling match the aim of each opponent is to force the other to submit to his will by 'throwing' him. An act of war is an act of force to compel an enemy to do one's will. It would seem to follow from his account that the enemy is an enemy before the first act of war takes place.

Clausewitz regarded the laws and customs of war with a certain degree of contempt.

> Attached to force are certain self-imposed imperceptible limitations hardly worth mentioning, known as international law and custom, but they scarcely weaken it ... Force—that is physical force, for moral force has no existence save as expressed in the state and the law—is thus the *means* of war; to impose our will on the enemy is its object ... the true aim of war is to render the enemy powerless ... The maximum use of force, force without compunction, while the other side refrains, means that the first will gain the upper hand (von Clausewitz, 1983, p. 83).

In spite of these words it is unlikely that Clausewitz would have thought well of the methods of war employed between 1914 and the present day. The historians and scholarly soldiers of 1819 could not have predicted the 'all-out' wars perpetrated by the nations of Europe, Asia and America during the twentieth and twenty-first centuries.

Although Clausewitz seemed unwilling to accept the idea that law and custom can influence the conduct of warfare his comments on the superior intelligence of certain nations suggests a different view. He said that wars between civilised nations are less cruel and destructive than wars between savages. He believed that civilised nations do not devastate cities—which was probably true in his time

— because intelligence plays a larger part in their methods of warfare and has taught them more effective ways of using force. He also said that differences between ways of waging war reflect the internal social conditions of different nations. What we might call moral standards Clausewitz described as social conditions but the lesson seems the same. As to the uncivilised, the nations that are cruel and destructive, he was thinking, perhaps, of certain Native tribes in North America whose warriors had a custom of collecting the scalps of prisoners as proofs and emblems of their courage and manhood. Some tribes tortured enemy captives, possibly in order to show their own young lads how *not* to react to pain. For in the thinking of those peoples to cry out in pain was deemed unmanly.

Clausewitz distinguished between two different motives for war, hostile intentions and hostile feelings. Hostile intentions are the fundamental motives because they can exist, and be acted on, in the absence of any hostile feelings. Yet even civilised nations sometimes develop passionate hatreds for their opponents since war, after all, is not a rational non-hating activity. Conflicting interests lead to war but war itself, or the threat of war, leads to hatred.

Lenin on war

In the latter part of the 19th century and the early years of the 20th the words 'Imperialism' and 'Imperialist' were not terms of abuse but of praise, moreover capitalism as such was not condemned except by the followers of Karl Marx.

According to V.I. Lenin free competition between capitalist firms in one country gives way to national monopolies. Monopolies then generate government interest in international adventures designed to find new markets and new exploitable workers. Because of this interest attacks are launched on under-developed countries and also on rival capitalist states.

Lenin refers to European coercion of the populations of India, Africa (including Egypt) and China, and also to President McKinley's successful wars against the Spanish colonies on the West Coast of North America. He asks: What drives imperialism? And answers: Not morality but capitalism and the profit motive. What drives men to war? Imperialism, he suggests, has always been a cause but by the 20th century it had become the main cause (Lenin, 1996).

After the first world war left-wing opinion rejected the claim that European and white American invasions of undeveloped countries were motivated by any desire to improve the lot of the native peoples. However it was not only on the left that hostility to imperialism appeared. Woodrow Wilson's Fourteen Principles included the right to self-determination.

Speculation: George Orwell and Aldous Huxley

George Orwell's famous last novel *Nineteen Eighty-Four* published shortly after his death, extrapolates from the early years of the Cold War and describes what might turn out to be the aim, the point, of war in the future. Aldous Huxley, in a now forgotten story, *Ape and Essence*, gives an account of the likely aims and causes of a possible future nuclear catastrophe.

Human beings, especially young ones, are very vulnerable to propaganda, as the advertising industry knows quite well. This vulnerability is probably related to the instinctual traits, whatever they are, that underlie gregarious behaviour. George Orwell was probably the first author to describe the effects of propaganda as disseminated through television. His novel postulates three huge future nations, Oceania, Eurasia and Eastasia, between which there obtains a persisting low-level state of war so that two of the three are always at war with a third, though not always the same two. Towns all over the world undergo unceasing but almost casual bomb attacks launched from military aircraft while every human being on the planet is subjected to unceasing propaganda directed against the current enemy. The identity of the enemy changes every few years, the warring groups make new alliances and overnight the propaganda changes.

On Orwell's account the preservation of an all-encompassing tyranny will be the real aim of warfare in the future. The point of making war will be to induce fear in the populace and thereby increase and deepen tyranny and make it more efficient. The lives led by the inhabitants of *Nineteen Eighty-Four* are directly affected by dictatorial systems of government but only indirectly affected by war so that the worst things about life in Orwell's horrible imaginary world result from the power of the state and its lying propaganda. In the year 1984 England is ruled by Big Brother and his minions, mysterious individuals who address the nation, not directly but through television broadcasts, and who arrange for the punishment or disappearance of anyone who tries to think for himself or herself (Orwell, 1949).

When *Nineteen Eighty-Four* was first published readers assumed that the author had intended it as a satire on the Soviet Union.

Orwell, partly I think in playfulness, denied that that was so; he claimed to be satirizing the BBC, an organisation he had worked for during the second world war. Partly but not entirely as a result of his experiences in the Spanish civil war he held a very low opinion of Soviet communism, but, on the other hand, he apparently thought it possible that the growth of mass-circulation newspapers and the increasing availability of television would tempt Western leaders to increase their control over ordinary citizens by instilling fears of external and internal enemies and fears of stepping out of line.

Orwell invented a special terminology to describe the world of the future. In his dystopia people are taught *Newspeak*, a language designed to replace English. The reason is that those who possess a natural language are capable of critical thinking which is condemned as *thoughtcrime*. Perpetrators of thoughtcrime are tracked down by Thought Police and subjected to rehabilitation (torture) or vapourisation (a bullet in the back of the neck). Orwell probably believed that fear of thoughtcrime is part of the human condition and explains why it is easy for rulers to lead people into aggressive wars.

Nineteen Eighty-Four is unrealistic in that its perpetually ongoing air war is a pretty low level affair. Atom bombs are left out of the story because the author wanted to attack government tyranny rather than military science. Aldous Huxley's novel, *Ape and Essence*, is more realistic in that it describes a possible future world devastated by nuclear bombs and chemical warfare.

Huxley considers both the aims of war and its cause: 'Surely it's obvious? Doesn't every schoolboy know it? Ends are ape-chosen; only the means are man's.' (Huxley, 1949, p. 32). In other words, human beings have high intelligence when thinking about techniques but like the beasts have very restricted ideas about the future and therefore cannot foresee any but the most immediate consequences of their own actions.

Aldous Huxley depicts the initiation of the third world war by baboonish military men launching chemical and nuclear weapons across the oceans with the help of scientists—Faraday, Pasteur and Einstein—who are dragged about on leashes. He believed, no doubt correctly, that chemical weapons, and the radiation emitted by atomic weapons, could cause diseases in the living and deformities in the unborn.

Ape and Essence describes Los Angeles as it might be in the 22nd century, three generations after the dropping of what the survivors in California call The Thing. In the year 2108 Los Angeles, formerly the home of millions of people, has only a few hundred human inhabitants, the descendants of those who survived a nuclear bombardment. The Thing was not a low level atomic weapon but the most deadly nuclear device that mankind could devise. The city is ruled by castrated priests who worship Belial. Belial has to be propitiated because it was he who sent The Thing. After The Thing the millions of dead could not be buried so the streets of Los Angeles are littered not only with the debris of smashed buildings but with huge quantities of human bones which the new Californians make into simple artifacts. A cohort of cemetery workers has the task of digging up pre-war coffins and undressing the corpses in order to provide clothing for important people.

Sex is forbidden except for a special two-week orgy held annually. After the orgy all the 3-month-old infants born as the outcome of the previous year's orgy are ceremoniously examined by the priests of Belial. Most infants are deformed: those with minor deformities are permitted to live, the rest are knifed by the priests. Then their mothers are whipped with bulls' pizzles. Women are referred to as 'vessels', short for 'vessels of deformity and enemies of the race.' The priests explain to a visitor that the number and the severity of the infantile deformities increase each year so that the population will eventually disappear altogether.

It is possible that the effects of a future nuclear war could be just as unfortunate as Huxley predicted. Although the 1945 atomic bomb attacks on Japan have not been repeated anywhere else the major powers still hold huge stockpiles of much more powerful weapons and have not been able to prevent the spread of nuclear technology to other nations. By 1987 Robert McNamara, once a very belligerent American Secretary of State for Defense, had come to believe that if a third world war were to be waged with nuclear weapons it would destroy all life on the planet.

Speculation: Sigmund Freud

Freud wrote about war more than once. One source is a 1915 paper 'Thoughts for Our Times' in which he tried to explain the origins of warfare. Another source is a letter he wrote to Albert Einstein in the 1920s. Einstein had been asked by the League of Nations to enter into correspondence with anyone he chose about any topic he chose. Einstein chose Freud and asked him whether he thought mankind could be delivered from the menace of war. Freud's reply is entitled

'Why War?'. The two essays are published together in a slim book (Freud, 1953).

Einstein had mentioned the difference between might and right. Freud substituted the idea of violence for the idea of might, and claimed that it is easy to prove that right evolves from violence. His so-called proof simply states that all conflicts of interest between man and man are resolved, in principle, by recourse to violence. This supposed proof merely restates the thesis waiting to be proved and the reference to principle fails to say what the principle *is*. I believe the founder of psychoanalytic theory, or rather his unconscious mind, was relying, not on any statistical or other empirical evidence, but on the old German proverb *'Gewalt geht vor Recht'* ('might precedes right').

Freud says that civilisation, in other words the community, the State, demands that the citizen renounces many instinctual gratifications. National leaders forbid individuals to engage in wrong-doing, not because States wish to abolish the practice but because they want to monopolise it in the same way that they monopolise taxes on tobacco and salt.

Another Freudian thesis is that every living thing has an impulse towards destruction, the Death Instinct. It is not clear whether he meant to refer only to animals or whether cabbages and parsley were covered by his generalistion, but be that as it may, the Death Instinct, he said, is quite a healthy thing — though only when it is turned outward as the instinct to kill, being morbid and unhealthy when turned inward, as in suicide. In the papers under discussion Freud maintains that the morbid unhealthy version of the Death Instinct is the origin of conscience thus suggesting that he thought of conscience either as a kind of illness or as an illusion or as both. He also said that right is simply the violence of the community and that law emerges when brute force is transferred from individuals to governments.

Well, is war caused by the destructive instincts or intentions of rulers? If so how do those relate to the motives of ordinary individual citizens? Does the larger entity, the community, the State, have instincts of its own, over and above those of individual rulers and subjects? How can that be? Or is the State somehow motivated by the instincts of those it is supposed to govern?

Freud is not worried about ambiguity and contradiction, hence he first implies that the State declares war at the urging of its citizens' instincts and then says that the relaxation of moral ties between different national communities during war affects the morality of individuals — all in the same book.

Some supporters of Freud, more logical than he, might here point out that individual rulers, individual heads of States, have often fought in wars. Once upon a time kings and princes were real soldiers who led their forces into battle. Even nowadays hereditary monarchs and their kin serve in armies and navies, for example three of Queen Elizabeth II's four children have served in the armed forces, two in peace time and one (the Duke of York) in a war zone during a war. In early 2006 both her grandsons were in training at Sandhurst. On the other hand Western monarchs today are merely nominal rulers, the real rulers — for example members of Parliament in Britain, Senators and Congressmen in the United States — do not join the military in time of war and rarely, if ever, encourage their children to serve in the armed forces.

Freud gives what he calls 'the illusion' of conscience two different explanations. In one explanation he says conscience originates in a morbid, that is, a suicidal, version of the Death Instinct. In the other he says conscience is nothing but fear of the community. Can conscience be both those things? He also suggests that the impulses of philanthropy and the impulses of kindness to animals are not genuine but really cloak quite different feelings. All the supposed friends of humanity, all the supposed champions of animals were as little children sadistic tormenters of their pet dogs and cats. There is no such thing as heroism, no such thing as genuine self-sacrifice. The real explanation of supposedly heroic acts is that no-one believes in his own death. Moreover the supposed dread of death is not real; it is caused by unconscious guilt. There is no such thing as genuine grieving. When anyone seems to grieve for the death of a loved person his real feelings are a mixture of hatred and gratification. There is no such thing as chivalry; it is a figment of the imagination. Enslaving an enemy is very gratifying and that fact explains the supposedly chivalrous practice of giving quarter.

It might be possible to agree with Freud about some things but nevertheless question his thesis that all human feelings, motives and actions are selfish and violent and cruel. His account of humanity, a gregarious species, is hostile and one-sided.

The beliefs expressed by Freud in these two papers evidently look plausible to his followers. But superficial plausibility cannot overcome the brute fact that Dr Freud never supports his theories with any evidence. He insists, repeatedly, that he is a scientist; he even compares his 'discovery' of psychoanalysis with Einstein's work on relativity. Yet in these essays he at no point alludes to history or anthropology or ethology or any other empirical enquiry. In other words his theories are unsupported.

A good example of an unsupported thesis is his claim that what is true of human violence is also true in the whole animal kingdom. That is simply false. For example the males of our nearest cousins, the apes, do not fight to the death as human beings do, they fight to establish dominance. Once the Alpha male ape is recognised as such the fighting ends. The Beta and Gamma males rarely get killed because they know it is better to submit or if need be to run away.
The big cats occasionally kill one another but that is not their ordinary way of resolving conflicts of interest. It only happens when things get out of hand, out of paw. Male crocodiles eat crocodile eggs and young crocs but that is not a way of resolving saurian conflicts. It seems more like a species-related eating disorder.

Parent birds protect their young by pretending to be wounded so that predators will be led away from the nestlings. They place their own lives at risk, just as chivalrous human beings do. Penguins of both sexes protect their young under their feet all through the Antarctic winter.

As with ethology so too with history and anthropology. None of Freud's amoral or anti-moral propositions are supported by empirical evidence apart from the obvious fact that mankind does indeed go in for killing members of its own species on a grand scale. Freud's attempts to explain war do not rest on genuine enquiries into causes. He ignores the fact that anthropology, like history, teaches that levels of violence vary a lot between different times, different places, different groups.

When Freud said that Eros and the death wish are both 'indispensable' was he talking only about males? Do women and female animals have the death wish, the desire to kill? Whatever other psychologists might teach Freud himself was not in a position to assert that women have a death wish because he, on his own say-so, was not in a position to apply any of his theories to women. In his well-known letter to Marie Bonaparte he said that in spite of all his years as a psychoanalyst he still did not know what women want. The confession surely shows that Freud's big generalisations have to do only with males. The remark to Marie Bonaparte is also a manifestation of his usual refusal to look at any kind of ordinary evidence. He had many women patients and could have at least made a statistical study of what they said they wanted in life. If the answers seemed insincere he could have tried hypnotism, one of his earlier tools of trade.

It is quite apparent that Freud actually had a real aversion to seeking evidence. That would explain some of his reckless generalisations: for example in the little volume under discussion he writes that after a war the soldier returns to his wife and children 'joyous, fulfilled and unconcerned'. Well, it is true that many men like to fight and it is quite probable that young inexperienced soldiers look forward to war. When they return — and of course not all do, people get killed in wars! — some will have been blinded, some will have lost limbs, some will have had their lungs or other organs damaged by chemicals and virtually all will have lost comrades. Soldiers returning from Japanese prisoner of war camps after the second world war felt anything but joyous.

Had Freud ever met any returning soldiers? Or was he simply obtuse? D.H. Lawrence said that pornography does the dirt on sex. In his essays on war Sigmund Freud does the dirt on the whole human race. He was a well-read man (for a doctor) and was doubtless familiar with the writings of Nietzsche and Darwin and Malthus. He seems anyway to have adopted the Nietzschean view that there are no moral facts. (Though Nietzsche, not a consistent thinker, also proposed a new set of 'oughts' and 'ought nots', as embodied in the theory of the Superman.)

Freud's contemptuous rejection of the human traits that you and I and others think of as benign, traits such as generosity, fellow-feeling, heroism, self-sacrifice, grief at the death of loved ones, and kindness to animals, is much worse than the superficially similar teachings of Nietzsche.

Wittgenstein says that Freud's 'science' lacks evidence because there cannot be any evidence for Freudian theories: 'What he gives us is speculation — something prior even to the formation of an hypothesis.' (Wittgenstein, 1966, p. 44). He notes that Freud felt that there must be some law explaining this or that human activity and quotes one of the psycho-analyst's best-known remarks ('Do you want to say, gentlemen, that changes in mental phenomena are guided by chance?') and remarks that in his opinion the fact that there aren't actually any laws here is important. According to Wittgenstein people are inclined to accept Freud's ideas because they are attractive in the way that myths and stories are attractive.

Freud's reply to Einstein ends with the unoriginal idea that a powerful world government might be able to do away with war. Was Einstein disappointed? Probably.

The most striking thing about Freud's reasoning in the two essays about war is its shockingly muddled and contradictory character. The muddle, and the failure to support conclusions with any evidence, indicate a lack of what one might call scientific morality, or scientific responsibility, or, more generally, the ethics of enquiry.

Ape and Essence and *Nineteen Eighty-Four* are works of the imagination. The contributions from Lenin and Freud are also imaginative in that Marxist-Leninism and Freudianism, contrary to the claims of their inventors, are not sciences but pseudo-sciences.

To my mind, however, the two novelists and the two pseudo-scientists have between them correctly located the ultimate causes of war as originating partly in the brains of men and partly in the institutions created by men. Like dragons the causes of war sometimes sleep and sometimes wake but they will not go away unless men can change or modify their institutions and at the same time overcome — somehow! — the natural propensity to aggression lurking inside their heads.

Chapter 2
Rules of War in the Ancient World

Even the jungle has laws
(Rudyard Kipling)

Customary law and the laws of war

The aspects of 19th and 20th century international law which have to do with warfare were inspired by humane ideas and by feelings of chivalry and pity and reflect to some extent the moral reasonings of the philosophers and jurists mentioned hereafter, in chapter 3. Yet the thesis that war should be constrained by ethical rules did not begin with the Christian thinkers of the middle ages. References to unwritten customary laws which governed the conduct of warfare — at least to some extent — between the tribes or States in parts of the ancient world can be found in the Old Testament and in Herodotus's *Histories* and in Plato. According to Coleman Phillipson (Phillipson, 1911) similar references appear in works from the scribes of ancient India.

It is necessary however to distinguish between rules and restraints on the one hand and actual practices on the other. In war expediency, utility, greed, haste, vengefulness and delusions very often over-ride ethical considerations and even ignore ordinary foresight and concern with consequences. In times of war not a few countries — including some of those von Clausewitz had in mind when he spoke of 'civilised influences' — will sooner or later begin to behave badly. During the second world war the uncivilised or decivilised nations of Germany, Japan and Soviet Russia all engaged in bestial practices and so did the Allied Forces on occasion. Cultural influences do not positively guarantee ethical or even rational behaviour in hot war or cold. Arthur 'Bomber' Harris was not restrained by the culture and civilisation of the West nor were the anti-morality opinions of the American General Curtis Le May affected by such influences (see chapter 25, *ibid.*). The extraordinary threats made by 'Cold War warriors' on both sides between 1946 and the 1980s were based on a degree of moral blindness amounting to serious delusion.

Israel and Greece

Coleman Phillipson's book does not mention the siege of Ilium, which — if it occurred at all — took place in about 1270 BC. The conduct there of the Greeks and Trojans as related by Homer (Homer, 1996) clearly gave expression to macho ideals of heroism but little evidence of any other ethical or quasi-ethical concepts. On the other hand the practice of occasionally arranging single combat between two prominent heroes was perhaps an indication of a desire to avoid widespread bloodshed; a huge blood-bath might have offended the gods.

The eventual victors perpetrated many crimes: they burnt the city, carried off loot, enslaved the Trojan women, killed children, desecrated dead bodies, and invaded a sanctuary in order to seize the Trojan princess Cassandra.

Did they have any customary laws regarding the conduct of warfare? Bad behaviour is certainly not conclusive evidence to the contrary, even in this case, particularly as Homer says that some of the Greeks were punished by the gods for their more offensive actions.

Asylum: According to Coleman Phillipson it was a customary law of Israel and Greece, and also of Egypt and Rome, that individuals seeking asylum must not be harmed. Local people threatened by other locals could take refuge in temples and in some cases foreigners fleeing from their own countrymen were also protected in this manner. Suppliants were inviolable and in some places harming a suppliant incurred the death penalty.

Nowadays asylum seekers still appeal to the laws of the lands they flee to. When their claims to asylum are recognised as genuine they will be protected and supported by governments and taxpayers rather than by Oracles and worshippers. The custom is perhaps an aspect of the duties relating to hospitality.

Envoys and Ambassadors: In Israel and Greece, and also in Persia and Rome, the persons of envoys and ambassadors were regarded as sacred, as inviolable. This rule about the proper treatment of envoys and heralds and ambassadors was widely accepted more or less since the earliest beginnings of civilisation and has survived until modern times. Nowadays it is enshrined in some of the protocols propounded in Geneva and The Hague.

Isaiah regarded war as a universal scourge and a universal punishment, the very worst thing that can happen to human beings, worse than illnesses, worse than slavery, worse even than the captivity of a whole nation. Yet even in those distant times envoys were inviolable. Isaiah describes how the enemies of King Hezekiah (715–687 BC) sent messengers who announced various plans and threats. Hezekiah ordered his own men to remain silent and following a customary rule allowed the messengers to go free (Holy Bible, *Isaiah*).

Darius (548–486 BC), a King of Persia who came to power in 521 BC, sent envoys to Athens and Sparta demanding they submit to his rule. According to Herodotus the messengers to Athens were killed by being thrown into a pit while those to Sparta were done away with by being thrown into a well. But Nemesis was waiting. The Spartans had a temple dedicated to Agememnon's envoy and for many years after they killed the Persian messengers their temple sacrifices gave no favourable signs. The Spartans therefore decided that two of their number must offer their lives to King Xerxes, the son of Darius, in payment of the debt owed to his father. Two volunteers, supposedly descendants of Agamemnon's messengers, traveled to Persia and addressed Xerxes as follows: 'King of the Medes, the Spartans have sent us here ... in reparation for the murder of the Persian messengers ...' (Herodotus, 2003, pp. 136–7)

But the King replied that he had no intention of behaving like Spartans who by killing the ambassadors of a foreign power had broken a law which all the world held sacred. Herodotus says that after the messengers returned from Persia the anger of Agamemnon's envoy was allayed, as indicated by the results of the sacrifices performed in his temple.

Treating the persons of envoys as sacred is demanded by reason, it is an example of the connection between morality and rationality, something perhaps best explained in Kantian terms. According to Kant the moral law, though often flouted, is nevertheless acknowledged by every human being. It does not have to be codified because it exists anyway in the human mind and in the form of customs governing relations between individuals and between tribes and States.

Plato and Aristotle

In Book II of *Republic* Plato assumes mankind will never be free from the threat of war. Women and men must be trained to fight side by side and children will have to be taken by their fathers to places where battles are occurring in order to learn and practice the work of soldiering.

He also suggests some special rules for warfare. There should be no exchange of prisoners: if a soldier allows himself to be captured alive he must be given to the enemy's army to treat in any way it likes. Outstanding bravery must be rewarded, the rewards to include embraces and kisses; no man or woman may refuse to embrace and kiss a valorous soldier. The populace must be told that death in battle is glorious and taught to worship dead soldiers as gods. Plunder should be forbidden, especially in wars between Greeks and Greeks; devastation of houses and villages is also forbidden (Plato, *Republic,* Bk. 7, 1998).

Plato seems to disapprove of wars between Greeks and suggests a verbal 'improvement' of the kind much used by politicians in our own times: he says that such episodes should be called *conflicts* not *wars.* He implies that when fighting against barbarians Greeks may do what they like, rather as some modern professionals — lawyers, military men, scientists, and even a few philosophers — like to tell us that no holds are barred in wars waged against those variously described as insurgents, guerillas or terrorists.

Aristotle remarks that warfare is a natural activity. It is a species of acquisition and acquisition is natural and necessary. Hunting beasts is profitable and is also good practice for hunting men, i.e., for war. War comes about when men born to rule hunt down those who refuse to submit to their natural masters. For the hunters such warfare is naturally just (Aristotle, *Politics,* 1984).

Rome

The Romans distinguished between justice in the conduct of war and conduct allowed by the gods. They sent envoys to demand recompense for alleged wrongs and did not approve of surprise attacks. Past injuries, not future intentions, were grounds for war.

The other customary laws of war accepted by Rome (and also by Greece) included the following:

- There had to be a valid reason for fighting and the reason had to be announced to the enemy in advance, for example by envoys. The Greeks always claimed they had just cause for fighting but sometimes forgot about sending warnings or envoys. The Spartans in particular were especially remiss in such matters.

- There had to be a formal declaration of war.

The Philosophy of War and Peace

- Certain people had to be given safe conduct and some were entitled to the rights of suppliants and the right to asylum.
- Proper arrangements had to be made for the burial of the dead.
- Temples, graves and sacred objects were inviolable.
- There were rules about neutrality.
- And rules about truces and armistices.
- And rules about prisoners of war and ransoms and exchanges
- And rules about hostages.
- Finally, of course, there were customs relating to peace negotiations and peace treaties.

The customary laws relating to war accepted by ancient Greece and Rome were not unlike some of those propounded by jurists and philosophers of the Christian Middle Ages and later. It can be assumed, of course, that Aquinas, Vitorio, Hugo Grotius, John Calvin and Thomas Hobbes would have read works by the ancient authors.

Chapter 3

The Just War I

Christian Philosophers & Jurists in the Middle Ages

In some cases it is plainly the will of God that a righteous man should fight in a war

(Augustine)

The thoughts of Saint Augustine

Only a minority of Christians have been pacifists yet it is characteristic of Christianity that its followers should be drawn to anti-militarism. The reasons can be traced firstly to what is taken to be the general tone of Christ's teachings, secondly to His own non-resistance to the men who arrested him and thirdly to various passages in the Gospels — including of course His words to Peter when the soldiers came for Him in the garden.

It is possible that Roman persecution of Christians was in part a result of the fact that converts to that religion refused to fight for the Roman polity.

The rejection of war was itself rejected by St. Augustine (354–430) who argued that the violence of war is similar to the necessary violence exercised by rulers against criminals. Rulers have a right and a duty to punish criminals and by analogy a Christian Emperor has a right and a duty, a duty assigned him by God, to wage war against barbarians (Augustine, 1887, 1870).

One way of reconciling the seemingly pacifistic leanings of the early Church with the teaching of Augustine was to interpret certain passages in the Gospels as applying not to everyone but only to 'those who would be perfect', which in turn was interpreted as referring to priests and monks.

In the 9th century Pope Leo IV (Pope 847–55) kindly promised to use his keys to open the Kingdom of Heaven for those who died in wars against infidels (Kelly, 1988).

War and the religious orders

In spite of the afore-mentioned idea that the clergy are 'those who wish to be perfect', it seems that some priests liked to fight. The Bayeux Tapestry shows Bishop Odo, a brother of William the Conqueror, taking part in the Battle of Hastings. He wields a sort of club, rather than a sword or lance, presumably in order to wound and kill while avoiding bloodshed.

According to Peter Brock Gratian, who was writing in the 12th century, held that canon law forbids the clergy to engage in battle; other Christians of the same time said the clergy may bear arms but only to frighten enemies; others again argued that all Christians, including priests, are permitted to fight in wars against heretics and infidels (Brock, 1972). This opinion was presumably adhered to by the men who created a specialised religious order of soldiers, the Knights Templar, also known as the Poor Knights of Christ and the Temple of Solomon. The order was founded in 1118 in France and then situated itself in Jerusalem from where the Templars took on the task of protecting Christian pilgrims on the roads of the Holy Land. When Jerusalem fell in 1187 they moved to Acre and later to Cyprus. The order became extremely wealthy and adopted a new profession, namely, as bankers to monarchs and the nobility. In 1307 they were accused of heresy and immorality, many were burnt at the stake and all their wealth was confiscated. It is believed by some authorities that the motives of the accusers were envy and greed.

Developing the idea of a just war

Thomas Aquinas (1225–74) condemned the killing of innocent people, giving four reasons: the destruction of innocent people shows contempt for God; it harms those who being harmless deserve no harm; it harms those to whom one has a duty of charity; and it deprives the community of something good (Aquinas, 1966).

Francisco Vitorio (1480–1545) wrote treatises on the laws of war. His second treatise begins with references to passages in the New Testament, for example chapters 5 and 26 in Matthew's Gospel, which appear to forbid self-defence. Vitorio was puzzled by those passages but solved the problem in part by arguing 'from the reason of the thing' and in part by adopting Augustine's view that there is a similarity between the necessary violence of the magistrate and the violence of war. Since the aim of war is to preserve the State everything necessary to that aim is permissible. On the other hand he also asserts that since killing innocent people is illicit within the State so killing the innocent during a war is also illicit. Yet as it turns out he also believes that a soldier must obey the orders of his prince even if the orders are wicked. For a prince does not owe the soldier an explanation. It can be seen, again 'from the reason of the thing', that if Monarchs always had to explain their orders war, and even ruling, would become impossible. Vitorio, in short, contradicts himself from time to time (Vitorio, 1917).

The Protestant Hugo Grotius (1583–1645) distinguishes five kinds of law: divine law, natural law, and three kinds of human law: civil law, international law and church law. He says that not all law is written down, much rests on precedent and custom or simply on what men want to happen, hence there are national and international laws or rules which are not backed by sanctions but are obeyed because some men like to have a good conscience and because they respect law and justice and fear God. Soldiers wish to believe their cause is just and when they do believe that they tend to avoid acts of brutality and cowardice. There is for example an unwritten law about the respectful disposal of dead bodies. Most nations, says Grotius, will allow enemies to bury their dead after a battle. Grotius, like some of the other authors, says the only good reason for initiating a war is to right wrongs. Thus fear of what is uncertain is not a good reason for fighting. Since everyone has the right of self defence and a right to build defensive structures it is wrong to tear down defensive walls erected by one's neighbours. War started for love of fighting, he said, is the war of savages and war started in order to seize land or property is the war of robbers. Taking land already inhabited by native peoples is wrong, and a claim to rule others for their own good is mere pretence. Even if a nation has been wronged and has a right to retaliate it should give up that right and try to negotiate if at all possible because even a just war is a disaster. Even surrender is usually better than war because peace is more important than freedom. The slaughter of a people is the worst possible evil (Grotius, 1825).

(Some slaughtered peoples, for example the Jews and the Australian aborigines, have not only been unable to fight they have not even been allowed to negotiate—such is the wickedness of the human race.)

Grotius says, surely rightly, that, although what one owns can be passed on to one's heirs, what one deserves is not heritable; thus Alexander's claim to be punishing the descendants of Xerxes' Persia was either foolish or a deliberately mendacious excuse or both. And surely it was mendacious and foolish for Nazi leaders to claim a right to punish the descendants of the peoples who fought against Germany in the war of 1914-1918.

It can be seen from the above that Christian ideas about justice in warfare developed gradually over two or three centuries.

In George Orwell's 1949 notebook there is an anecdote about an antiques dealer in Italy who wished to sell a crucifix to J.P. Morgan the American millionaire. It wasn't a particularly attractive crucifix; its value was due to the fact that it could be taken to pieces to reveal a stiletto inside.

Orwell commented 'What a perfect symbol of the Christian religion!' (Orwell, 1968, p. 32)

The conditions needed for a war to be just

The aims and methods which distinguish just wars from unjust ones can be tabulated roughly as follows:

> First: there are some men, namely priests and monks, who may not bear arms.—It seems to have been assumed that women do not and should not engage in warfare.
>
> Second: if a war is to be just it must be initiated by, and led by, a proper authority.
>
> Third: such a war must be fought for a just cause and with right intentions.
>
> Fourth: such a war must not use illicit means.

These rules are still accepted by the Catholic Church today, though with certain ambivalent modifications relating to conscription and conscientious objection expressed during Vatican II.

The second condition for justice in war raises questions as to what counts as a proper authority in initiating war and leading in war. What are the necessary and sufficient conditions?

It seems reasonable to suppose a proper authority would have to be either the constitutional or the *de facto* ruler of a political unit which is independent of other similar or larger units. Thus a city council cannot rightly wage war on a central government or on other

The Philosophy of War and Peace

city councils. Nor can groups of private individuals rightfully wage war on each other or on States or cities. Mercenary armies employed by millionaire drug dealers can indeed wage war but drug dealers are surely not proper authorities.

What of the sufficient conditions? For most of human history, including most of the Christian era, the right to rule and hence to wage war, has depended on inheritance. On the other hand revolutionaries, including those who rejected the rule of George III, include in their rhetoric or in their later justifications various denunciations of old ideas about the inherited right to rule. The first version of the American Constitution, for example, allotted the right to rule to a body of men elected by the male citizens. Since most blacks in America were slaves and native Americans were not citizens an elector usually had to be white.

Usurpers have been recognised, either in the long run or the short run, as having acquired the right to rule. Oliver Cromwell is one example and members of the Bonaparte family are others.

For two centuries or thereabouts colonial administrators were accepted by the European powers and by the peoples of Europe as having a right to rule in India, the Far East and Africa. White men in North and South America assumed they had a right to rule the native peoples and indeed to kill them off if they got in the way. In North America the native 'Indians' were moved from their lands and pushed into reservations. The native population of Uruguay was killed off more than 100 years ago (according to local tour guides in Montevideo).

In modern times it is widely believed that only governments elected by the people have genuine authority. Proponents of this view tend to ignore the fact that until the middle of the 20th century the electorates of so-called democratic countries were all-male and in America all-white. Such defenders of democracy also tend to forget awkward matters like rigged elections in South America and Hitler's electoral successes in Germany. These awkward matters raise two important questions viz: Is there any such thing as a just revolution? If so how is to be distinguished from a criminal rebellion? (Possible answers will be considered in Part IV *ibid.*)

As to the third condition listed above, violence, including the violence of warfare, was held to satisfy the need for proper intention if the intention was self-defence — a natural right needing no external authority — or defence of the homeland, or the defence of allies, or the reclaiming of stolen goods and expropriated land, or the conversion of infidels, or the punishment of guilty persons. In modern times certain ex-rulers and their minions have been war criminals and are taken to have been guilty in the required sense. But only some have been punished.

These Christian justifications of violence can be found not only in Augustine and the decrees of popes, they have also been appealed to by modern rulers in modern times. Self-defence was the rationale of the huge military alliances of the twentieth century: the North Atlantic Treaty Organisation, the South-East Asia Treaty Organisation and the communist Warsaw Pact. Return of stolen land was the reason given (by both sides) in the Falklands War. In this the twenty-first century the destruction of terrorist threats was the reason given by America and its allies for invading Afghanistan and Iraq. In the case of Iraq the overthrow of a dictator thought to be armed with nuclear and chemical weapons was another stated motive for the invasion.

The fourth traditional condition for justice in war has to do with methods. It covers several different matters: truces, deceptions, types of weapon, treatment of prisoners, treatment of allies, and treatment of civilian populations.

Thomas Hobbes (1588–1679) says that keeping promises and truces is a fundamental natural law. If truces cannot be relied on protagonists will not surrender until they are defeated utterly, every battle will be a battle to the death, and every war will be an all-out war. As noted in chapter 1 all-out war was not inevitable in the ancient world. The Greeks made truces in order to allow both sides to bury their dead, the Romans made truces with cities which offered to surrender, heralds, who carried important messages, including offers of truce, were protected and given safe conduct and temples and churches were supposed to be sacrosanct.

Feudal practice included holding prisoners for ransom (current opinions about ransom arrangements will be discussed below, in chapter 12).

War and punishment

How apt is Augustine's comparison between the violence of war and the necessary violence exercised by rulers against criminals?

Because rulers (he says) have both a right and a duty to punish criminals it can be argued from analogy that God has assigned to Christian Emperors the right and the duty to wage war against barbarians. Punishment and war are both all right if pursued in a spirit of compassion and with the motive of helping, improving, and if need be converting, the criminal or the enemy nation, as the case may be. Presumably the compassion and the help and the improvement apply only to those who actually survive the war.

Augustine's followers included the 15th century canonist Alfonso Tostado who said that just war is simply a mode of legal execution.

How close is the analogy between punishment and war? In Augustine's time the functions of police work and military work were carried out by the same people, namely soldiers. But that does not prove that the work done is all of the same kind — or ever was. Secondly, police work and police forces are not invariably benign. Sometimes, as in Haiti under 'Papa Doc' Duvalier, police forces have been so evil that the people would have greatly benefitted from their abolition. In Papa Doc's Haiti, and other places too, the police have been above the law. It is only in civilised countries that the citizens have a legal right to sue a policeman, only in civilised countries that policemen can be questioned in court by lawyers acting for alleged criminals. More importantly in civilised countries catching criminals, convicting them, and punishing them, are three separate functions, carried out by, respectively, the police, the courts and the prison service. In war there can be no parallel division of roles. There is no true analogy with punishment because when active warfare is being carried on it can happen that the roles of courts, gaols and execution blocks are all rolled into one, ending up in the hands the military forces.

Wars are initiated by States or by rebels. Rebels can sometimes be caught and punished but victorious States cannot. Vanquished rulers can be punished though that doesn't invariably happen. The threat made during the first world war to hang the Kaiser was not carried out; instead the victors imposed a blockade on the German *people* during which thousands are said to have died of starvation.

Aggression, defence, uncertainty

The right of self-defence is accepted almost universally, the only exceptions being absolute pacifists. As already noted, Hugo Grotius said that since everyone has the right of self defence and a right to build defensive structures it is wrong to tear down the fortresses and other defensive walls erected by one's neighbours. He also said that since the only good reason for initiating a war is to right wrongs fear of what is uncertain does not justify fighting. Does it justify making bloodthirsty threats? (A question raised again in chapter 9.)

Who has the right to self-defence? Do colonial powers faced with aggression from other colonial powers have the right? Or does the right pertain only to native peoples?

Can a distinction be drawn between different kinds of weapons: between aggressive weapons and weapons of self-defence? In the days when knights donned armour those knights were sometimes intending to attack people or places but was the actual armour essentially defensive or essentially aggressive? If a country anticipates a war by building fortresses is that aggression or defence? If towns being bombed from the air instal anti-aircraft batteries is that aggression? American military men thought so in 1961: they advised the President to continue nuclear testing then because they feared the Soviet Union might develop an anti-missile missile system, that is, a system of defensive weapons.

Chapter 4

The Just War II

Philosophers & Clergy in the Twentieth Century

Every act of war directed to the indiscriminate destruction of whole cities or vast areas together with their inhabitants is a crime against God and man

(*Vatican II* 1963, English translation 1974)

Several modern philosophers have written about just and unjust warfare; they include G.E.M. Anscombe, Anthony Kenny and John Finnis (with Germain Grisez and Joseph Boyle).

Elizabeth Anscombe (1918–2001) published three papers on the topic; all three are reprinted in the third volume of her *Collected Papers* (Anscombe, 1981). During the 1960s Anthony Kenny discussed the topic of modern war in many letters to Catholic journals. He quotes from the correspondence in the first volume of his autobiography, *A Path from Rome* (Kenny, 1986).

Elizabeth Anscombe's papers on war

The first of Anscombe's three papers about war was written at the end of 1939 when she was 20. She and another student, Norman Daniels, published a pamphlet made up of two essays, giving it the title *The Justice of the Present War Examined: a Catholic View*. Anscombe's contribution has an amusingly insouciant footnote about a papal encyclical which had been translated first in the Vatican and then by Mgr. Ronald Knox. The footnote runs as follows: '… comparing these with the Latin original we have often found cause to alter the translation ourselves' (Anscombe, 1981, p. 80).

Her essay outlines seven conditions needed before a war can be just and insists that even if only one is absent then the war is morally forbidden. She correctly predicted that the Allies would eventually use aerial bombardment to attack the civilian populations of Germany; and attacking civilians is a mortal sin, it is murder. The fact that the enemy's air force is also murderous does not make it all right.

The subtitle of the pamphlet, 'A Catholic View', caused the Bishop of Birmingham to tell the young authors that only works carrying an *imprimatur* may rightly be called Catholic. He did not give it an *imprimatur*.

The origin of Elizabeth Anscombe's second paper on war was as follows. Before moving to the Chair of Philosophy in Cambridge in 1970 she had been a senior member of Somerville College Oxford with voting rights in the University's governing body (Convocation) which consists of the professors, lecturers and tutors of the University. The only occasion (as far as I know) in which she exercised the right was in 1956 when academics in Oxford proposed that Harry S. Truman be given an honorary degree. Anscombe held the view that President Truman's decision to drop atomic bombs on Japanese centres of civilian population was very wicked. She decided to make a formal protest at a meeting of Convocation and asked the Senior Proctor how she might do that. He referred her to the Registrar, who informed the Vice Chancellor of her intention, as was his duty. She wrote later that 'cautious enquiries' were made as to whether she had 'got up a party'. She replied No. It seems that word had got round so that many dons turned up to the meeting. Some came along to support Mr Truman, others to foil what they suspected was a plot concocted by certain inherently incomprehensible people, namely, the female academics.

When the proposal for the honorary degree was put to the meeting Elizabeth said *non placet* (it does not please), the formula used both for demanding a vote and for voting No. Alan Bullock, of St. Catherine's College, had the task of defending Mr Truman in a speech at which Anscombe later poked some rather grim fun. When the matter was put to the vote a large majority were in favour of giving the President his degree. Four people voted against: Elizabeth herself, her Somerville colleagues Philippa Foot and Margaret Hubbard, and a man with a fine war record, the historian M.R.D. Foot *croix de guerre*.

In 1957 Elizabeth Anscombe published a pamphlet, *Mr Truman's Degree*, which explains her *non placet*.

A third paper, 'War and Murder', first appeared in America in 1961 and later, like the other two, in her *Collected Papers III*. It begins with the statement that without law human life is a jungle and adds that laws not backed by force are useless. Following St. Augustine Anscombe compares the right to make war with a civil authority's right to control crime and violence. Criminals who are prepared to kill must be prevented from doing that, if need be by killing them, from which it follows that the exercise of mortal force by rulers cannot be bad in all circumstances. Hence the State has a right to use force in protecting its citizens against external violence, the violence of pirates, for example, and the violence of other States. It also has a right and possibly a duty, to seek the common good of mankind by attacking external evil-doers such as foreign slavers.

The present day conception of aggression, she says, is a bad one. 'Why *must* it be wrong to strike the first blow in a struggle? The only question is, who is in the right, if anyone is'. (Here one might give some thought to comparing Saddam Hussein's first strike against Kuwait and George W. Bush's first strike against Saddam's Iraq.) On the other hand, however, she insists that most wars have been 'mere wickedness on both sides'. It is probable that the soldier's life is a bad life: '*Militia* or rather *malitia*' as Anselm says ('military service, or rather malice').

The wickedness so often seen in warfare stems from the fact that States themselves are parties to the dispute and so are not subject to any temporal authority which could prevent or limit their behaviour.

Anscombe allows the possibility of rightful rebellion but only against usurpers. Unfortunately, as Peter Geach has pointed out, some of the royal houses of England and Scotland have been founded on earlier usurpations, including, perhaps, his own favourite, the House of Stuart.

In her 1961 paper Anscombe asserts that the principal wickedness in war is killing the innocent, a type of evil behaviour for which conquerors are praised. She does not mention the passage in the book of Samuel which describes how exultant dancers sang and shouted: 'Saul has killed his thousands and David his tens of thousands' but does refer in passing to the destruction of the Canaanites ordered by God and attempted by the Children of Israel, adding a somewhat ambiguous qualification: 'according to the Old Testament'.

The meaning of innocence

Elizabeth Anscombe explains that in the context of warfare the meaning of 'innocent' is not 'good' or 'moral' or 'without sin'. It simply means 'not harming'. Those who harm and therefore may be targeted, and if need be killed, include soldiers, munitions workers and transporters of arms; those who may not be targeted include farmers, housewives and children. Yet collateral damage can and does occur in wars fought with permissible means, as when attacks on military targets kill harmless individuals who happen to be passing nearby. Such deaths are properly called collateral because they are accidental. But the same cannot be said when harmless people were killed in Dresden and Hiroshima (and, one might add, in Guernica). It would be ridiculous to describe such deaths as *accidents*.

In 1984 Anscombe said in conversation that she lacked the skills of a Jonathan Swift and for that reason regretted the somewhat intemperate tone of 'War and Murder'. Her language is certainly pretty vigorous, to say the least. Although no-one is mentioned by name anonymous persons who *might* disagree with her are severely castigated, and as it were in advance, before they had put pen to paper. The attacks appear usually but not always in footnotes. Some people are said to be ignorant of the New Testament or just ignorant generally. Others are directly described as supporters of wickedness. High-sounding hypocrisy is mentioned. An unnamed judge is said to be 'talking nonsense'. Some of the author's fellow Catholics get it in the neck too. She makes no allowance for stupidity but in effect insists that all her unnamed opponents are bad people, not fools but knaves.

Anthony Kenny and others on war and deterrence

In 1962–3 a Catholic priest, Father Anthony Kenny, became involved in a series of controversies about atomic and nuclear weapons. He had been influenced by Elizabeth Anscombe's pamphlet *Mr Truman's Degree* which was still in circulation when he went up to Oxford to study for a D.Phil. Unlike Anscombe, however, he tends to abjure strong language and usually prefers words like 'mistaken' and 'immoral' to her word 'wicked'.

Anthony Kenny's concerns with just war teachings mirror those of Elizabeth Anscombe insofar as they have to do with means rather than with ends. However he added a new dimension to the discussion in that as well as condemning the *use* of weapons aimed at civilians he also considered, and attacked, the role of such weapons as *deterrents.* He did not join the Campaign for Nuclear Disarmament but occasionally addressed meetings under its auspices, arguing there and elsewhere against those of his fellow clergy who held that dropping two atomic bombs on Japan was justified because it shortened the war and saved allied lives. Those clergy, of course, were appealing to principles of utility and patriotism and not to Christian teaching about just and unjust war. In his autobiography Kenny writes:

> The dropping of bombs on Hiroshima and Nagasaki had shocked some of my priest friends but in the years of the Cold War the majority of clergy had come to accept as legitimate the possession, and perhaps even the use, of nuclear weapons. Certainly, attachment to the cause of nuclear disarmament was something regarded as eccentric and dangerous ...' (Kenny, 1986, p. 169)

Kenny believed that other clergy — 'a majority of the minority who bothered to reflect on the matter at all' — would agree that using atomic weapons to attack cities was wrong while nevertheless claiming that to possess such weapons as a deterrent was permitted. It seemed possible, to them, to imagine such weapons being used in lawful ways, perhaps when directing the bombs at armies rather than at towns. At first Kenny supposed that theologians who had studied the matter — as distinct from ordinary parish clergy perhaps — could not but agree with him but he soon had to give up that supposition. It transpired that Catholic theologians were not only loth to condemn the nuclear deterrent but also unwilling to explicitly condemn using the bombs to target civilians. Their reason seems to have been connected with a fear that the stance taken against the Soviet Union by nations in the West might be weakened if nuclear deterrence were to be condemned. The theologians naturally regarded atheistic communism as the Church's worst enemy. One clergyman tried to have it both ways, claiming that the enslavement of whole nations, the destruction of faith and the corruption of morals which would follow on domination by a ruthless atheistic power, would far outweigh the material destruction and moral evil resulting from the use of the bomb adding that the bomb could anyway be lawfully used against a naval fleet at sea.

It seems that in the 1960s most Catholic clergy never imagined for one single moment that the destruction of faith and the corruption of morals could or would be brought about in the West as a result, not of communist conquest or teachings, but as an outcome of the West's own ideology. They did not, and no doubt could not, predict that consumerism, and profitable developments in pharmaceutical science (contraception), and the law case of *Roe v. Wade*, and a free press, and freely reported scandals in the Church itself, would quite quickly lead to what has seemed to many a pretty steep decline in Christian faith and traditional Catholic moral teaching.

Kenny argued that Christian teaching on war condemns attacks on non-harmful folk whether they be Russians or Japanese, Christians or Communists. His words hark back to those of Vitorio who said the children of enemies must not be killed — 'not even the children of Turks'. In a long letter to the editor of the *Catholic Gazette* he said the theory that deterrence works as a bluff is idle, it does not rule out the possibility or even the probability that if war broke out cities full of civilians would be targeted with enormously destructive weapons. It will not stand against the sheer fact that western nations had already shown no compunction about devastating centres of population with ordinary weapons, for example as in Dresden, or with atomic bombs, as in Japan. The editor was unwilling to publish the letter and asked Kenny to avoid political questions. A similar letter to another Catholic organ, *The Tablet*, was not printed and received no acknowledgement.

In an article accepted by the *Clergy Review*, Kenny argued, further, that the deterrent would not work unless the democratic powers can convince the enemy that they are willing and able to use it. Clearly they cannot so convince the enemy unless they have military units willing and able to fire the bombs and, in the case of Britain, parliamentary sanction to do so.

Vatican II and pacem in terris

In 1962-3 Pope John XXIII convened the second Vatican Council. Vatican II considered very many matters; the English translation of its report has 1,024 pages. Of those 1,014 pages 9 are devoted to the topics of war and peace. It was rumoured that discussion of nuclear weapons was curtailed for fear of alienating the United States. Still, the document does include the words quoted at the beginning of this chapter and also the following passage:

> ... in this age of ours ... it is irrational to think that war is a proper way to obtain justice for violated rights ... the development of armaments by modern science has immeasurably magnified the horrors and wickedness of war. Warfare conducted by these weapons [atomic weapons] can inflict immense and indiscrimi-

nate havoc which goes far beyond the bounds of legitimate defence ... Providence urgently demands of us that we free ourselves from the age-old slavery of war (Flannery, 1974, p. 991).

Finnis *et al* in their book *Nuclear Deterrence* describe the Vatican debate on choosing between the evils of nuclear war and the evils of Soviet domination as 'inconclusive'.

When the Cuban missile crisis boiled up in October 1962 Anthony Kenny noted that President Kennedy's threat to bombard the Soviet Union with a full panoply of nuclear weapons was not seen as a bluff. In a crisis deterrence was replaced by *genuine* threats. Kenny preached a sermon denouncing Nikita Khrushchev and J.F. Kennedy as 'wicked men who prefer to risk the destruction of the world rather than accept any diminution of national prestige or interest'. The sermon offended those of his hearers who regarded President Kennedy as a good Catholic and a hero of anti-communism.

In 1963, just a few weeks before his death, Pope John XXIII issued his encyclical *pacem in terris*. It was translated into English by Vatican Polyglot Press, and printed in the United States as *Peace on Earth*; the American publisher added sub-headings (John XXIII, 1963).

The peace the Pope discussed was not restricted to peace as the opposite of war. His topics included human rights, human duties, the nature of human persons, the relationship between citizens and the State, the divine origins of authority, the common good, the responsibilities of the State, the rights and duties of citizens, the relations between States, the reciprocal rights and duties of States *vis à vis* each other, including the duties to be truthful, to be just, to treat minorities fairly, to help under-developed nations, to seek active inter-State solidarity, to foster freedom, and to support the world community including the United Nations Organisation. The English translation has 21 pages of text of which about half a page is devoted to disarmament. In that half-page the Pope argued that nuclear weapons should be banned. Justice, humanity and right reason urgently require an end to the arms race. The stockpiles of nuclear weapons which exist in various countries should be reduced equally and simultaneously by the parties concerned and a general agreement should eventually be reached about progressive disarmament and an effective method of control (John XXIII, 1963).

In the months following the publication of *pacem in terris* Anthony Kenny defended unilateralism again, first in an essay published in the *Clergy Review*, then, in a popular paper, in a review of the new encyclical. In the latter case he treated the encyclical as a serious contribution to thinking about war and peace but privately believed it was 'muddled, ambiguous, and unworthy of the importance of the subject it dealt with.' These thoughts were among the doubts which led him to seek laicisation. He ceased to be a priest in the Autumn of 1963. Later he was knighted, but not, one surmises, for his work on nuclear disarmament.

Two decades later some clergy were still supporting deterrent threats in spite of the Vatican statement quoted at the head of this chapter. Thus in 1982 Fr. James Schall S.J. gave what seems to be a merely utilitarian reason in support of using deterrent threats: he said that the indiscriminate and even a possibly unnecessary bombing of civilian targets was a lesser evil in comparison with Soviet tyranny. He is also thought to have coined the anti-disarmament slogan: *Better Dead than Red.* In 1983 Fr. David Hollenbach S.J. speaking in a similar utilitarian mode said that no just war argument against deterrent threats could be relevant to the then current situation because the Cold War faced the West with a choice between two evils. In that same year the Catholic bishops of France announced that when a nation is faced with the choice between two unstoppable evils, namely, capitulation to Soviet Russia or making counter-threats, it should choose the lesser evil but without claiming to make a good of it.

The views of the two members of the Society of Jesus and the statement made by the Catholic bishops of France are quoted by Finnis and his colleagues in their book *Nuclear Deterrence* (Finnis *et al.*, 1987, pp. 195f). Finnis *et al.* argue that Christian morality does not admit the possibility of objectively irresolvable moral perplexity. Following a ruling of the 16th century Council of Trent they argue that sin is never inevitable, in other words, there is no such thing as a forced choice between a greater and a lesser sin (*Council of Trent*, 1858).

Is choosing between evils the same thing as choosing between sins? Not necessarily: there can be choices demanded of one by others as well as choices between one's own possible future deeds. The Council of Trent's ruling surely applies to sins not to outcomes.

Elizabeth Anscombe and Anthony Kenny appear to have supposed that the rules for a just war which they discuss in their writings reflect the official teachings of the Catholic Church. But is the assumption correct and absolutely beyond doubt? Noble ideas about justice and injustice in war have come to us from saints and philosophers and jurists. Has any Pope or conclave set out detailed rules regarding warfare? Has any Pope or conclave directly ratified the rules enunciated by saints and philosophers?

Some difficulties

Is it an easy matter to distinguish between self-defence and aggression, between domestic crime and revolution, between guerilla war and war proper? The answer No is silently assumed or openly stated by leaders, and even by some philosophers, who think that ignoring the Geneva protocols and the laws of war will bring victory and even win hearts and minds.

Slippery slope arguments are used against those who accept the traditional Christian account of justice *in* war. At the practical level, it is argued, it is impossible to know whether a war with a just cause will be fought with just means. There is reason to accept this point: the war against Hitler, Mussolini and the Emperor of Japan was fought for just causes but, as will be noted in Part II of this book, some of the means eventually chosen, for example by Bomber Harris and President Truman, certainly failed to conform to the traditional account of what counts as justice *in bello*. On the other hand those who condemn Harris's and Truman's decision to launch massive attacks on civilians are faced with the question: what if the second world war could not be won except by those means? Those who object to unjust means are often faced with the slogan 'he who wills the end wills the means' — but that slogan, even if true, does not *justify* evil means.

According to some thinkers it is never right for a leader to engage his country in military conflict if he is sure the other side is bound to win. This raises the following question: when a nation faces aggression from a tyrannical regime what degree of risk (risk of failure) may its rulers take when deciding to fight back or not as the case may be?

A different kind of problem is that the account given by Christian philosophers of the differences between just and unjust wars contains internal inconsistencies. If a ruler is deemed legitimate according to the criteria of his time then any revolutionary or other serious opposition must be unjust because lacking proper authority, a thesis which is at cross purposes with other ideas about justice. It is possible in principle and indeed in fact for kings and presidents and elected assemblies to choose courses of action the wickedness of which outweighs the evil of revolution. Moreover opposition to rulers is not invariably revolutionary. Many civil protests carried out in

England during the twentieth century were quite peaceful. That they were mostly unsuccessful is another matter.

During the war between America and North Vietnam (1964–1973) the actress Jane Fonda was known as Hanoi Jane because of her support for North Vietnam. In April 2005 a London paper, *The Week*, reproduced a news report from Washington as follows:

> Jane Fonda has apologised for posing with a North Vietnamese anti-aircraft battery during her infamous visit to Hanoi in 1972. The actress described the photograph as a 'betrayal' and as 'the largest lapse of judgement I can ever imagine.' ... Many US veterans still think Hanoi Jane should be tried for treason.

The report notes without comment that Ms Fonda made the apology while promoting a forthcoming book of her memoirs. Be that as it may, her choice of where to pose is relevant to the debate about the right to self defence (see p. 29); surely an anti-aircraft gun is a defensive weapon.

At some time in 2005 Ms Fonda reverted to form and decided to take part in demonstrations against the war in Iraq.

Chapter 5
The Laws of War and the Red Cross

The right of belligerents to adopt means of injuring the enemy is not unlimited

(The Hague Convention of 1907)

International law and the law of war

Hugo Grotius created the first systematic treatise of international law. First published in 1625 his book *De Juri Belli et Pacis* (*The Law of War and Peace*) (Grotius, 1825) is largely concerned with the conduct of warfare, the reason being that he was moved to write by the horrors of the Thirty Years War (1618–48), a long-running series of conflicts involving several European countries and concerned partly with constitutional issues and partly with power struggles between Protestantism and Catholicism.

Like Grotius the modern authors of documented international law also give priority to the laws of war. The first codification of international law relating to warfare was promulgated in Paris in 1856 and took the form of a Declaration signed by a number of national governments. Its title is *The Paris Declaration Respecting Maritime Law* and its main aim was to protect neutral shipping in time of war (Roberts, and Guelff, 1982; unless otherwise stated the facts referred to in this chapter are taken from Roberts and Guelff).

The Red Cross

International laws relating to aggression, defence, and most especially to the possibility of encouraging ethical conduct in war, are a result of the work of Henri Dunant (1828–1910), a citizen of Switzerland, who founded the organisation now known as the Red Cross. The organisation came into being after France and Piedmont invaded Lombardy. During the ensuing war there was a battle at

Solferino (June 20 1859) which resulted in such terrible casualties on both sides that Napoleon III, the main aggressor, sued for peace.

After these events Henri Dunant proposed the formation of voluntary societies the aim of which would be to rescue soldiers left injured on battle fields. In 1863 the International Committee of the Red Cross was founded for this purpose, adopting as its flag a red cross on a white ground (the Swiss flag reversed) in honour of Dunant.

International declarations

The creation of the Red Cross organisation was followed by international declarations most of which outlaw inhumane methods of fighting.

Signatories to the St Petersburg Declaration of 1868 renounced the use of 'Explosive Projectiles Under 400 Grammes Weight'. Signatories to the Hague Declaration of 1899 renounced the use of asphyxiating gases and expanding bullets (dum-dum bullets). In 1907 the Hague Conventions covered a very long list of the rights and duties of countries at war; its provisos re-appear in many later documents.

Nations accepting international proclamations about war first signed then ratified. In some cases many years passed between signing and ratification. Signatories could add reservations to their signatures; it was not unusual to add words to the following effect: *We will obey but only if the other side does too.*

Three principles were intended to limit the ways in which war is waged:

1. Military necessity
2. Humanitarian considerations
3. Chivalry.

The concept of military necessity follows Clausewitz: it is the need to get complete submission from the enemy as quickly as possible and with the least expenditure of time, lives and resources while nevertheless having regard to principles of humanity and chivalry.

Humanity forbids the use of means which are not strictly necessary.

What is chivalry? It is the behaviour of the ideal knight, the Chevalier or horseman who is brave, courteous, disinterested, willing to defend or help the weak. St George of England, he who fought the dragon, is the epitome. Chivalry forbids the use of dishonourable means, dishonourable expedients and dishonourable conduct.

Breaking treaties, killing envoys and peace-makers, killing prisoners of war and attacking helpless individuals such as women and children and old men and those once described by Grotius as 'harmless agricultural folk', are all dishonourable.

Codified law has to deal with the balance to be obtained between the three principles above and especially with the relationship , or possible clashes, between military necessity on the one hand and the demands of humanity and chivalry on the other.

It is held that if forbidden acts are carried out and then defended as military necessities the defence should normally be rejected. However an exception is made in such case as when the law itself states that humanity and chivalry are only relevant if military circumstances permit.

The resort to war and the methods of war

The 'laws of war' as codified in the 19th and 20th centuries include

Agreements governing the resort to war, namely:
The Hague Conventions on The Pacific Settlement of Disputes (1899 and 1907);
the *Covenant of the League of Nations* of 1919;
the *General Treaty for the Renunciation of War* of 1928, also known as *The Kellogg Pact*; and
the *Charter* of the United Nations, 1945.

Agreements governing the conduct of war:
There are many of these and in general they accept, and in some cases repeat, Article 22 of *The Hague Convention* of 1907 which states that the rights of belligerents to adopt means of injuring the enemy are not unlimited.

As well as the agreements reached at The Hague, Geneva and elsewhere the General Assembly of the United Nations has issued a number of declarations relating to particular conflicts and to war generally.

Opinions differ as to the status of modern codified laws of war. It has been argued that some of the protocols, conventions and agreements, especially those signed and ratified by many nations, have acquired the force of customary law. Others deny this. The question is not unimportant, for while international codified laws are binding on *all signatories* customary law is regarded as binding on *all States*.

The Hague Convention of 1907 runs to many pages. Articles 22–30 ban poisons, treacherous ways of killing, killing people who have surrendered, using arms causing unnecessary suffering, misusing flags of truce, attacks on undefended towns, bombing without warning, pillage, and punishing spies without first making them stand trial. The destruction of churches, art works, charities, hospitals, and historic monuments is forbidden. Article 32 asserts the inviolability of persons carrying a flag of truce unless it can be shown he is misusing it as a ruse. Article 35 says that capitulations should be handled with regard to military honour. The convention forbids nations and armies to declare that no quarter will be given. The demands for unconditional surrender made by the eventual victors of the second world war seem to have come perilously close to violating that rule. Other provisos forbid torture and collective punishments.

The Hague Rules for Aerial Warfare promulgated in 1923 forbid attacks on non-combatants; ban the shooting of parachutists escaping from damaged planes; and forbid the use of incendiary bombs. Bomber Harris's arrangements for dropping phosphorous bombs on Dresden were surely a clear violation of that rule.

The 1925 *Geneva Protocol* prohibits the use of asphyxiating and poisonous gases and of bacteriological warfare. It was ratified by Britain in 1930 but that did not prevent British scientists from experimenting on military personnel at the chemical warfare laboratories at Porton Down. Moreover some signatories added a proviso, viz, that they would refrain from using such weapons only if the enemy also refrained — though since biological weapons have the capacity to destroy civilians as well as combatants the proviso amounts to saying 'We will kill your harmless bystanders if you kill ours.'

America's use of Agent Orange and Napalm in 1964–73 in Vietnam would certainly have counted as clear violations of the Protocol, however although the United States signed the Protocol in 1925 it did not ratify it until 1975, that is to say, two years after the end of the Vietnam war.

According to Donald Rumsfeld, President George W. Bush's chief legal and military advisor, the President of the United States can over-ride by fiat any international protocols the nation has signed and ratified. However that all depends on what is meant by the word 'can'. I 'can' over-ride laws against destruction of property by throwing a brick though my neighbour's window. Whether or not I were to be punished for the deed is a separate matter and one that depends on factors that do not affect the 'can'.

The *London Protocol* of 1930–36 forbade the use of submarines and other warships to attack merchant shipping, but with two provisos:

merchant ships may only be attacked if they refuse to stop and be searched. If in such case it is decided to attack a non-military ship the attacker must first place the passengers, ship's crew and ship's papers in a place of safety. For that purpose the ship's lifeboats were not regarded as places of safety except in the proximity of land and in a calm sea. The *Protocol* was signed by Germany in 1936, three years after Hitler came to power. His submarines and warships attacked convoys and passenger ships as well as Royal Navy vessels and did not stop to rescue survivors.

1948 saw the United Nations' *Convention on Prevention and Punishment of Genocide*. In 1949 there were four *Geneva Conventions* dealing with the amelioration of sick and wounded armed forces in the field, the amelioration of sick and wounded armed forces at sea, the treatment of prisoners of war, and the protection of civilian populations in time of war.

Many nations signed these conventions, but a large number had reservations about various details.

1954 saw *The Hague Convention for the Protection of Cultural Property*. In 1961 the General Assembly of the United Nations Organisation issued a *Declaration on the Prohibition of the Use of Nuclear and Thermo-nuclear Weapons*. In 1972 a *Biological Weapons Convention* prohibited the development, production and storing of biological weapons.

There have been many armed conflicts since the end of the second world war, some of which were not international in character and were therefore not covered by internationally accepted protocols. An extension of the laws of war to cover informal conflicts conducted by rebels, insurgents, guerillas and so on, came about as a result of a Swiss initiative which eventually led to the new *Geneva Protocols* of 1977.

In 1974 the Swiss convened a Diplomatic Conference on the Reaffirmation and Development of International Humanitarian Law Applicable in Armed Conflicts which dealt with this matter among others. It held several sessions between 1974 and 1977, generating additions to the *Geneva Conventions* of 1949. The number of States represented at the meetings dropped by 15 from 124 to 109, some doubtless removing themselves because of matters of principle, others probably for reasons of *realpolitik*. When national liberation movements made up of guerillas were invited to join the deliberations of the conference that no doubt decided some of the original participants to depart.

The two *Geneva Protocols* of 1977 include as well as add to those of 1949. Taken together they re-affirm the principle that the right of belligerents to adopt means of injuring the enemy is not unlimited. It states that parties to a conflict shall at all times distinguish between the civilian population and combatants; that the civilian population shall not be the object of attack; and that indiscriminate attacks are prohibited. They prohibit the use of weapons causing unnecessary suffering, including any weapons which cause starvation by destroying crops and flocks, prohibit weapons likely to cause widespread and/or permanent damage to the environment. The authors presumably had defoliants and nuclear weapons in mind.

Parties to a conflict are prohibited from declaring or threatening that there will be no enemy survivors.

Some of the additions to the 1949 document were controversial. One addition rules that the protocols shall apply to 'armed conflicts in which people are fighting against colonial domination and alien occupation and against racist regimes in the exercise of their right of self determination'. Thus the armed forces of a party to a conflict are defined as consisting of all organized armed forces, groups and units which are under a command responsible to that party for the conduct of subordinates even if that party is represented by a government or an authority not recognised by an adverse party. Such armed forces should be subject to an internal disciplinary system which amongst other things should enforce compliance with the rules of international law applicable to armed conflicts.

The account evidently refers not only to regular forces but also to guerilla fighters provided they are organised along lines roughly similar to those seen in ordinary armies. On the other hand, and equally controversially, *Geneva 1977* also ruled that mercenaries do not have the same rights as ordinary combatants.

Of those countries which signed in 1977 a number had still not ratified by 1982. Several signatories, including important nations, added reservations.

The 1981 *United Nations Convention* again affirmed that the right of belligerents to adopt means of injuring the enemy is not unlimited. It also made a ruling on the use of certain conventional weapons condemning various kinds of booby trap (mines). It stated that the locations of mines must be recorded by the mine-laying power and the enemy must be warned of the presence of mines in those locations and the United Nations must also be informed. At the end of hostilities the two sides must work together to remove the mines. International mine-clearing efforts might be needed. There are still thousands of mines strewn across much of south-east Asia. The late Princess of Wales tried to organise projects to get rid of the mine fields but to little avail.

An interesting and important decision was taken about the education of soldiers. The contracting parties had to undertake to disseminate the terms of the Convention as widely as possible and in times of peace as well as in times of war. They had to include the study of the rules laid down by the convention in programmes of military instruction so that those rules become known to the armed forces of all the signatories.

In Britain officers give short courses of lectures about the rules of war to the Other Ranks. To judge from the behaviour of British soldiers in Northern Ireland, where for years they have been faced with two terrorist organisations, the Irish Republican Army and the Ulster Defence Association, the they have indeed been so instructed. In Northern Ireland when — as happens rather rarely — a soldier appears to have targeted and killed or wounded a civilian he is court-martialled.

American military forces are issued with a handbook of instructions.

Savagery

It is a sad fact that international attempts to reduce the savagery of warfare have mostly failed. Clausewitz remarked that when and if a country behaves reasonably decently during a war that is because its culture rests on certain moral standards. In the 20th century even (previously) civilised peoples were taught by example and persuaded by their leaders to accept evil ways of fighting. Germany is a prime example of course but the Allied Nations are open to condemnation too because of their use of area bombing.

It is arguable as to whether Russia and Japan counted as civilised during the first half of the twentieth century. Be that as it may, the Japanese certainly behaved with extraordinary cruelty in their wars against China and Korea. Chinese and Korean people were beheaded or cut in half while alive and the dismembered body parts publicly displayed in order to discourage local resistance. Korean prisoners of war were used as targets for Japanese bayonet practice. British and Australian prisoners of war were used as slave labour while being deliberately starved to death and suffering insanely cruel punishments for failing to work hard enough. According to the

London *Daily Telegraph* of April 6 2005 fifteen thousand Australian soldiers were captured after the fall of Singapore in 1942. Of those 15,000 people 8,000, more than half the total, died in prison as the result of ill-treatment.

As to the Russians, Solzhenitsyn reports as follows in *Gulag Archipelago I*:

> For three weeks the war had been going on inside Germany, and all of us knew very well that if the girls were German they could be raped and then shot. This was almost a combat distinction. Had they been Polish girls or our own displaced Russian girls, they could have been chased naked around the garden and slapped on the behind — an amusement, no more (Solzhenitsyn, 1974, p. 21).

The Nuremberg judgement

The Nuremberg judgement confirmed the ruling that national leaders are responsible for the behaviour of national armies. The judgement was based on the Nuremberg Charter which incorporated many of the laws of war adopted at The Hague in 1907 and at Geneva in 1929. Not all the parties to the conflict were parties to The Hague directives of 1907 but Germany certainly was. On the other hand it would seem that neither Britain nor France could be bound by the directives of 1907 unless those directives were to count as customary law and therefore binding on all nations. The reason is that Britain denounced the 1907 convention in 1925 and France denounced it in 1929.

The judgement against Nazi leaders and Japanese military men listed crimes against peace, war crimes, and crimes against humanity.

The crimes against peace: aggressive war and war in violation of international treaties

The war crimes: violations of the laws and customs of war; the murder of civilians and prisoners of war; the ill treatment of civilians and prisoners of war (universal in Japanese prison camps); slave labour; deportation of populations; wanton destruction of towns and villages; and devastation not required by military necessity — all of which were ordered by the German and Japanese governments and practised by German and Japanese forces.

The crimes against humanity which in Germany were perpetrated both before and during the war: murder, enslavement, extermination, deportation, and persecution for religious, racial and political reasons.

The Nuremberg Judgement was perhaps thought of as a precedent which in the future would allow the punishment of those who ordered or carried out genocide, or attacked civilians, or chose to use cruel weapons and weapons which damaged the environment, or tortured prisoners and spies.

Elizabeth Anscombe held that the Nuremberg judgements embodied truly scandalous examples of retrospective law-making. It would have been better, she said, to hunt down the Nazi and Japanese criminals in a sort of open season rather than appeal to a retrospective law . She was wrong as to facts because the Nuremberg judgements were not based entirely on retrospective law-making. They referred to the definitions of war crimes which appear in The Hague Convention of 1907 and the Geneva Convention of 1929, agreements which had been signed and ratified by some of the Axis Powers in their earlier incarnations. On the other hand the judgements regarding crimes against humanity were not, and could not be, supported by reference to any existing laws since it was not until 1949 that an international convention first mentioned the crime of genocide.

The Red Cross fundamental rules

Let us return to the Red Cross. Because the codified laws of war are complex the Red Cross issued a short summary in 1978, as follows:

(1) Persons *hors de combat* and those who do not take a direct part in hostilities are entitled to respect for their lives and physical and moral integrity. They shall in all circumstances be protected and treated humanely without any adverse distinction.

(2) It is forbidden to kill or injure an enemy who surrenders or who is *hors de combat*.

(3) The wounded and sick shall be collected and cared for by the party to the conflict which has them in its power. Protection also covers medical personnel, establishments, transports and *materiel*.

(4) Captured combatants and civilians under the authority of an adverse party are entitled to respect for their lives and dignity, personal rights and convictions. They shall be protected against all acts of violence and reprisals. They shall have the right to correspond with their families and to receive relief.

(5) Everyone shall be entitled to benefit from fundamental judicial guarantees. No one shall be held responsible for an act he has not committed. No one shall be subjected to physical or mental torture, corporal punishment or cruel or degrading treatment.

(6) Parties to a conflict and members of their armed forces do not have an unlimited choice of methods and means of warfare. It is prohibited to employ weapons or methods of warfare of a nature to cause unnecessary losses or excessive suffering.

(7) Parties to a conflict shall at all times distinguish between the civilian population and combatants in order to spare civilian population and property. Neither the civilian population as such nor civilian persons shall be the object of attack. Attacks shall be directed solely at military objectives.

PART II
THE LAWS OF WAR IGNORED

Chapter 6
All-out Aerial Warfare

Power is the opium of politicians
(Ephraim Avneri, quoted by Amos Oz.)

Opium ... a stimulant and a narcotic
(*Oxford English Dictionary*)

Hitler's Blitzkrieg and 'Gott straf England!'

In 1938 German forces marched into Austria, the Sudetenland (in Czechoslovakia), Bohemia, Moravia and part of Lithuania. In 1939 Hitler demanded that Poland surrender a corridor of land leading to the port of Danzig and when Poland refused it too was invaded. On September 3 1939 the British Government under Neville Chamberlain declared war on Germany. In 1940 Nazi Germany continued its policy of 'blitzkrieg' (lightning war) by making rapid marches into Holland, Denmark, Norway and Belgium and by initiating the aerial bombardment of Britain. For a short time the Luftwaffe's attacks were aimed only at aircraft factories and shipping but Hitler soon directed the pilots to bomb civilian targets, a policy he called 'Gott straf England!' ('God punish England!') . Civilian centres in Russia were also bombed after Germany invaded its erstwhile ally in 1941. By 1943 a new invention, the German V1 bomb, also called a buzz bomb, was being aimed at residential areas of London. Buzz bombs were pilotless explosive aircraft, soon to be superceded by the V2 bomb, the 'doodle bug', a rocket designed by Werner von Braun (see chapter 8, *ibid*.). Germany's research into unmanned bombing devices was carried out at Peenemunde in Friesland and there were 63, later 96, launching pads all along the coast. In May 1943 the Royal Air Force took photos of Peenemunde and bombed it in August of the same year. About 20 of the 96 launching pads were also eventually destroyed. After Arthur Harris ordered the assault on German cities, Goebbels, in charge of Nazi propaganda, gave the

V2 rockets the title *Vergeltungswaffen*, reprisal weapons (Churchill, 1949, *passim*).

'Bomber' Harris

Sir Arthur Harris as Chief Air Marshal directed the attacks on German cities which began in 1943. His *Despatch on War Operations*, written during the second world war, was placed in the Public Records Office but withheld from public view until the 1990s.

Harris's policy was to divide a map of a German city into numbered areas. Each and every night one of more of those areas would be 'blanketed' by high explosive bombs and fire bombs.

Sebastian Cox, who wrote the 'Introduction' to Arthur Harris's *Despatch on War Operations*, remarks as follows:

> Harris held to his own deep-seated conviction that the area attack of German cities was the only sensible method of attack for his Command in the face of heavy pressure from the Air Staff and others to ... devote more effort to precision attacks (Cox, in Harris (1), 1995, p. x).

'Precision attacks' meant attacks on military targets, arms factories, and oil storage depots. Armaments factories and other industrial plants were situated on the outskirts of German cities. In 1943 Harris ordered massive attacks on Hamburg in which not a single bomb was aimed at the industrial areas, docks or railways; all were aimed at residential areas. On January 10 1944 *The Times* newspaper reported that the proclaimed intention of Bomber Command was 'to proceed with systematic obliteration'. The report was not true; the Bomber Command Directorate had ordered Harris to target military objectives, i.e. arms factories, aeroplane factories and oil terminals, but he simply ignored the order.

Later a leading article in *The Times* urged that the project of area bombing be abandoned.

Members of the Air Staff put considerable pressure on Harris to target industrial sites such as arms factories, aircraft factories, ball bearings factories and oil terminals either as well as or instead of civilians. Even those members of the Air Staff who supported him held that area bombing, though necessary, should only be a temporary measure. They hoped that when new radio navigation aids became available to Royal Air Force pilots the area bombing would cease so that industrial areas could be targeted. Some thought the *intention* was always to return to the bombing of precise targets as soon as possible.

Although Harris did not comply with the directions given him by the Air Staff of the Directorate of Bomber Operations Sebastian Cox states that the *Official History of Bomber Command* accepts Harris's version of what he was permitted to do. Harris defended targeting civilians on the grounds that it would make an invasion unnecessary. He opposed the official policy, the invasion plan *OVERLORD*, labelling it 'a diversion'. Because of his belief that invasion was not necessary he never targeted aircraft factories—no German town associated with fighter plane production was ever bombed—yet it was essential, of course, that the Allied air forces not be denied air superiority over the Luftwaffe during a land invasion. That superiority was achieved not by the Harris policy but by men of the Royal Air Force in the fighter planes which intercepted enemy bombers.

Cox tries hard to be even-handed but nevertheless describes Harris as 'dogmatic', 'rude', 'suffering from tunnel vision' and holding an unbalanced view about the importance of attacking real military targets. He also hints that Harris was devious and distorted facts as when he claimed the Air Staff had agreed with him about the central importance of destroying German morale.

According to a German author cited by Cox, Winston Churchill supported Harris at first but then dropped him and dissociated himself from a policy of bombing German cities simply for the sake of inducing terror. After seeing photographs of Dresden when the city had been obliterated Churchill is said to have asked: 'Gentlemen, have we become beasts?'

Could German civilians have surrendered? Anyone can surrender to soldiers on the ground but it is impossible for targeted civilians (or soldiers) to surrender to air crews flying 100's or 1,000's of feet above them. Only those in command can parley with forces that attack from the air, and then only through the men who ordered the attack. It follows that talk about breaking the will of a civilian population doesn't make much sense.

Hitler himself never issued orders to surrender, nor, it seems, did he ever consider doing so. In the end he committed suicide and left the German people to their fate. Admiral Doenitz, his second-in-command took over and surrendered almost immediately.

After the war the new British Prime Minister, Clement Attlee, elevated a number of military leaders (including Bernard Montgomery for instance) to the House of Lords. According to the German newspapers cited by Cox he 'refused' to ennoble Harris.

In 1992 a statue to Harris was unveiled outside the Royal Air Force church (St. Clement Danes) in London in defiance of direct appeals from Germany not to do so (Cox/Harris, 1995, pp. x, xi). The monument has been attacked physically by English people and in print by German newspapers. One such paper said its construction was a revenge taken by veterans who resented being condemned by public opinion after the bombing of Dresden.

Bishop George Bell

Complaints about Arthur Harris's programme came from those who believed precision bombing would be more effective, for example many members of the Air Staff and several air crews — though the air crews, of course, had to obey orders anyway. Members of the other military forces, the Navy and the Army, believed Harris's policy, which mimicked Hitler's 'Gott straf England!' would not be more effective than the German bombing of London.

Others had moral objections to targeting civilians. George Bell, Bishop of Chichester, Cosmo Lang, Archbishop of Canterbury and John Collins, Air Force Chaplain at Harris's station, all strenuously opposed Harris.

On February 9 1944 Bishop George Bell moved in the House of Lords that the Government be challenged on its policy of bombing cities rather than military targets. He agreed, of course, that the Luftwaffe had already bombed many centres of civilian population, including Belgrade, Warsaw, Rotterdam, London, Portsmouth, Canterbury and Coventry. But he argued that Britain should not imitate Hitler's Germany — a move somewhat reminiscent of Xerxes' refusal to imitate the Spartans. In his address to the House of Lords he concentrated on the moral odiousness of area bombing but also mentioned practical points, noting that bombing residential centres wasted ammunition which should have been aimed at arms factories and thereby put at risk the lives of air crews for no military reason. His speech ran as follows:

> If long-sustained and public opposition to Hitler and the Nazis is any credential I would humbly claim to be one of the most convinced and consistent anti-Nazis in Britain. But I desire to challenge the government on the policy which directs the bombing of enemy towns on the present scale, especially with reference to civilian, non-combatants and non-military objectives ... in anything I say on this issue of policy no criticism is intended of the pilots, the gunners, and the air crews, who, in circumstances of tremendous danger, with supreme courage and skill, carry out

the simple duty of obeying their superiors' orders ... At the outbreak of war, in response to an appeal by President Roosevelt, the governments of the United Kingdom and France issued a joint declaration of their intention to conduct hostilities with a firm desire to spare the civilian populations and to preserve in every way possible those monuments of human achievement which are treasured in all civilised countries ... explicit instructions were issued to the Commanders of the Armed Forces prohibiting the bombardment of any except strictly military objectives (Bell, *Hansard (Lords)*, February 9, 1944).

Unfortunately the Government of the United Kingdom had added a proviso to the effect that if the enemy failed to observe similar restrictions then the Governments of the United Kingdom and France reserved the right to take all such actions as they may consider appropriate. Bishop Bell remarked that even in this proviso the distinction between military and non-military objectives is accepted as a genuine one, as is also clear from international law and the fundamental principles accepted by all civilized nations.

Bell went on to quote a number of civilized sources including the following: first, the Hague Convention of 1907; then a work by A.L. Goodhart, an Oxford Law don who wrote that any direct attack on non-combatants is an unjustifiable act of war; then a French jurist, M. Bonfils, who asked a sarcastic question which Bishop Bell quoted: 'If it is permissible to drive inhabitants to desire peace by making them suffer, why not allow pillage, burning, torture, murder, rape?'

Bell noted that the policy of total obliteration of residential areas was openly acknowledged by Sir Arthur Harris and that Harris's targets included towns with no military potential of any kind. He condemned the policy for its blindness to human psychology, its inability to reckon with moral and spiritual facts, its forgetfulness of the ideals which inspired British resistance to Nazi Germany, its refusal to understand that the progressive devastation of cities threatened the roots of civilisation. There will be a long-term harvest, he said, of terrible desolation.

Cosmo Lang, the Archbishop of Canterbury, made a speech in which he clearly intended to support his colleague of Chichester though his effort might seem rather muted to post-war readers.

Viscount Fitzalan of Derwent, who appears to have been a rather Woosterish man, declared himself to be an out-and-out bomber and hoped that many more aerial attacks would be made on enemy cities. He went on to make some strange remarks about the character, career and safety or otherwise of the Pope and ended by demanding that Rome not be bombed because of its cultural and historical importance.

The Secretary of State for the Dominions (why he rather than someone representing the Foreign Office?) answered on behalf of the government with a brief statement to the effect that the Royal Air Force did not engage in terror bombing. Bell replied politely to the obvious lie and withdrew his motion. An important point was made by the bishop when he remarked that terrible methods of war are not adopted in historical isolation. Their defenders appeal to precedents and the new methods are later cited as new precedents for perpetrating deeds of appalling inhumanity.

Bell was proved right quite soon when Arthur Harris in his book *Bomber Offensive* defended his decisions by citing what he (wrongly) took to be a precedent. He said that all wars caused civilian casualties adding that the victors' blockade of Germany after the first world war caused nearly 800,000 deaths. He ignored the fact that the blockade was perpetrated in peace time, after the Armistice (Harris (2), 1995).

The order to drop phosphorous bombs on Dresden created a new precedent which perhaps partly explains why the American fire bombs dropped on Tokyo were not condemned. Those attacks in turn gave President Truman a reason, or an excuse, to order that atomic weapons be aimed at Hiroshima and Nagasaki.

Hiroshima, Nagasaki

The decision to use atomic bombs on Japan might not have been taken if America and Britain had agreed to accept conditions of surrender.

The policy of unconditional surrender was adopted almost by accident. In 1943 there was a conference at Casablanca attended by F.D. Roosevelt, Winston Churchill and Josef Stalin. President Roosevelt urged that Germany and Japan be made to surrender unconditionally, an idea that Churchill rejected. However at a press conference Roosevelt referred to a policy of unconditional surrender as if it had been agreed on and Churchill felt he could not publicly oppose his colleague (Finnis *et al.*, 1986).

Germany surrendered on May 8 1945. The Allied leaders met at Potsdam in July and issued a Declaration regarding Japan which made no reference to unconditional surrender. The Declaration did however list some non-negotiable terms; Churchill, who argued for more flexibility, was over-ridden once again. The non-negotiable terms did not mention the future of the Emperor.

The Japanese leaders were divided on surrender but decided that if unconditional surrender were to be demanded they would not comply. Soon afterwards Japan asked the Soviet Union to negotiate peace terms on their behalf. The message was intercepted by the United States.

On July 29 1945 Japan rejected the Potsdam Declaration.

General Eisenhower tried to persuade President Truman to demonstrate the power of the atomic bomb by dropping one on a target where it could do no or little damage. Truman rejected the proposal because fire bombs had earlier been dropped on Kobe, Tokyo, Nagoya and Osaka without apparently inducing a mood of surrender. Eisenhower, though, thought it clear that the Japanese would soon surrender anyway, basing his opinion, presumably, on the fact that they had asked the Soviet Union to negotiate peace terms.

Eisenhower said later that he hated to see his country to be the first to use such a weapon, yet like other Presidents during the Cold War he allowed his staff to threaten Soviet Russia with nuclear annihilation. The likely reason is that between 1945 and 1989 American leaders — and Russian leaders too — were under immense pressure from their military, political and scientific advisors.

When Eisenhower reached the end of his second term as President he issued a warning to the people of the United States. He said that the policies of their country were coming under an increasing and increasingly ominous influence from what he described as 'a military-industrial complex' (Eisenhower, 1965).

On August 6th 1945, eight days after Japan rejected the Potsdam Declaration, the first atomic bomb was dropped, on Hiroshima. On the same day the American government issued a statement describing Hiroshima as 'an important army base'. On August 9th President Truman said that Hiroshima was a military base chosen to avoid as far as possible the killing of civilians .

When the bomb fell on Hiroshima the Japanese leaders pleaded only for the life of the Emperor. Their appeal was not accepted and on August 15 a second atomic bomb was dropped, on Nagasaki. Japan surrendered unconditionally on the same day. The United States installed General Douglas MacArthur as military ruler of Japan and allowed the Emperor to remain.

Four years after the war ended the 1949 Geneva Convention was signed and ratified by 147 nations including Great Britain, the

United States of America, and the Soviet Union. It was noted in chapter 5 (*op. cit.*) that part IV of that Convention includes a section, Article IV, according to which signatories must agree to disseminate the text of the convention as widely as possible in their respective countries and in particular to include the study thereof in their programmes of military and if possible civil instruction.

It seems rather a pity that Article IV did not suggest politicians and scientists also be made to study the text of the Convention. Jonathan Glover says in his book *Humanity* that the scientists who worked on the bomb and the politicians who decided to use it behaved throughout as if walking in their sleep.

Chapter 7
All-out War and the Ordinary Soldier

Accursed be he who first invented war
(Christopher Marlowe)

Soviet soldiers in Afghanistan

In 1978 there was a communist coup in Afghanistan followed in late 1979 by an attempted Muslim anti-communist coup. The Soviet Union then sent in 30,000 troops, a number which eventually grew to 100,000. America, China and Saudi Arabia all supported the Muslim (Taliban) side and sent aid consisting in the main of arms and technical (military) advisors.

By 1981 the fighting between Soviet communists and Afghani Muslims had led to a stalemate. The Russian leaders announced that Soviet troops would be withdrawn soon though in the end they did not leave until 1989. By that time the Soviet Union had installed a pro-communist collective government led by Mohammed Najibullah. The collective was called the Peoples' Democratic Party and was supported by Russian troops. That government collapsed in 1992, less than three years after the Russians had left. It was replaced by a coalition representing various extremist elements. Western sources said that fifteen thousand Russian soldiers died in the fighting and 37,000 were wounded. The number of Afghans killed was estimated at one million.

In 1989 or 1990 Svetlana Alexeivitch, a journalist, conducted interviews of 'Afgantsis', veterans of the 1979–1989 war (Alexeivitch, 1992). The title of her book, *Zinky Boys,* comes from the name Soviet soldiers gave themselves and their dead comrades after learning that men killed in the war were sent home in zinc coffins and buried at night. Although parents were told of the deaths and were presumably allowed to attend the funerals they were not permitted to see the bodies of their sons. Causes of death were often said by officials to be malaria or typhoid. Surviving soldiers believed, or knew, that in some cases the coffins would not contain complete or even semi-complete bodies but lumps of flesh and shattered bones — or even just a military uniform and a few handfuls of earth. No casualty figures were published in Russia.

Conscripted men and volunteers were informed that the aims of the invasion were to introduce socialism, build houses, instruct the people in new farming techniques and generally modernise the country for its own benefit. When the young soldiers arrived in Kabul they saw posters which said: 'Communism — Our Bright Future !' Their families were always told that their sons had volunteered though not many did in fact volunteer after the first few years.

In the 19th century British attempts to conquer Afghanistan did not go well. Afghan fighters and their womenfolk were notorious for ruthlessness and brutality. For example after battles the women sought out wounded enemy soldiers and castrated them. When the Afghans captured wounded men during their anti-Soviet war of 1979–89 they cut off their hands and feet and applied tourniquets so the captives would not bleed to death. Presumably they sometimes continued the old practice of castrating enemy fighters. In the circumstances it is perhaps not very surprising that Russian soldiers accepted the commands of their NCOs, which as well as the usual Soviet demand for total obedience, included such instructions as: 'forget your conscience, you have no right to a conscience.'

The Russians took no prisoners.

One Soviet soldier said to Alexeivitch: 'You shoot first and find out later if it was a woman or a kid.' Another told her: 'I shot up an Afghan wedding. I got the happy couple, the bride and groom. I'm not sorry for them.' A nurse said: 'Often our soldiers massacred a whole village. I remember one little girl lying in the dust like a broken doll with no arms or legs.' A Soviet officer returned from the war explained that killing people had become a pleasure, he said he wanted to go on doing it. Some veterans insisted they felt proud about kicking children to death. Like American soldiers in Vietnam the Russian fighters made necklaces of dried human ears.

Following the usual communist practice Soviet army instructors and officers ordered young men to inform on one another — not a good way to encourage military comradeship. Matters were made worse by the shameful bullying, incompetence and corruption at all levels of Russian military and civil authority. The men in command treated soldiers as nineteenth century landowners had treated their serfs so it is not surprising that some officers and non-commissioned officers died in action as the result of being shot in the back. Medical equipment was inadequate or was stolen by members of the invading forces and sold in market places in Kabul. One nurse said Russian officers had drunk up all the surgical spirit in her hospital. Opium, of course, was readily available in Afghanistan and perhaps helped men to fight without too much fear. Blankets and other army issues were stolen and exchanged for opium.

The young soldiers were amazed to find that primitive Afghan shops and markets had goods unobtainable in the Soviet Union; not only luxuries like watches and perfume and jewellery but also weapons greatly superior to the Russian issue. For the Afghan military force, the Taliban army, had been supplied with equipment from the United States and Pakistan and Britain. Looting took place, of course, but was re-looted from returning soldiers by greedy Soviet customs officers.

It is surprising that such a regime and such a badly-equipped army was able to defeat the German Wehrmacht in 1944–45. The reason must be that defending a homeland is a much more serious business than invading a neighbour.

From the London *Daily Telegraph* in June 2005:

> Sixteen years after the last Red Army tank left Afghanistan three ghosts of the Soviet Union's 10-year occupation are still hiding among the country's northern hills. ... Until 1981 Naseratullah was a Red Army officer called Nikolai. Nikolai, Rahmatullah and Amintullah ... are the last survivors of five Soviet soldiers who were captured or deserted, converted to Islam and fought with the mujahideen against their former comrades ... one soldier, Nikolai, said he served for three months before deserting in 1981 after witnessing a massacre of more than 70 civilians at the village of Kaligai.

American soldiers in South-East Asia and Iraq

On March 16 1968 an American military unit attacked My Lai, a village in Vietnam, and killed all the inhabitants, about 400 people. Some soldiers later said they were told the villagers were Viet Cong fighters, others were told, they said, that the civilians were Cong supporters. It turned out that the victims were old men, women, and small children. When the news finally got back to the United States some people were very shocked. They could not understand why young men reared in the free world treated Vietnamese civilians in much the same way that Nazi soldiers had treated Jews.

The power of words is immense. Most human beings, especially young ones, are easily moved by propaganda. Hitler came to power in 1933 and within seven years or less his speeches and those of his propaganda minister Joseph Goebbels had convinced thousands upon thousands of young Germans that killing Jews was a military duty.

The American soldiers who devastated My Lai were mostly aged between 18 and 20. They had been reared during the Cold War period when American citizens and the citizens of allied nations were bombarded by political speeches about the evils of 'commies' at home and abroad. Political speeches in the free world are not quite as poisonous as those to be heard in unfree countries but they certainly have an effect. Killing 'commie' women and children must have seemed *almost* all right to many of the teenage soldiers at My Lai. Lieutenant Calley, the leader of the assault, repeated words which he had probably heard from Cold War speeches made in his homeland; he said that American soldiers were not sent to Vietnam in order to kill *people* but were sent there to kill an *ideology*. In spite of which killing people, any people, was exactly what he ordered to be done in My Lai.

Lieutenant Calley was the only man to be court-martialled as an outcome of the massacre. It was known that he had already committed similar crimes such as shooting an old man after throwing him into a well, and he repeated the performance in My Lai when he disposed of a small baby he saw crawling away from the slaughter. Calley was not brought to justice until 1971. At his court-martial he was sentenced to life imprisonment with hard labour but three days later President Richard Nixon ordered he be released from prison pending an appeal. He then spent nearly three years in a bachelor apartment at his base at Fort Benning where he was often visited by a girl friend. After noticing that he was kind to his dog the girl friend told inquisitive reporters that she knew 'deep down' that he would not hurt anyone.

In 1974 Calley was released on parole after a judge ruled that 'War is war and it is not unusual for innocent civilians such as those in My Lai to be killed.' The learned judge ruled that Joshua's storming of Jericho was similar to the storming of My Lai and did not fail to learnedly point out that Joshua was never court-martialled: an interesting appeal to precedent and as it turned out an entirely successful one. On the other hand the good judge did not remember that the Book of Joshua, unlike reports about events at My Lai, makes no mention of living people being scalped nor does it say that little children were raped and sodomized before they were killed.

After his release Calley moved to a small town in Georgia where he was still living in 1992. He refused to talk about the past and according to one interviewer appeared to feel no guilt. But some of the other soldiers involved felt terrible remorse (Bilton and Sim, 1992).

One such was Robert T'Souvas, who was moved to a base in Korea where for a time he tried to wear an armband reading: 'Ashamed of American Murders'. The armband was removed by military police. After leaving the army T'Souvas became a drop-out living under cardboard and would have drunk himself to death had he not been murdered by another drop-out.

When another soldier, Paul Meadlo, lost a leg in Vietnam he decided he was being punished by God for the things he had done in My Lai.

Varnardo Simpson was aged 18 at the time of the attack. After the war he became delusional and believed that the people of My Lai were not really dead but were coming back to kill him. When his own young son died in a car accident he held the boy in his arms — and said: 'his face was the same face as a child I had killed. And I said "this is the punishment for killing the people I killed."' (Bilton and Sim, 1992, p. 6).

Medical treatment, which went on for a long time, did not help Simpson. In the 1980's he was living alone in a house with locked and barred doors and windows and according to an interviewer his eyes were puffy with perpetual crying and his body never stopped shuddering. Simpson told the interviewer that he wanted to die in spite of his belief that on Judgement Day he is certain to be sent to everlasting damnation. His fate gives good reason to reject Freud's idea that after a war the surviving soldiers return to their families 'joyous and unconcerned'. It is quite possible that some of the other men who obeyed Lieutenant Calley suffered similar though less spectacular feelings of guilt and fear.

According to a news report from Iraq, American soldiers about to return from the war there are being 're-programmed by therapists in the battle to retain sanity'. The report explains just how and why as follows:

> It is time to go home for US marines who stormed Fallujah last year, killing more than 2,000 insurgents in house to house fighting ... Brains are being re-programmed, from kill-without-

hesitation mode to one more attuned to hugging wives, paying bills and drinking beers at parties in the back yard ... group therapy in confessional sessions is the Marine Corps's new remedy for the mental scars of battle ... sixteen per cent of army personnel who served in the invasion of Iraq in 2003 report combat mental illness ... therapy sessions are now compulsory ... One group was asked: 'what would you do if you're in a bar and someone made disparaging remarks about the war in Iraq?' The answer came back: 'Smash him [i.e., the "someone"] over the head with a beer bottle.' ... During the coming months America will discover how many men can follow the official advice ... [which is to] simply walk away (*Daily Telegraph*, March 7 2005).

Chapter 8

War and Science

> *It is of little use trying to suppress terrorism if the production of deadly devices continues to be deemed a legitimate employment of man's creative powers.*
>
> (E.F. Schumacher)

Scientists and war

It is thought that Leonardo da Vinci drew up plans for an underwater ship but destroyed them when it occurred to him that submarine vessels could be used in war to attack an enemy's shipping. Presumably he had some opinions as to what constitutes unjust conduct in war.

It is unlikely that any of Leonardo's patrons could themselves have invented or built a submarine, or a new gun, or indeed any other reasonably complicated device. It not likely that many Presidents or Prime Ministers or Generalissimos known to history could have invented or built such items; Benjamin Franklin, an early President of the State of Pennsylvania, is one of the very few possible candidates in this context. Since some discoveries are useful and some are surely harmful, scientists on occasion carry the moral responsibility of harming people to order, that is, on the orders of politicians. Such moral responsibility is rarely if ever mentioned either by scientists or by politicians.

Aeroplanes

The men who invented and built the first aeroplanes were not much like Leonardo, they had no thoughts about the possible results of their work. It could be said that the future fate of civilians in wartime was sealed when the aeroplane was invented. Small aeroplanes were used by Britain to suppress anti-colonialist risings in the early part of the 20th century when air-crews were ordered to drop fire-bombs on recalcitrant native villages. However, the first aerial strike to make headlines all over the civilised world was the bombing of the Basque capital Guernica, an undefended city in Northern Spain. The attack was carried out by the German Luftwaffe after an appeal from General Franco and remains to this day a notorious example of terror tactics. After the practice run in Spain Nazi Germany soon adopted a policy of aiming bombs directly at civilian targets: Warsaw, Belgrade, Portsmouth, London, Coventry and Canterbury were all hit by the Luftwaffe. Arthur Harris, 'Bomber Harris', commander-in-chief of the Royal Air Force between 1942 and 1945, retaliated by organising massive bombings of German civilian centres. Aerial bombardment has an important role in America's war in Iraq. According to a news report published on 29/10/2004 in the London paper, *The Independent* an estimated 100,000 Iraqis had been killed in the war up to that date. On the same day *The Guardian* estimated, or guessed, that more than half the dead must have been women and children.

Chemical warfare

Mustard gas was synthesized in 1860 by Frederick Guthrie but its use in war did not come about until 57 years later. Two German scientists, Lommel and Steinkopf, who presumably for reasons of German national security were referred to collectively by the sinister acronym LOST, developed a process for mass producing the gas as a weapon (http//www.answers.com/topic/mustard-gas — accessed on 13/12/05). The process was carried out by the Bayer company and employed in the first world war. It was first directed against Canadian soldiers, in 1917. The French and British retaliated by developing the same gas, using it in 1918 to break through the Hindenberg Line. Chlorine gas and phosgene were also used in that war.

Mustard gas has made several re-appearances since 1918. Mussolini's forces used it in his aggressive war against Ethiopia in 1923–26, Soviet Russia used it in parts of China in 1930, Japan used it against China for 8 years, from 1937 until 1945. Egypt employed it against North Yemen in 1963–1967 and Iraq first used it during its war against Iran (1984 to 1988) and then against the Iraqi Kurds in 1988.

Napalm is made of petrol ('gasoline') mixed with other substances to form a jelly. The first attempts to create it needed rubber as a component and were not 'satisfactory'. In 1942, a Harvard scientist, Dr Louis Fieser, working with a team at the American Army Chemical Warfare Service, discovered how to make a usable rubberless jellied gasoline compound. It is highly inflammable ('flammable') but also slow burning and is designed to stick to any target it comes into contact with (http//www.medicine.com [*re* napalm] — accessed on 13/12/05). It was used in the second world war in the bombing of Dresden, also against Japanese cities, and later by the United States' Army in Vietnam. A news photograph of a small naked Vietnamese child covered with napalm and screaming down a village street convinced not a few Americans that their government had led them into a very cruel war.

A scientific experiment

On 16/11/2004 the London *Daily Telegraph* ran a story about a death which had occurred in 1953 in a British research establishment:

> A young airman who died in secret nerve gas experiments at Porton Down, the Government's chemical and biological warfare research establishment, was unlawfully killed, an inquest jury found yesterday. The verdict (was) delivered half a century after Leading Aircraftman Ronald Maddison died ... He was 20 when he stepped into a sealed gas chamber at Porton Down (and) died in agony minutes later when sarin gas was dripped onto his arm. Although Britain was not at war at the time the Home office ordered that Maddison's inquest be held in secret, on grounds of national security. His father John was sworn to secrecy. The official verdict was death by misadventure. Michael Cox, who also volunteered to attend Porton Down, actually saw Maddison die. In 2004 he described Porton Down as 'the most closed society you had ever come across ... lots of people were working on secret projects ... there were high walls guarded by War Office military police'.

Maddison believed he was taking part in an experiment to find a cure for the common cold. Many other servicemen and women who were also told they were participating in experiments to find a cure for the common cold were exposed to CS gas, mustard gas and hallucinogens. In 2004 Lord Justice Woolf quashed the original verdict into Corporal Maddison's fate. He said it was 'a death which occurred at the hands of the State'.

Engineers and physicists

Werner von Braun (1912–77), the physicist who invented the V2 rocket aimed at civilian centres in England during the second world war was captured by American forces in 1945 and taken to the United States where he helped to develop ways of sending satellites into space and new rockets for making moon shots. In 1969 when he was congratulated on the forthcoming landing of men on the moon he asked as a favour that the event be accompanied by a performance of Richard Strauss's work *Thus Spake Zarathustra*, a tone poem set to Nietzsche's words in the book of that title. Von Braun's request was happily accepted. It is unlikely that he can have forgotten the fact that Hitler's ideas about the German Master Race were in part inspired by Friedrich Nietzsche's doctrine of the Superman.

During the second world war President Roosevelt invited American scientists to develop an atomic bomb. He feared that Hitler's scientists were engaged on the same task and the fear was well-grounded, though as it turned out the work planned by German atom scientists was frustrated by the Norwegian resistance movement (see below, chapter 15).

Roosevelt's decision resulted in fame for Edward Teller, one of the two or three men known thereafter as '*the* Father of the Atomic Bomb'. Were they proud of that title one wonders.

German scientists made several contributions to nuclear physics and some were awarded Nobel Prizes for their work. In 1942 Werner Heisenberg (1901–76), well-known to philosophers and physicists as the propounder of the Heisenberg Uncertainty Principle, was put in charge of the programme for developing a German atomic bomb (Rhodes, 1988). The dangerous work of handling uranium was carried out by women held in the Sachsenhausen death camp, in other words, by Jewish slave labour. Did Heisenberg know that? Did he know where his instructions were going? Did he know who had to carry them out? Or was he kept in the dark about those details?

It is possible that Heisenberg hoped for patriotic reasons that an atomic bomb would help Germany win the war. On the other hand he is said to have told people in America that he deliberately slowed down work on the project because he wanted the Allies to defeat Germany. In other words he denied having supported Hitler. Well, he would, wouldn't he ...

Perhaps a clue to his intentions might be gleaned from the fact that early in the war he travelled to Denmark in order to meet the Danish physicist, Niels Bohr (1885–1962). The reasons as to why he wanted to meet Bohr have not become clear, mainly because the two men gave somewhat different accounts of what they talked about. It is known, however, that Heisenberg questioned Bohr about various technical and scientific problems and then gave him a sketch of the reactor he himself was in the process of designing. Bohr, an anti-Nazi, escaped from Denmark in 1943, taking the sketch with him.

Did nuclear scientists in the West warn politicians and civilians about the dangers of radioactive fall-out? William Penney, the scientist in charge of British atomic tests at Maralinga in the Australian desert, said he did not give any order to make sure the soldiers guarding the area had protective clothing and agreed that they had been exposed, unprotected, to radiation from the tests. When questioned about this by an Australian newspaper some time later he acknowledged the facts, laughed lightly, and said 'I was rather a strange young man in those days'.

Physicians and psychiatrists

It is well-known that psychiatrists in the Soviet Union connived at the incarceration of dissidents, treating them, or rather mistreating them, with electric shocks and chemical 'therapy' in a kind of game-playing, a lucrative game about 'curing or controlling severe cases of insanity'.

The Lancet (Britain) of August 28 2004 contains a paper by Stephen Miles which has 59 references in its two and a half pages. It is based on American sources: the Senate and House Armed Services Committee, the Department of Defense, the Office of the Deputy Assistant Attorney General, memos to President George W. Bush, the United States Military Police website and the United States' military Field Manual for 1987.

Miles' paper shows that medical personnel — physicians, psychiatrists and nurses — have co-operated with torturers in the prisons at Abu Ghraib and Guantanamo. He alleges that the current Bush administration has been reluctant to admit that the Geneva Convention on Prisoners of War applies to al-Qaeda forces because al-Qaeda is not a signatory to the Convention (*The Lancet*, 21/8/04 8). It would seem to follow that al-Qaeda could in its turn now excuse its refusal to treat American and other captives correctly, firstly because it is not itself a signatory to the Convention and secondly because the United States has rejected the relevance of the Convention to the present bout of fighting. Such a discussion however is not likely to happen because al-Qaeda presumably recognises only Koranic law which some say allows the killing of anyone who refuses to convert to Islam. A Declaration signed in Tokyo in 1975 included a passage about medical personnel which was re-emphasized by the World Medical Association in June 2004. The Association stated that military doctors are bound by medical ethics and must not countenance, condone or participate in torture or in degrading procedures even during armed conflicts and civil strife.

The London paper *The Week*, which provides readers with digests of articles from news sources all over the world, contained an item on 15/1/2005 taken from *The New England Journal of Medicine* . The journal had interviewed more than two dozen military personnel and concluded that American doctors helped develop a number of interrogation techniques (including for example sleep deprivation) at the prison in Guantanamo Bay, techniques which the *NEJM* said 'breached the laws of war'.

Many similar news stories from 2004 and 2005 stated that no medical personnel serving in Iraq had ever issued any reports about the treatment of prisoners at Abu Ghraib prison until an investigation was ordered into happenings at that place; and also that at Guantanamo Bay the prisoners' medical records were shared with their interrogators despite objections from the International Committee of the Red Cross.

Abu Ghraib was closed down in April 2006.

Science and politics

Does a sense of responsibility require unusual intelligence? Surely not; it is imagination not braininess that is needed if a person is to develop the idea that some of the things he contemplates doing, or has already done, might be blameworthy.

If imagination is in short supply we can anyway ask: Would politicians and scientists act differently if they could see, close up, the results of their decisions and their research? Or are they too ambitious or too wedded to the doctrine of 'anything goes' to be moved by anything they know or see?

Seeing the results of actions and decisions has on occasion affected some people very strongly. Napoleon III called off a war after witnessing the aftermath of the battle of Solferino. Quite a few nuclear physicists felt an anguished responsibility for the closing events of the second world war and for the radio-active fall-out sent into the atmosphere by weapons' tests during the 1940s, 1950s and 1960s. Visual evidence of burning cities and dying children affected many other people too.

The Vietnam war ended with victory for the Viet Minh and the Viet Cong probably because they were fighting in their own country. The end result was also partly due to the fact that young men in the United States refused to obey the draft and, also, too, because they and other Americans were horrified by news photographs of the effects of the defoliant Agent Orange (deformed babies) and the effects of Napalm (children being burnt alive).

There is no evidence that the chemists who invented mustard gas and napalm and Agent Orange ever felt repentance. On the other hand there is no evidence that they didn't. Let us suppose the men responsible for inventing those weapons could have looked into the future and seen the actual results, or even just photographs of the results, of their proposed research. Might they then have taken up different projects or turned to cultivating their gardens? One rather hopes so.

In the West many scientists opposed the political and military decisions which led to the continued testing of bigger and bigger nuclear weapons. They then had to suffer the consequences of opposition, consequences which included accusations of treason quickly followed by loss of employment. In Russia dissenting scientists were imprisoned or exiled to distant parts of the Soviet Union.

Frederic Joliot-Curie (1900–1958), son-in-law of Pierre and Marie Curie, worked in their laboratory in Paris and with his wife Irene Joliot-Curie discovered the possibility of artificially creating radio-activity. For this work Frederic and Irene were awarded the Nobel Prize for chemistry in 1935. During the second world war they supported the French Resistance and joined the local communist party. In 1946 Frederic was appointed to the French High Commission for Atomic Energy, at that time devoted to peaceful uses of radio-activity. He was dismissed from the post in 1950 when the government diverted the commission to the task of developing atomic weapons. It seems likely that he was sacked before he had time to resign.

Marie, Frederic and Irene, all died of cancer caused by exposure to radiation.

Otto Hahn (1879–1968) showed that nuclear fission is possible. He was shattered by news of the atomic bombs dropped on Japan because he felt he was responsible for those events—as indeed he was in part. In 1957 Hahn was one of the instigators of *The Gottingen Declaration,* a document stating that none of its eighteen signatories would co-operate in a possible German project for developing nuclear weapons.

Julius Rotblat who was born in Poland in 1908 moved to Liverpool University in 1939 and then to America where he participated in the atomic bomb project. According to an obituary notice published in the London *Daily Telegraph* in August 2005 he joined the Manhattan Project at Los Alamos in 1944 but resigned after hearing an after-dinner speech by a serving American General. The General said the real purpose of developing an atomic bomb was to subdue the Soviet Union, then an ally of Britain and America. Rotblat was shocked. According to the same obituary the authorities in the United States of America suspected him of being a communist spy but were unable to find any evidence against him. After returning to England he worked only on medical and other peaceful applications of atomic research. He joined with other scientists in the Pugwash conferences organised by Bertrand Russell (see chapter 22).

The American physicist Robert Oppenheimer (1904–1967) joined the atomic bomb project in 1942 and was director at Los Alamos between 1943 and 1945. He became chairman of the Advisory Committee of the United States' Atomic Energy Commission in 1952. Oppenheimer believed that America and the Soviet Union should arrange to hold joint control of atomic energy. He also unsuccessfully advised the American Government not to develop the hydrogen bomb. In 1953, during the McCarthyite witch hunts, he was accused of having communist sympathies and was suspended from secret nuclear research by a security review board. The real reason for his suspension, according to George Kennan (1984, chapter 9), was that he opposed the continuing military use of atomic energy.

After witnessing the 1945 atomic bomb test on July 16 Oppenheimer said: 'I remembered the line from Hindu scripture ... "I am become death, the destroyer of worlds".' In a lecture given in 1947 at the Massachusetts Institute of Technology he made the following ambiguous assertion: 'The physicists have known sin; and this is a knowledge which they cannot lose.'

Philip Morrison (1915–2005), a polio victim who lived to a great age, worked first with Enrico Fermi in Chicago, then later at Los Alamos. He helped to assemble the bomb intended for Nagasaki and in 1945 was one of the scientists who flew over Hiroshima to assess the damage there. He was horrified at what he had done and began to campaign for the bomb to come under international control. In 1953 he was summoned to appear before Senator McCarthy's Senate Security Sub-Committee where he was accused of being a secret communist (see below, Appendix ii). McCarthy's investigations were eventually abandoned but according to an obituary in *The Daily Telegraph* (London) on April 27 2005 Philip Morrison remained under suspicion for the rest of his life.

Andrei Sakharov (1921–89) took part in developing the Soviet hydrogen bomb but later announced his opposition to nuclear tests. In 1980 he was accused of treachery and exiled to Nizhni-Novgorod, causing influential individuals in the West to carry out a long campaign for his release. He was freed shortly after Mikhail Gorbachev succeeded Leonid Brezhnev in 1985. Sakharov was awarded the Nobel Peace Prize in 1975 when he was still in exile.

Some scientists have been real traitors, as was the case with David Greenglass and possibly also the case with Ethel and Julius Rosenberg. Julius Rosenberg was a member of the signals corps in the United States' army and Ethel's brother Greenglass worked at Los Alamos. In 1951 Greenglass was found to have passed atom secrets to the Soviet vice-consul *via* an intermediary; he and the Rosenbergs were accused of treason. Greenglass turned State's witness in return for a promise that he would not be executed. He told his interrogators that his sister and brother-in-law were the go-betweens who had carried atom secrets to a Russian diplomat. Julius and Ethel were convicted of treason and in 1953 executed in Sing Sing prison. There were world-wide appeals against the sentence, and especially against the execution of Ethel, the mother of two young children. Some protesters believed Greenglass had bought his life by incriminating people he knew to be innocent.

Is it possible that some scientists, horrified at the prospect of a nuclear war, decided that a policy of deterrence could only work if the Cold War protagonists were equally matched? Is it possible that some traitors set out to make the balance as even as possible by working for the seemingly weaker side, the side with fewer or less powerful weapons?

Science and truth

Although scientists are not necessarily more ethical than other people they can incur very heavy moral responsibilities. When the researches of physicists and chemists get mixed up with war and when the practices of psychiatrists and physicians become entangled with politics it can happen that they forget to ask themselves any questions about outcomes or about morality. And although scientists seek the truth they don't always tell the truth, as can be seen from what happened at Porton Down and at Maralinga. Even in peacetime some scientists are willing to carry out researches involving horrible outcomes. An example was described by the London *Daily Telegraph* in a report with the headline: 'US developing "pain from a distance" weapon'. The item was written by the newspaper's science correspondent, Nic Fleming:

> The US military is developing a weapon that delivers a bout of excruciating pain from afar to use against protesters and rioters. Documents released under the United States' Freedom of Information Act show that scientists have received funding to investigate how much pain can be induced in individuals hit by electromagnetic pulses created by lasers without killing them. Due to be ready for use in 2007, the Pulsed Energy Projectile weapon (PEP), is designed to trigger extreme pain from a distance of one and a quarter miles. It fires a laser pulse that generates a burst of plasma — electrically charged gas — when it hits something solid. Tests on animals showed that it produced 'pain and temporary paralysis'. Pain researchers told today's *New Scientist* magazine that the technology could end up being used for torture and that it was unethical.
>
> Andrew Rice, a consultant in pain medicine in London, said, 'I am deeply concerned about the ethical aspects of this research.'

Chapter 9

Deterrent Threats in the Cold War

> *The nation which indulges toward another an habitual hatred ...*
> *is to some extent a slave.*
>
> (George Washington)

The Cold War and deterrent threats

The 'Cold' War between the Soviet Union and the Western powers began soon after the capitulation of Japan. The Western powers feared Russia and that is what explains why James Byrnes, public official, Supreme Court Judge and Secretary of State under Presidents F.D. Roosevelt and Harry S. Truman, said that possessing and demonstrating the bomb would make the Russians more manageable in Europe.

As the Cold War grew more ominous the nations of the world began to issue very blood-thirsty threats. The threats discussed below are described by Finnis *et al* in their book *Nuclear Deterrence* (Finnis *et al.*, 1987, pp. 3–35).

Britain, France and America all expressed a willingness to see the annihilation of Soviet Russia and hinted that if necessary they would be prepared to destroy most of the rest of the world as well. In Britain on January 1st 1946, i.e., less than seven months after the end of the second world war, the newly elected Prime Minister, Mr Clement Attlee, said the West must be prepared for aggressors who have widely dispersed industries and populations. In order to be effective against the Soviet Union it was necessary for Britain to have a considerable number of atom bombs.

In March 1955 the next Prime Minister, Winston Churchill, said the value of having hydrogen bombs lay in the fact that such a policy would increase the deterrent effect on Soviet Russia by putting her scattered population on an equality with the small densely populated island of Great Britain.

Giscard d'Estaing, President of France 1974–81, was reported as saying that France's aim if attacked was to destroy an area of the enemy equivalent to the total area of France (*Figaro*, 12/12/1983) and in 1977 the Prime Minister of France, M. Barre, said:

> We have adopted and will maintain the most effective and *least costly* solution, the only one that really matters, that is, to threaten the great urban centres of the adversary nation, where the greatest part of its *demographic* and economic strengths are concentrated.

(My italics. No doubt attacking 'the demographic strengths' is the same thing as attacking 'the largest possible number of people'.)

British politicians had at first expressed a rigid determination to bomb centres of population but later began to engage in a certain amount of devious mealy-mouthed double-talk. Perhaps they were worried about the large numbers of protesters marching to and from Aldermaston (below, chapter 20). Or perhaps the French view of Albion as perfidious is partly right. However that might be it came about that in 1958 the British defence secretary referred ambiguously to 'retaliation' as 'the massive nuclear bombardment of *the sources of power* in Russia' (my italics). But what *are* 'the sources of power'? The army? The factories? The Kremlin? Or the population?

American threats included the following: On September 30 1950 President Truman said that the only deterrent his country could present to the Kremlin is the evidence America will give that it will or may make *any* of the critical areas it cannot hold to be the occasion for a war of annihilation against Russia. President Eisenhower, in his State of the Union Address of January 9 1958 said that the United States intended to face an aggressor with the prospect of the virtual annihilation of its own country (Kennan, 1983, p. xvi).

Under President J.F. Kennedy American statesmen and scientists explored the possibility of creating tactical nuclear weapons which could be used in a series of graduated responses beginning with relatively small strikes on real military targets but leading if necessary to the destruction of cities. On the other hand, Kennedy's defence secretary, Robert McNamara, said in September 1967 that America must:

> ... retain the capability of destroying the aggressor to the point that his society is simply no longer viable in any meaningful 20th century terms.

In October of the same year he expanded his point:

> ... we must be able to absorb the total weight of a nuclear attack on our country — on our retaliatory forces, on our industrial capacity, *on our cities and on our population* — and still be capable of

damaging the aggressor to the point where his society would simply be no longer viable in 20th century terms.(my italics).

John Finnis and colleagues remark:

> The positive character of final retaliation, after one's own society has been crushed, was thus officially expressed with a vividness not often found in such official statements.

McNamara claimed that the damage which the Soviet Union would probably consider unacceptable would involve:

> ... the destruction of between one quarter and one-third of the total population and up to two-thirds of the industrial capacity.

Possible nuclear futures which were not officially discussed in the West in the 1960's include:

(1) A future in which Europe, and possibly even the United States, suffered enormous devastation *and* eventual Soviet domination, or

(2) A future in which both sides suffered a degree of destruction which exceeded the one envisaged by political and military advisors, or

(3) The death of Planet Earth.

Some people, though not many politicians or soldiers, were beginning to discuss the third possibility.

The uselessness of nuclear weapons: George F. Kennan

George F. Kennan, an American diplomat and historian, was posted to Moscow in 1945 as deputy Ambassador and became Ambassador there in 1952. After leaving the diplomatic service he joined the Princeton Institute for Advanced Studies as professor of history (1956-1977). His book *The Nuclear Delusion* is a collection of speeches, broadcasts and essays on nuclear weapons and the Soviet threat in which he attacked America's political thinking on deterrence, arguing that nuclear weapons are obviously suicidal. The earliest item reprinted in the book dates from 1950 and the latest from 1983.

Kennan believed that the use of atomic bombs against Japan in 1945 should be seen as 'a regrettable abnormality'. To rely on such weapons in military planning, he said, is to commit very serious errors.

In the book's 'Introduction' (written in 1958) Kennan suggested the public position of the American government ought to be as follows:

> We deplore the existence and abhor the use of these weapons and we have no intention of initiating their use against anyone. We would use them with the greatest reluctance and only if we were forced to by the methods used against us ... (Kennan, 1987, p. xvi).

In a later chapter, based on a paper of 1982, Kennan argued that it is going to be necessary to make governments and peoples understand that warfare, a 'time-honoured institution of the European past' is no longer a rational way of settling disputes between governments. It is not even a rational means of self-defence.

Kennan also believed that there is no evidence at all that the Soviet Union was seeking world domination by military means. He pointed out, however, that everyone in the government of the United States disagreed with his views. The scientists working on the American nuclear project also disagreed with him.

After leaving government service in the 1950s Kennan continued to argue against nuclear armaments in lectures in Princeton in 1954 and again in his Reith lectures for the BBC in 1958. In the Reith lectures he suggested that America should seek an agreement with the Soviet Union according to which both sides would withdraw all their troops from Europe, Germany would be de-militarised (which ought to please the Russians who had suffered great losses during the German invasion), and would be re-unified (which ought to please America and Germany itself).

Kennan said that these suggestions, made during President Truman's second term, provoked a violently adverse official reaction, especially in the United States and Germany but also elsewhere in the West.

He deplored what he called the 'hysterical war scares' expressed or promoted by political leaders, especially during the Truman presidency. In his opinion the scares, though without rational foundation, were genuine from an emotional point of view. Some politicians were provoked by a need to feel virtuous in comparison with real or imaginary external enemies, others were panicked by the hostage crisis in Iran (see chapter 12 below), others again were seriously upset by America's frustrations in Vietnam. Last but not least the political leaders of the United States were badly spooked by the behaviour of American students who refused to accept the draft to serve in Vietnam ('Heck, No, We Won't Go'). Many ordinary citizens, too, found the students' behaviour inexplicable.

In 1977 Kennan expressed disgust at the fact that the anti-nuclear SALT treaty of 1975 was ratified by the Russians but not by his own country. He wrote:

> The principle of first use (of nuclear weapons by the United States) is more deeply embedded in the theory and practice of ourselves and our allies than it was in 1950 (Kennan, 1983, p. 106).

He claimed that the American assumption that the Soviet Union had belligerent intentions was either completely incorrect or at best highly improbable. He himself, he said, had never seen any evidence that the Soviet leaders seriously considered attacking Western Europe at any time during the years after the second world war.

George Kennan held that nuclear weapons have no rational purpose; they are sterile and suicidal and completely useless.

He also believed the history of the United States in the twentieth century showed that whenever the country was involved in any kind of military project it became seriously disoriented. For example (he said), during the first world war the United States decided that the Menshevik parliamentary party in Russia was an enthusiastic supporter of the British and American war effort, an opinion which he, Kennan, regarded as wholly incorrect and even absurd. America also thought the members of the Bolshevik party were German agents — also not true of course. Kennan described the 1920 decision to send three American battalions to Archangel under a British command as pathetic, confused and myopic.

All hostility to Russia mysteriously disappeared after Pearl Harbour but had returned, apparently spontaneously, by the end 1945. Anti-Soviet anxieties rose to a peak in 1950–53 under President Truman and another peak under President Reagan. Kennan suggested that there was more than one reason for American anxiety and hostility. He listed the following sources:

First, the American belief that Soviet ideology positively demanded an attack on the West. The fact that Russia was capable of launching an attack on the West was taken as proof of its intention to do so, an inference which according to Kennan involved a considerable degree of disorientation.

Secondly, unreal anxieties about Russia's intentions were stimulated by the mundane fact or tradition that peace-time military training and planning requires teachers and planners to assume the existence of an adversary with evil intentions. Otherwise the plans make no sense. Kennan remarked that to feel frightened of an adversary merely because he has been depicted as an enemy *in lessons* and *in the imagination* is another sign of serious disorientation.

Thirdly, the hostility between the two countries had an inner competitive momentum.

Finally, Western political leaders regarded as somewhat left-wing — for example Labour politicians in Britain, the Democrats in America — were frightened of being labelled 'soft on communism'. It was because journalists and others regarded President Richard Nixon as a hard-line right-winger that he was able to visit communist China. It also explains, perhaps, why Nixon was not seriously criticised for making the humiliating decision to abandon South Vietnam. On the other hand some conspiracy theorists think the Watergate crisis would not have dislodged Nixon from the White House if it had not been preceded by those two foreign policy decisions.

Kennan believed that the Khrushchev era, especially the years 1955-60, provided a favourable situation for improving the relations between East and West. Khrushchev, said Kennan, was 'primitive and naive ... a peasant parvenu', quite different from Stalin, who was imbued with 'crafty cynicism'. Khrushchev's speech at the 20th Communist Party Conference dealt Stalinism a blow from which it never recovered, yet in Kennan's opinion America insisted on behaving as if the Korean war (1950–54) was still in progress and as if Stalin had never died.

In 1981, during the presidency of Jimmy Carter, the United States and the Soviet Union were on a collision course and a nuclear holocaust seemed to be on the agenda.

Kennan agreed that there were real difficulties in Khrushchev's idea of detente. He noted that compromise is alien to the Russian character and that gross intolerance has always existed at every level of Russian society. Nevertheless the Russian character does not explain why the communist Russia decided to develop nuclear weapons. The explanation had to do with fear. Soviet Russia was very frightened of America.

The ethics of deterrence: John Finnis and colleagues

John Finnis and his colleagues Joseph Boyle and Germain Grisez described the Western nuclear arsenal as of 1986, the year before the publication of their book *Nuclear Deterrence*: They listed:

One thousand American missiles on standby, each one between 50 and 100 times more powerful than the Hiroshima bomb and two hundred and fifty American aeroplanes carrying the bombs. In Germany there were fifty American missiles which could be delivered by rockets. Thirty-five American submarines were equipped with nuclear missiles; half the vessels were on patrol and half on full alert. There were more such bombs on surface vessels. America also had an Early Warning System. Great Britain had one hundred aeroplanes and four submarines for delivering its nuclear bombs. France had four submarines and 18 land-based missile stations.

Eisenhower introduced a system whereby the President of the USA was accompanied everywhere by a courier with a satchel containing war orders in code and a 'decision book' containing pre-planned presidential options and 'go-codes' for major attack options including pre-emptive strikes, selective attack options, military targets only options and regional options aimed at armies invading at different points. By 1986 more than 700 Soviet cities with populations of 25,000 were targeted by one or more of the above options. The total number of targets in the Soviet Union was 40,000 and the major attack option targeted the largest 200 cities. Crews were given the codes but not the names of the targets so did not know where their missiles would be falling.

By 1986 Soviet Russia had its own nuclear arsenal but Finnis *et al* do not give a detailed account of that arsenal. Presumably the details are hard to come by.

According to George Kennan Henry Kissinger became worried about the permanent state of high alert and about the uncertainty as to who would give orders if the President was incapacitated by illness or killed by an enemy strike. Kennan states that before the Soviet Union acquired its own nuclear weapons a certain American military commander said he would not wait for presidential permission to launch missiles if Russia looked like invading its neighbours.

Finnis *et al* claim that there are two equally bad utilitarian considerations concerning the rationale of deterrence, one for it and one against. Supporters of the first consideration say that the evil of the world or a large part of the world being conquered and governed by Soviet Communism would be a worse evil than a nuclear war. Supporters of the second say a nuclear war would be a worse evil than conquest and rule by Soviet Communism. According to Finnis and his colleagues consequentialism cannot tell us how to decide between the two evils. These philosophical critics believe that to rank the results of future enormous disasters, was, and is, quite impossible. Such rankings could not be based either on facts or on reason. In the world of politics they were based on guesswork and propaganda and what Robert McNamara eventually came to describe as 'institutionalised hostility'.

Stalin not immortal

Looking back to those days it seems that the Western powers became subject to certain unthinking assumptions including a seemingly unconscious assumption that the actions and policies of Stalin's successor and of all the successors of his successor would resemble Stalin's own. This thinking, insofar as it was empirical, was based on too few cases, indeed on only one case, namely the fact that Stalin's policies were like those of Lenin (only even worse). Otherwise the reasoning was *a priori* guesswork.

In those days the leaders of the West in sometimes spoke as if they thought Stalin would live forever, they seemed to forget that one day he would have to die and be buried and be eaten by worms. They did not remotely guess that soon after his demise his statue would be removed from Russian cities, they did not guess that the towns of Stalingrad and Leningrad would eventually be re-named. There is even talk nowadays about removing Lenin's body or effigy from its shrine in Red Square and having it buried (if a body) or destroyed (if made of wax).

Stalin's immediate successors were Nikita Khrushchev and Georgi Malenkov. Malenkov disappeared after a short while though it seems he was not imprisoned or exiled. Khrushchev began to made anti-Stalin speeches almost at once. And he had a very different personality from his predecessor. Khrushchev ordered that Solzhenitsyn be released from prison and ruled that his *samizdat* novel, *One Day in the Life of Ivan Denisovich* could be published. Mrs Khrushchev reported that the KGB people subjected 'us', that is, the Khrushchev couple, to enormous pressure and pestering in unsuccessful attempts to reverse the relaxation of bans on previously forbidden books.

Khrushchev was succeeded, that is to say he was painlessly ousted in a surprisingly non-murderous and non-Stalinist manner, by Leonid Brezhnev, described by George Kennan as 'outstandingly cautious' in his dealings with the West. Other authors have called Brezhnev 'an inert member of Russia's Gerontocracy'.

Mikhail Gorbachov, quite youthful in comparison with some of those who went before, was both cautious and creative. He said he wanted *Glasnost* ('openness') to govern the relationship between his country and the West. Moreover he was alleged to have had romantic feelings about Britain's Conservative Prime Minister, Mrs Margaret Thatcher.

George Kennan said that some of the predictions made in the West about the probable behaviour of Soviet Russia immediately after the second world war were *a priori* deductions from Marxist-Leninist theory. If that is so it is clear that those making the predictions held a faulty interpretation of the Marxist-Leninist gospel. According to that gospel capitalism is doomed to be overthrown by a workers' revolution rather than by war.

Whether Soviet policy after the second world war was really inspired by Marxism is another matter.

Western analysts also pointed to the fact that the land mass comprising the Soviet Union, a large part of the most extensive land mass in the world, had increased in size during the war because of Russian incursions into its Western and Northern neighbours. In fact though the incursions were not the result of Soviet *aggression*, the facts are much more complicated than that. The Baltic States, Latvia, Lithuania and Estonia, were all ceded to Russia in the 18th century; Germany invaded them during the first world war; then they became independent nations after Germany's defeat in 1918. In August 1939 the Nazi-Soviet Pact was negotiated by Ribbentrop and Molotov and one of its provisions was that the Baltic States and Eastern Poland would thereafter belong to Soviet Russia. However the Pact lasted less than two years and when Germany invaded Russia in June 1941 the German armies occupied the Baltic States on their way to Leningrad. The Germans cannot have read von Clausewitz who said in chapter 17 of *On War* that the vast area of Russia means the country can not be conquered. Field Marshal Bernard Montgomery, on the other hand, might well have studied von Clausewitz for when he was asked what he took to be the first law of war he said 'The first law of war is: "Do not invade Russia."'

During the second world war Stalin told Churchill that he wanted to incorporate the Baltic States into the Soviet Union and apparently this was agreed. It was also agreed that Poland should remain within the Russian sphere of influence. Churchill insisted that the Poles be allowed free elections but of course they weren't.

The German retreat from Russia began after the battle of Stalingrad in 1943. Leningrad was besieged but never taken. By 1945 Hitler's forces had been driven all the way back to Berlin by the Soviet army and all the way from the English Channel to the outskirts of West Berlin by British, Canadian, French and American forces.

In short, the Baltic States were occupied by Russia as the result of a wartime agreement and the East European States were occupied by right of conquest (if there is such a thing). It can hardly be said that the situation was the ultimate result of Marxist theory. Nor of course does it follow that the Soviet system was not malignant *qua* system.

Another reason the Western nations feared an attack by the Soviet Union and therefore opposed nuclear disarmament was their belief that strong nations have a natural tendency to take advantage of weak or peaceable neighbours. There is of course plenty of historical evidence for that proposition, including the excursions of Napoleon and President McKinley's God-demanded seizures of Spanish territories in North America, the Pacific Ocean and the Carribean. Was Russia about to behave in that way immediately after the second world war ? George Kennan said he had not been able to find any evidence that Stalin ever made explicit or even implicit threats against the West.

It seems probable that people in the West would regard the effects of a nuclear war as much worse than Soviet domination if they had ever been in the unlikely position of experiencing (and surviving) both. The preference would not be due to cowardice but in part to the idea that the survival of the human race was something to be thankful for and in part, perhaps, to a well-founded belief that Westerners in general would not behave as slavishly as many Russians did under Lenin and Stalin. Westerners trapped in tyrannical regimes would surely include some who would try to undermine the tyranny in cunning ways, rather as the French Resistance and the people of Norway did when invaded by German Nazis. Westerners under tyranny might well follow the examples set by courageous Russians like the poet Anna Akhmatova, the novelist Alexander Solzhenitsyn and the scientist Andrei Sakharov.

In any case it seems clear that the threat of nuclear retaliation, if carried out, could not achieve the end for which the threat was made. Revenge is not the same thing as deterrence.

On choosing between evils

Finnis and his colleagues hold that Soviet domination might indeed be a worse evil than nuclear war. They conclude that the West had a practical moral obligation to keep the nuclear deterrent and to be prepared to use it. Then they point out that having an obligation is not the same thing as being obliged to do *anything at all*, however barbaric, as a means to its fulfilment. It follows that there are situations in which it is morally forbidden to fulfill an obligation. That proposition might seem paradoxical yet a simple example shows that it is true. Parents have a moral obligation to feed their children but they are morally forbidden to kill some *other* parents in order to steal food from *their* children. What is morally obligatory is not morally permissible in every possible circumstance.

Could the situation just described be interpreted as a case of choosing between two evils? Or a case of choosing between two sins?

Choosing between evils is a fact of everyday life and does not of itself always involve sin. Catholic teaching follows the 16th century Council of Trent in ruling that although it is not possible for human beings to avoid all sin there are no situations in which someone is ineluctably forced to choose between sins. It is always possible to resist the temptation to sin (Council of Trent, 1858).

The conclusion drawn by Finnis *et al.* is related to the moral necessity of deterring enemies. There was, perhaps, a moral requirement to oppose the Soviet Union but to do so by destroying between a quarter and a third of its population was not permissible. Nor was it permissible to make genuine threats to carry out that kind of destruction.

The authors finally argue that innocents must not be killed or targeted because life is both a basic human good and also the necessary condition for all other human goods. Most of our rational activities are designed to promote or save or protect or hand on human life. A threat to destroy whole cities or to engage in a nuclear 'city-swap' is a threat to destroy most or all human life and the good things dependent on human life.

In Britain the Conservative Party has been clear about its policy. During the election campaign of April-May 2005 Nicholas Soames, an elderly Tory Member of Parliament, told the *Daily Telegraph* that his party, if elected, would spend £2.7 million more on front-line defence between 2005 and 2008 than Labour intended to spend. He pointed out that the Conservatives have always been publicly and consistently committed to the nuclear deterrent.

The election was won by the New Labour party. However Prime Minister Tony Blair is equally clear about his own policy and has implied that he will not allow parliament to thwart his wishes. On October 19 2005 he informed the House of Commons that he is in favour of updating the country's nuclear weapons system, adding that although he will arrange for the matter to be discussed in Parliament he will not permit it to be put to a vote (*Daily Telegraph*, October 20, 2005).

PART III
TERRORISM, TORTURE, HOSTAGES

Chapter 10

Terrorism

> *Your terrorist is my freedom fighter*

('Anon' is responsible for this saying and for the falsehood it implies.)

Politics and terrorism

When used by politicians and other politically motivated people the word *terrorism* has very little descriptive meaning. It is merely a term of abuse or what once upon a time used to be called an 'emotive' word. The primary function of an emotive word is to inflame passions, usually hostile passions, with the result that description lies in the background. The descriptive function of the word *terrorism* lies so far in the background that not even jurists are always able to provide it with a coherent explanation. As to politicians, it must be very difficult for anyone to persuade them to explain what they mean by terrorism, the only way they handle the word is as an anathema.

A prime example of emotive thinking can be found in the words of Alan Dershowitz, an American academic author who in 2002 published a book called *Why Terrorism Works* (Dershowitz, 2002). Dershowitz explicitly declines to offer a definition of terrorism, not even a working definition nor even an *ad hoc* stipulative definition. By refusing to say what he means he leaves open the question as to which people count as terrorists and thereby allows every government and every rebel group to decide for itself what does so count. The questions as to who shall be captured and who shall be punished are thereby also left open.

The main reason why Professor Dershowitz cannot give a clear account of terrorism is that he makes no effort to describe the character of actions. He claims that the anti-Nazi resistance movements in France and Norway engaged in terrorism even though he agrees that they only attacked military and police targets. But he doesn't say *why* he thinks the people in the resistance movements were terrorists. He rejects dictionary definitions of terrorism which mention the deliberate killing of innocent civilians as a criterion because in his view the bombing of Dresden, and of Hiroshima, and of Nagasaki were definitely not acts of terror. Here he does in fact say *why* he thinks what he thinks: he thinks what he thinks because 'most people' would agree with him. Now, that is a piece of localised Orwellian *groupthink*. Most people where? In Japan? In Germany?

Dershowitz's approach to the notion of terrorism is an outstanding example of what happens to concepts when they have been infected by political viruses: they become meaningless pieces of mental elastic.

Types of terror

Terrorism is thought to be difficult to define but if we conclude that definition here is *impossible* it will also be impossible to decide on the moral status of people and groups who have been accused of engaging in it.

Any attempt at a definition of the word should recognise that the phenomenon is multi-faceted and needs a multi-faceted description. There is nothing wrong with multi-faceted accounts, seemingly untidy definitions are all right if they suit the term defined.

The essence of terrorism does not consist solely in its aims, which usually have to do with political or religious change. Political change is also a possible aim of legitimate elections and religious change is a possible aim of preaching. Terrorism is typified by its practices more than by its hoped-for results.

Reigns of terror: any government which engages in torture or imprisons its subjects without trial is a reign of terror. There have been plenty such in the history of the human race.

Wars of terror: can warfare be terroristic? Yes, it certainly can. During the second world war some politicians and military leaders said quite openly that they intended to inspire terror in enemy civilians and indeed proceeded to do so. Area bombing is terroristic.

Non-government practices sometimes held to be terroristic include insurgency, attacking civilians, hostage taking, torture, political assassinations, and destruction of property. To my mind insurgency as such is not terroristic whereas torture is. Hostage-taking is a borderline case, much depends on how the hostages are treated and only a little on the aims of the perpetrators. Yet aims are relevant, after all hostage-takers include criminals whose aims are merely financial; and if they treat their victims cruelly that counts as serious bodily harm or torture but not as terrorism.

Destruction of property is sometimes terroristic and sometimes not, it depends on what kind of property it is and also on the motive. Blowing up an empty bank building is not necessarily a cause of terror whereas a political or military threat to destroy an important item of cultural heritage, Vatican City for instance, or the great buildings in the centre of Washington, would inspire fear (as well as rage). It would cause fear for, on behalf of, a way of life, a culture.

On definitions

Definitions explain the meanings of words and since the world contains very many different entities there are very many different words and several different kinds of definition.

Definitions in geometry, such as 'a *triangle* is a plane figure enclosed by three straight lines' are short and accurate and work well for any intelligent learner with an adequate visual or tactual imagination.

Definitions in the life sciences — in botany for example — are traditionally constructed by referring to genus, species, sub-species. This kind of explanation is short and accurate but doesn't get very far without supplementary descriptions and visual aids. 'A tiger is a carnivorous feline mammal' won't always enable a traveller in the jungle to avoid the creature, he needs to know that the carnivore hunts by day, sometimes attacks human beings, is stripey and is large enough to eat him. For practical purposes it is necessary to know what the animal actually looks like.

Some words cannot be defined solely with other words: *red* for instance requires ostensive definition, definition by pointing.

There are hundreds of words which can only be defined by means of fairly wide-ranging explanations. Some of these describe ambiguous nouns (for example *revolution*), others designate abstractions (for example *politics, philosophy, memorability*), others again refer to complicated concrete objects (e.g. *cathedral, osteopath, camera obscura*).

It can be seen from the above that not all good definitions, not even all the very best dictionary definitions, are tidy. One reason is that a too tidy definition will surely be ambiguous if the word it defines has a number of different — though related — senses. The problem can be reduced, at least to some extent, when untidinesses, such as lists and explanations, are allowed.

How to define the word terrorism

In attempting a definition we might begin by considering the way the term is used in everyday speech and thereby construct an *ordinary language definition*. However, since everyday speech is influenced by political speeches and newspaper editorials any ordinary language definition is likely to be horribly muddled, for the reasons mentioned earlier in this chapter.

We might next try to devise a philosophical definition. But looking for a philosophical definition could involve relying on philosophy professors and unfortunately such people tend to disagree with one another. Thus Noam Chomsky seems to think that governments are the main, perhaps the only, perpetrators of terrorism, and, as is well known, he places the rulers of the United States, his own country, at the top of the list of such wrong-doers. Other authors hold that terrorism is best understood as a type of unjust rebellion. Others again, including Professor C.A.J. Coady believe terrorism is evil by definition but what definition do they have in mind? Coady also says terrorism can consist in damaging property: perhaps he is right about that but doesn't it depend on who owns the property, and on what kind of property it is, and on how much is destroyed, and on whether terror is likely to be caused? Before the first world war British suffragettes destroyed letter boxes, the property of the government, surely that essentially non-terrifying kind of non-lethal action wasn't terrorism (Coady, 1985).

Several national and international bodies have attempted to define terrorism.

The phenomenon has been defined as *criminal acts directed against a State* – which appears to rule out reigns of terror (perhaps deliberately) but not acts of war perpetrated by army rebels like General Franco. It is unsatisfactory for the further reason that although revolutionary war can be terroristic not all revolutions have unjust aims.

Another definition: terrorism is *a variety of criminal activity involving the unlawful use of force* – another unsatisfactory account. The repetition of the reference to illegality is otiose, the specific variety of criminality is left in doubt, and there is no mention of methods.

A third attempt states that terrorism is *a use of force by revolutionary organisations*. This too ignores reigns of terror (perhaps deliberately) since it refers only to acts of war made by citizens against the State. It thereby fails to cover acts of war of the kind that destroyed the New York World Trade Center and the Pentagon in Washington, deeds carried out by private individuals from a foreign country, possibly

Saudi Arabia. The definition also ignores the question of methods. Moreover whoever framed it failed to notice that their words *a use of force by revolutionary organisations* applies to the American Revolution of 1775–76.

Terrorism has been described as *the use of violence for political ends including the use of violence for the purpose of putting the public or any section of the public in fear*. This does at least mention fear but otherwise is too broad. Whoever drafted it must have been in a careless frame of mind because his definition covers far too many different kinds of behaviour, including the State's own punishment of treason.

These unsatisfactory accounts suggest that we might do better to look at history and etymology and then stipulate as to how much emphasis is to be placed on each. Some stipulations will yield a relatively narrow list of terrorisms, others a relatively wider one. This approach to the task of devising a useful account of the nature of terrorism is the most promising. It might start with and build on a disjunctive description which at the same time rules out obvious non-starters — such as laws which explain how and where and when convicted criminals are to be punished:

> Terrorism can be a way of ruling or a way of fighting; in either case it involves a coercive use of force or terror-inspiring threats of force against ordinary non-criminal civilians. As a way of ruling it is employed by governments and government agencies. In other situations it is used by anti-government forces such as local rebels or foreign agents. Hence it can be aimed either at sustaining a *status quo* or at achieving political or religious change. It can also be motivated by revenge for real or imaginary injustices.

That is still too tidy because different agents of terror sometimes act together even when not sharing precisely the same aims as when members of the German Baader-Meinhof gang co-operated with elements of the Palestine Liberation Organisation in order to hi-jack an air France plane and take it to Entebbe (see chapter 12, *ibid.*). Then again if news reports are correct some agents of violent political change pay ordinary criminals to help them, as when the Mafia was paid to co-operate with terroristic government agencies working in South and Central America or when in 2005 the Irish Republican Army paid professional thieves to steal millions of pounds sterling from a bank. However these occasional slight complications are perhaps not very important.

The *Oxford English Dictionary* has the following brief but historically accurate short definition:

> *Government by intimidation as carried out by the party in power in France 1789-1794. Generally, a policy intended to cause terror in those against whom it is adopted.*

Two hundred years ago the word *terrorism* did indeed refer to actions carried out by governments whereas the second, more general, meaning was probably developed in the years following the European revolutions of 1848. In those decades self-confessed terrorists claimed their aim was not to run a revolution but to kill tyrants.

A multi-faceted definition

Here is an explanatory account of terrorism as derived from the foregoing considerations:

Terrorist actions or threats must terrify or tend to terrify their targets. Broadly speaking the motives of terrorism are either political or religious or both. The killing of politicians for other reasons can be included since they are presumably targeted because of their status as powerful public figures. Some terrorist actions aim to harm and terrify innocent people, in other words harmless people.

There are three strands or varieties of terrorism:

First, State terrorism as practised by the Nazis against the peoples the Germans had conquered and also against certain German citizens; and as directed at the Russian people by Stalin's government; and as used against Chinese and Korean citizens and military captives by the Japanese armies at the behest of the Japanese government during the 1930s and 1940s.

Second, political assassination of individual rulers and other important people. Victims of political assassination include Alexander II of Russia, murdered by an anarchist in 1881; the Archduke of Austria, killed by another anarchist in 1914; Leon Trotsky, murdered in Mexico on Stalin's orders in 1940; and Airey Neave MP, assassinated by means of a bomb in the car park of the House of Commons in 1979, a deed for which the Irish Republican Army is believed to have been responsible. President Abraham Lincoln was presumably murdered for political reasons, so too was President McKinley. Non-political assassins of politicians include the man who killed President Garfield, a man variously described as a disappointed place-seeker and as a madman inspired by an imaginary divine mission. Perhaps he was both those things. The British Prime Minister Spencer Perceval was assassinated in 1812 by a bankrupt businessman who was later hanged for the crime.

As to President Kennedy, people say 'Choose your own conspiracy theory'. One colourful but in parts somewhat improbable account was written by a Mafia man in an autobiography, probably ghosted by a journalist, in which he claimed that he and his colleagues were responsible not only for the assassination of President Kennedy and his brother Robert but also for the earlier death of Kennedy's erstwhile girl friend, Marilyn Monroe. Miss Monroe, said the author, was killed on the president's orders, while the president himself and his brother both met their deaths because they had not paid a debt of honour owed to the crime bosses who had fixed the 1960 election by cooking the Chicago vote.

Salvador Allende (1908–73), was elected President of Chile in 1970 on a left-wing agenda but overthrown in 1973 in a military coup after which General Pinochet was installed. Pinochet is currently awaiting trial for his alleged abuse of human rights. News reports at the time agreed that Allende died after falling from a tall building. Some journalists said it was suicide, others that he was thrown out by Pinochet's men accompanied by members of the American Central Intelligence Agency (CIA). The only elements of the explanations which are obviously correct is that he died during a *coup d'etat*. General Pinochet's later victims included several members of the clergy both high and low.

To my mind Pinochet and his cohorts were terrorists on two counts, political assassination and maltreatment of the populace.

Thirdly, there is revolutionary group terrorism, a contemporary variety of organised violence carried out by *ad hoc* or organised non-government groups inspired by political or religious beliefs or by a desire for revenge for real or imagined wrongs. The Palestine Liberation Army and the Irish Republican Army are entities of this kind. Both are associated with attacks on harmless civilians. The PLO also hi-jacks aeroplanes and ships and one of its branches persuades young people to carry out suicide bombings.

The Ku Klux Klan, the IRA and the Ulster Defence Association clearly count as terrorist organisations. However although the KKK received widespread support in the Southern States of the USA and although the IRA has had a lot of money from Catholic Irish folk in Boston — and for all I know the UDA might also have had some monetary support, from American Protestants — it is indeed the case, of course, that none of these organisations are literally sponsored by the White House. So they don't count as State terrorism. The label *group terrorism* is more accurate.

Although the Ku Klux Klan and the Irish Republican Army and the Ulster Defence Association would doubtless like to kill a lot of important politicians they mostly attack civilians. The IRA also attacks soldiers sent to defend those civilians.

We can conclude that judgments about the morality of otherwise of terrorism will be impossible if the term is allowed to remain woolly. On the other hand the word *terrorism* need not remain in clouds of wool because it can be defined as follows:

> Terrorism has distinguishable varieties: it is either State terrorism (including wars of terror) involving cruel treatment of critics and/or ordinary civilians; or political assassination carried out by individuals; or cruel activities by groups aiming at political or religious change; or a combination of these. It is called *terrorism* because cruelty causes terror.

However since the word *terrorism* — for reasons of blind inchoate political prejudice — is always a contested term the account just proposed will doubtless be found objectionable by many people.

Chapter 11
Torture

The greater the power the greater the abuse
(Edmund Burke)

Torture and the Inquisition

Torture is a practice used both to extract information and to punish people for heresy (*thoughtcrime*). Heretics who confessed to the Italian and Spanish Inquisitions were imprisoned or burnt; surely burning people alive because they have wrong ideas is torture *qua* punishment.

Lucius III (Pope 1181–1185) formulated a programme for suppressing heresy which was established as a permanent entity in Italy by Innocent IV (Pope 1243–1254). Innocent sanctioned the use of torture to extract confessions. Alexander VI (Pope 1492–1503), the Borgia who ordered the burning of Savanarola, also told the Inquisition in Germany to proceed 'with the utmost severity' against witches.

Those overseeing torture had to be familiar with doctrines and heresies, in other words they had to be priests. Paul IV (Pope 1554–1559) headed the Italian Inquisition himself and is said to have acted with inhuman severity (Kelly, 1988).

Protestants as well as Catholics tortured people. In Massachusetts at the time of the witch hunts suspected women were pressed to death.

The Potala Palace in Buddhist Tibet has a windowless room once used as a torture chamber. (According to a tour guide in Lhasa. It is possible that the story is a piece of Chinese communist propaganda.)

Numberless Hindu widows were burnt alive on the funeral pyres of their husbands until British Empire-builders suppressed the practice in the 19th century.

Dershowitz on torture

In his book on terrorism Alan Dershowitz agrees the history of the word *terrorism* shows that the phenomenon was originally attributed to States but he is not interested in government terror. Nor is he interested in the Irish Republican Army or the Ulster Volunteer Force or the Ku Klux Klan. His concern is limited to the Islamic factions al-Qaeda and the PLO (Palestine Liberation Organisation).

Dershowitz says terrorism 'works because it succeeds' — which is like saying it succeeds because it works, succeeds because it succeeds or works because it works. What he means is that terrorism is rewarded. Terrorism generates free publicity for certain causes and thereby persuades governments to accept terrorist leaders as important players on the stage of international politics. Secondly, when an act of terror leads to the capture and incarceration of the perpetrators another attack by the same faction will sometimes be followed by bargaining and the release of the imprisoned men. Aeroplane hijackers, for example, have been freed after their colleagues managed to hi-jack another plane. He fails to notice that hi-jacking ceases when security checks are efficiently carried out. When was the last time an El Al plane was hi-jacked in the air? Statistics indicate that hi-jacking has been declining elsewhere too, and for the same reason.

Is it really the case that Islamic terrorism is achieving its aims? What *are* its aims? The long term aim of the only groups Dershowitz cares about is the destruction of Christian and Jewish persons and polities. As to their short term aims, well, those are not always very clear. Some terrorist spokesmen speak about avenging past wrongs, others about a desire to punish decadence, others are more or less incoherent.

Dershowitz suggests ways of making terrorism less successful and some of his suggestions are fairly sensible. On the other hand his book has become famous — or infamous — because he wants measures to deal with terrorism to include the legalisation, by and in the United States, of the torture of suspected terrorists. It doesn't bother him that such a move might require American voters and lawgivers to overturn the constitutional rule against cruel and unusual punishments. Or does that rule apply only to citizens of the USA and not to foreigners or migrants or visitors?

Dershowitz's first reason for recommending torture depends on his belief that the United States already encourages the practice. He says the USA makes torture arrangements by secretly sending foreign suspects to countries where they are tortured to extract information. He lists Egypt and Jordan and the Philippines as places whose governments are willing to help America in this way. His second claim is that torture has been practiced by American soldiers in Iraq and by American prison guards in the United States' base at Guantanamo Bay in Cuba. His third allegation is that prison guards in America itself are able to arrange for recalcitrant inmates — not terrorists but ordinary prisoners — to be tormented by other inmates with beatings and anal rape. Finally he claims that prosecutors in American courts openly hint that convicted people who have pleaded Not Guilty are more likely to suffer rape and beatings in gaol than those who pleaded Guilty. Dershowitz fails to give any references to support what he says about the courts in his country but since he was a practising lawyer before he became a professor he probably knows how prosecutors talk and behave.

Official and unofficial torture

Dershowitz's comments on the behaviour of American interrogators are un-referenced and so could be untrue. On the other hand John Finnis *et al.*, whose book contains a vast number of references, agree that the abuse of legal procedures, especially by the rich and influential, does occur in Western societies. However they point out that in the countries of the North Atlantic community the abuse does not include *official* murder or *official* torture. These authors do not contradict Dershowitz's claim that America has secret *unofficial* torture organisations (Finnis *et al.*, 1987).

It is unlikely that free citizens of the United States are tortured by their fellow-countrymen either at home or abroad. Perhaps unfree Americans are treated badly in prisons, especially if they are black, but the bad treatment is condoned by government officials rather than organized by them. Dershowitz's unreferenced allegations to what has come to be called the export of torture are supported by news items in what can probably be regarded as reliable journals and newspapers.

In *The New York Times* in March 2005, Thomas L. Friedman wrote about 'a troubling report' which he summarised as follows:

> ... 26 prisoners have died in custody in Iraq and Afghanistan since 2002 in what Army and Navy investigators have concluded were acts of criminal homicide ... 'presumably in the act of torture.'

On April 3 2005 *The Independent on Sunday* (London) reported that the American Civil Liberties Union (ACLU) had used the Freedom of Information Act to obtain documents indicating that General Ricardo Sanchez, American military chief in Iraq, had authorised the use in Abu Ghraib prison of techniques outlawed by the Geneva conventions. Do the orders of a General constitute *official* authorisation? According to the documents obtained by ACLU, General Sanchez admitted that the techniques he sanctioned 'would not be sanctioned by other countries'. When Sanchez appeared before a Congressional Committee he denied that he had ever authorised such techniques: this caused the ACLU to ask (unavailingly) that he be tried for perjury.

If the General *had* faced a court he could have appealed to a political authority, namely, Donald Rumsfeld. In late 2002 'counter-resistance techniques' approved by Secretary of State Rumsfield included the use of dogs, nudity and isolation. Is the word of a Secretary of State enough to make a decision *official*? Perhaps not but in this case Mr Rumsfield was backed up by an even higher authority for it is known that in February 2002 President G.W. Bush signed an executive order stating that the Geneva conventions on torture do not apply to al-Qaeda or Taliban detainees.

On June 23 2005, the following op-ed item appeared in *The New York Times*:

> Defense Secretary Donald Rumsfeld is considering new top command assignments that could include promoting Lieutenant General Ricardo Sanchez, the American commander in Iraq during the Abu Ghraib prison abuse scandal ... It is one of two changes being considered that would involve new posts for senior generals who had previously been ruled out because of Senate outrage over (torture in) Abu Ghraib ... the Abu Ghraib scandal provoked global outrage ... many at the Pentagon and in the military believe that the scandal may be receding in public opinion.

It seems then that Dershowitz's account of torture might not be completely inaccurate. On the other hand President Bush's refusal in October 2005 to sign up to an anti-torture convention caused another high authority, namely, a majority of American Congressmen, to insist he sign. Even Representatives from his own party, the Republicans, wanted him to sign.

Reasons, good and bad, against advocating torture

Some reasons against advocating torture refer to the fact that allied nations might disapprove. This is not a very noble reason but it had some practical relevance, especially after journalists from Britain and other European countries began to express doubts about the way the war in Iraq was being conducted. On November 7 2005 the military historian Max Hastings wrote as follows in *The Sunday Telegraph* (London):

> ... many British soldiers dislike American tactics ... a senior advisor said to me 'It is very uncomfortable to fight as partners with allies who have a completely different attitude to the value of civilian lives from our own.'

On January 12 2006 the London *Daily Telegraph* reported that a British Brigadier had accused the United States forces in Iraq of 'a catastrophic inability to understand local values', heavy-handed tactics, failure to respect the people of Iraq, and cultural ignorance and insensitivity. The Brigadier published his comments in the US army journal *Military Review* and thereby caused a backlash from its usual readers one of whom described his article as the work of an 'insufferable British snob'.

The unfavourable opinions of allies and international organisations regarding torture were mentioned by members of the current administration after the International Committee of the Red Cross visited prisons in Iraq and Guantanamo Bay and reported that prisoners were being tortured in both places. Secretary of State Rumsfield responded to American reactions to the Red Cross report by advising President George W. Bush to give some consideration to the views of other countries when over-riding the Geneva Convention on torture. But he added:

> ... nothing in this memo ... restricts your existing authority to maintain order and discipline among detainees.

A Justice Department memo sent in August 2002 to President Bush and another which went to a Defense Department working group in March 2003 distinguished torture (not permitted) from cruel, inhuman and degrading treatment (which the document said is permitted). Even so, said the memos, torture as such is permitted whenever the President of the United States sets aside the Geneva convention.

Another reason for the American government to disallow the torture of captives is the fact that there are legal experts in the United States who reject the opinions of Dershowitz and Rumsfield and the authors of the memos referred to above. Dershowitz responded to his critics by saying that if the practice of torture were to be written into law then policemen, soldiers and prison guards would have to apply to the authorities for 'torture warrants'. It would follow, he thinks, that less torture would then occur, at least inside the United States itself. Policemen make fewer house searches when search warrants are required.

It is not clear that torture is less common when it is is part of an official policy. It was not exactly rare in the days of the Spanish Inquisition.

Professor Dershowitz's reasoning glosses over important differences between having your house searched and having your body subjected to severe pain. There are no Geneva conventions forbidding policemen from conducting house searches and in the United States itself the practice is governed by laws which reflect Article IV of the Constitution. Torture is quite another matter, in civilised countries it has been regarded as a terrible moral crime for at least 150 years. Article VIII of the American Constitution, which relates to trial by jury and was ratified shortly after the War of Independence, states that 'cruel and unusual punishment shall not be inflicted ...'.

It might be possible to interpret the ban on cruel punishments as applying only to citizens of the United States. The framers of the Constitution could not, of course, forsee that after slightly more than 200 years America would be the world's sole super-power. Is it likely that the signatories of Article VIII would have excluded everyone except American citizens from its provisions if they *had* predicted the events of the 1980s and 1990s? Who can say? On the one hand the authors of the Constitution lauded human freedom even though some of them owned slaves, on the other hand it is not inconceivable that they would regard the status of super-power as undeserved, even as immoral, if the rights enshrined in Article VIII were not extended to those living under the dominance of a world government.

Dershowitz and Bentham

Dershowitz defends his ethics by assuming that Jeremy Bentham is an important authority in moral philosophy — even though he seems not to have read Bentham's works. He is only able to cite a secondary source, one probably dug up for him by a student assistant whereas a proper researcher would have located the primary source.

Dershowitz notes that Bentham supported torture on utilitarian grounds, grounds which he, Dershowitz, approvingly compares with cost-benefit calculations in economics. He takes the outcomes of correct cost-benefit calculations to be bench-marks of rationality.

His first premise is that America's right to protect itself over-rides all other moral considerations. He does not consider the question as to whether a similar over-riding right is held by all the other nations in the world. If every country comes to believe it has a right to use any means at all in self-defence, if every country thinks its own right over-rides all other moral considerations, how will that affect the future of the human race?

Utilitarians tend to argue from extreme and imaginary cases and Dershowitz is no exception. He reasons that if the United States were threatened by terrorists armed with a nuclear weapon it would be allowable, even mandatory, to extract information as to the whereabouts of the bomb by torturing captured suspects. It would be allowable, or even mandatory, to impose collective punishments on people living where terrorists live. The young children of suspected terrorists could be captured and tortured in front of their fathers in order to persuade the parents to divulge information. Children of terrorists have no special rights.

Would the legal warrants to torture suspects and their neighbours and their children be used only in one extreme case, only when terrorists issued a nuclear threat? Is it likely that America would train torturers, and enact new laws about search warrants, simply to deal with the rare occasions when a terrorist group issued a nuclear threat? How often would guerillas be in a position to make such a threat? Are search warrants issued only when *very* large quantities of bullion have been stolen? Of course not. A new law made on the basis of an *a priori* argument taken from an extreme case will not be confined to the extreme case. Laws have to have some degree of generality, they apply to more than a single situation.

Finally, is it likely that American voters would approve a decision to overturn the Constitutional rule against cruel and/or unusual punishments?

In his book Dershowitz defends collective punishment by offering the fallacious reasoning already mentioned: if something is already happening it must be all right. He says that although collective punishment is prohibited by international law it is widely practiced, including in all the most democratic and liberally minded countries. He gives no references to support his claim that such punishment is 'widely practiced' (it probably is), nor his claim that it is used by all the most democratic freedom-loving countries (it probably isn't).

The inference that torture is all right because it is already happening is a parody of rationality. The conclusion does not follow from the premise and taken separately is completely at odds with religious and philosophical ideas. Even hard line utilitarians might have reasons to condemn torture. It is very strange that a real live lawyer should propose such a flawed reason in favour of anything at all, let alone torture. In this world all kinds of bad things happen or have happened: company fraud, child abuse and the assassination of several American Presidents, but that does not mean those activities should be legalised.

Some opinions of scholars, clergy, physicians

Let us compare Dershowitz's opinions on torture with the thoughts of a Jewish scholar, a Christian cleric, an agnostic philosopher, and a war historian.

According to *The Principles of Jewish Law* (ed. Menachem Elon) the traditional sources of such law do not allow confessions as evidence in criminal cases. Although nowhere stated it is likely that the rule against confessions was due to a desire to make sure they were not extracted under torture (Elon, 1975 — item on Criminal Law). Modern Jewish law, namely the civil and criminal law of the State of Israel, is based on English law. English law does not condone torture.

In his autobiography the late Canon Collins said that no civilised person of real integrity would accept torture as justifiable in any circumstances — even to prevent a nuclear holocaust (Collins, 1966).

The distinguished Oxford philosopher Philippa Foot says in her book *Natural Goodness* that:

> ... certain actions such as torture must always and everywhere be beyond the pale ... it is only when we think as consequentialists that we go wrong ... If the frequently unchallengeable description 'torture' belongs to an action then, whatever the circumstances, it is in my firm opinion morally 'out' (Foot, 2001, p. 49).

Newspapers expressing an interest in the question of torture include the *Los Angeles Times*. One of its articles was quoted on December 10 2005 in the London paper *The Week:*

> Torture may sometimes squeeze out a drop of truth, but more often it creates a flood of dangerous misinformation ... In 2001 Ibn al-Shaykh al Libi, who was thought to be an al-Qaeda official, was captured in Pakistan, taken to Egypt and subjected to [tor-

ture] ... he 'confessed' that Iraq had offered to supply and train al-Qaeda in chemical and biological warfare. ... Libi later recanted and said he had spoken falsehoods in order to stop the torture ...

Explaining torture and torturers

Using torture to extract information is a paradoxical activity because tortured people, people in agony, will say anything they think their persecutors want them to say. Even comparatively un-intelligent folk can recognise the paradox. Why then do men engage in torture and why do professors support the practice? Getting information cannot be the only motive.

In his book *Humanity* Jonathan Glover lists countries in which torture is or has been routine; they include Argentina, China, the Lebanon and apartheid South Africa. It was in this connection that he opined that moral philosophy could be more empirical than it is.

Glover asks: Why do torturers torture? A query to which we might add two riders: Why do law professors support the practice of torture? And: Why do medical men and science professors invent new ways of causing pain? Glover's answer deals both with empirical facts and with rational morality, it is a multi-layered explanation (Glover, 1999). His diagnoses are convincing because they lie close to the surface of consciousness in virtually all human beings. In other words we know some of the answers already.

The explanation of modern torture partly has to do with the world-wide training carried out by what Primo Levi called 'the silent Nazi diaspora'. Following Levi Glover says that the torturers who worked for Saddam Hussein had been trained by communist East Germany's secret police, the Stasi, who had themselves originally been trained by Hitler's Gestapo.

Other facts mentioned by Glover include the following:

There is a sex difference in cruelty: more men engage in torture than women. Glover does not mention the chromosomal abnormality which causes some males to grow very tall and to be very violent — to be *very* male, as it were — but perhaps that abnormality is occasionally to blame. The Old Norse word *Berserker*, which appears in Icelandic folk tales, refers to unusually tall, unusually dangerous men.

There is another kind of sexual dimension to torture. There exist heterosexual men who like sex, enjoy sex, but absolutely hate women. That can be verified by anyone who cares to consider the 'lyrics' of a kind of popular 'entertainment' called Gangsta Rap.

Glover believes torturing people gives the perpetrator a delicious feeling of omnipotence. That is one reason why torturers often laugh at their victims, for laughter indicates to the sufferer that his agony is of no importance in the eyes of the all-powerful tormenter. Jokes and jollity in the torture chamber are also defensive. Mocking the victim distances the torturer's actions from his consciousness while at the same time distancing the victims from humanity. The victims are 'them', not 'us', and ready-made labels provided by politicians and newspapers are used to reinforce the distinction. The people being tortured are not *people*, they are *Communists* or *Fascists* or *Goons* or *niggers* or *terrorists* or *towel-heads* or *Yids* or *cockroaches* or *freaks*. If the torture victim is a woman it is even easier to create a distance because she is obviously not a man. To a male torturer she is already different enough to be labelled not a person but a *dog* or a *slag* or a *whore*. Glover says that when girls and women are being tormented various 'amusing' humiliations designed especially for use on females are not uncommon.

Another layer of explanation has to do with the way soldiers are trained. Carl von Clausewitz described armies as made up of automata; he believed that soldiers must learn to obey orders without asking questions; a soldier, he said, cannot be permitted to reject his officer's orders and cannot be permitted to have independent ideas about which actions are allowable and which are not. It follows from this doctrine that soldiers must try to forget civilian ideas about good and evil.

Nowadays, that is, during the twentieth and twenty-first centuries, British law follows the Geneva conventions which by implication require soldiers to disobey their officers under certain circumstances. Unfortunately the Geneva conventions are ignored by some of the other signatories.

An important layer of Glover's explanation consists in his account of the ways in which the ambience of warfare and the ambience of regular armies undermine the mixture of fellow-feeling, affection and social discipline that supports ethical standards during peace-time. Soldiers are trained in camps and — usually — at some distance from their homes. They serve in foreign countries where everything is strange, especially the speech and the appearance of the inhabitants.

Glover's multi-layered explanation of the ways in which morality is undermined during a war is surely correct. The *degree* to which morality is undermined probably depends on a number of other factors: national character, fear, propaganda, and politics. When police forces in South and Central America secretly torture people *to death* that is not motivated by utility or cost-effectivesness, it is a form of capital punishment motivated by sadism and permitted by the culture found in dictatorships.

Finally, for some torturers torture is fun. The ignorant men and women who tormented Iraqi captives must have thought everyone else would agree that such behaviour is nothing but fun. They took photographs of their behaviour just as they would have photographed one another on visits to Disneyland. And just as photos of parties and picnics and visits to Disneyland are taken home to be developed in a shop, so too the films showing how captives had been treated were ignorantly made public in the same way.

Chapter 12

Hostages and Ransoms

I was in prison and ye came to me
(Gospel according to St Matthew, chapter 25)

Hostages in Entebbe, 1976

In June 1976 an Air France aeroplane carrying 146 passengers left Tel Aviv on a flight to Paris *via* Athens when it was hi-jacked and diverted to Libya. It happened during a period when Libya's long-term leader, Colonel Gaddafi, was sympathetic to the PLO (Palestine Liberation Organisation) and other anti-Western organisations.

After leaving Libya the Air France plane turned up at Entebbe airport near Kampala, the capital of Uganda. The terrorists separated the 104 Jewish and Israeli passengers from the 42 French passengers and allowed the French air-crew and French passengers to go free. The passengers flew to France and the air-crew, fine people in my opinion, decided it was their moral and professional duty to stay with the imprisoned Jews and Israelis.

In exchange for the lives of the Jewish and Israeli hostages the hi-jackers demanded five million dollars in cash and the release of PLO and Red Army Faction fighters held in prisons in Israel, Kenya, France, Switzerland and Germany. The German Red Army Faction was a group similar to the Italian Red Brigades which later, in 1978, captured an Italian politician, Aldo Moro, and killed him. The Faction's two most prominent members, Andreas Baader (1943-1977) and Ulricke Meinhof (1934-1976) had been captured and imprisoned in 1976 and were no doubt two of the individuals whom the hi-jackers wanted to have released.

Itzak Rabin, Prime Minister of Israel, announced his country's willingness to negotiate but pointed out that the PLO and Red Army Faction captives were imprisoned in several different parts of the world so that negotiations could not be concluded very rapidly. The hi-jackers accepted his reasoning and extended their 24-hour deadline to 72 hours.

As the result of an extraordinary ability to analyse intelligence and the extraordinary efficiency and daring of its commandos the Israel Defence Force was able to secure the release all but three of the 104 hostages. If Colonel Moshe Betser's book is accurate about timing, the rescuers' task was completed with nearly 20 hours to spare (Betser and Rosenberg, 1996). The incident shows that intelligence, in both senses of the word, was much more effective than a Dershowitz 'torture warrant' would have been.

Some of the information needed for the rescue operations was obtained from Colonel Betser who had helped train the Ugandan army before being thrown out of the country by the dictator, Idi Amin; some from the Israeli firm which had designed and built Entebbe airport; some from one of the French hostages who the hi-jackers had released and sent back to Paris; and some from a Jewish woman travelling on a British passport who when the plane landed for re-fuelling in Libya pretended to be having a miscarriage. She was supported in her claim by a doctor on board the plane and was released in Libya. She immediately flew to London and contacted the Israeli Embassy.

Israeli intelligence was able to establish that Idi Amin's forces were supporting the hi-jackers and that the original four terrorists, two adult Germans and two Palestinian teenagers, had been joined in Uganda by six more supporters.

On the night of the rescue four aircraft flew from Israel to Uganda. The flight path was kept low so as not to be detected by radar. The aeroplanes carried two commando officers, Yonni Netanyahu (a brother of one of Israel's later Prime Ministers) and Betser himself together with 40 other soldiers from the commando unit. All were wearing Ugandan army uniforms. There were also doctors, medical equipment, several jeeps and a Mercedes limousine disguised to look like those used by Idi Amin and his generals.

The plane landed at Entebbe in darkness. The Mercedes car, carrying Betser, his superior officer Netanyahu and six other commandos, drove off onto the unlit runway and were immediately followed by the other soldiers in jeeps. The convoy moved at a sedate speed to the building where the 104 hostages were being held. In spite of a blunder by Netanyahu the vehicles all reached the building.

Six terrorists were killed almost at once—the other four were in Kampala. Two of the 104 hostages died in the crossfire and a third, an elderly woman called Dora Bloch, who had earlier been taken to a hospital in Kampala, was murdered the following day on Idi Amin's orders. The other 101 people were driven in jeeps to the aircraft immediately after the gun battle. Some of the Israeli commandos were wounded though not killed but their leader, Netanyahu, sustained very serious wounds and died on the return flight (Betser, 1996).

Hostages in Iran, 1979-1981

The Shah of Persia (Iran) was pro-Western and by some standards rather right-wing. However he allowed elections and in 1951 a socialist, Mohammed Mossadeq (1881-1964), who was somewhat anti-Western, became Premier. The Iranian oil industry was owned by the Anglo-Iranian Oil Company. Mossadeq wanted to nationalise the industry but when he attempted to do so in 1953 the Shah sacked him and put him in prison, allegedly at the instigation of the American Central Intelligence Agency.

In 1979 the Shah was forced into exile after being toppled by the Muslim clergy who were led, from Paris, by Ayatollah Khomeini. The Ayatollah then came home to Iran and began to accuse America of plotting to return the Shah. He and other Iranians also alleged that after the fall of Mossadeq the Shah had arranged for the CIA to train the Iranian secret police in torture practices. As a result of his preaching a large crowd of students and other young men surrounded the American Embassy in Teheran in 1979, holding the 66 occupants hostage from November 11 1979 until January 20 1981. The Embassy phone lines were cut but the people inside were sent food and other necessities and apparently suffered no ill-treatment apart from the incarceration itself. The soldiers guarding the Embassy were perhaps not treated so well.

President Jimmy Carter first tried to end the crisis by imposing economic sanctions on Iran but when that didn't work he sent in a rescue squad of helicopters. The helicopters ran into sand storms and had to make emergency landings in the desert, an outcome which caused serious damage to Carter's reputation as leader of the free world.

The Ayatollah and his followers said they were prepared to negotiate the release of the hostages but refused to have any dealings with Jimmy Carter. In 1980 Ronald Reagan beat Carter in the presidential election. The hostages were released, unharmed, on January 1st 1981.

Since that time Iran has been governed by religious Muslims of the Shi-ite persuasion.

Hostages in London, 1980

Like the guerilla armies of the SOE, Norway and Cuba (see Part IV, below), the young people who surrounded the American Embassy in Teheran were relatively benign. They did not harm their civilian hostages though it is not clear how they treated the Embassy guards who would have been patrolling the grounds of the building.

All in all the people who besieged the building in Teheran were not much like the men who invaded the Iranian Embassy in London in 1980. On that occasion six armed men burst into the Embassy building in Princess Gate and threatened to kill the 26 people in their power unless their demands were met. Two of the captives were British, one a journalist and the other a policeman who had been guarding the main door. The terrorists were Iranian Arabs demanding autonomy for their region of Persia, demands which reflected the internal power struggles following the fall of the Shah.

After six days the invaders shot and killed a hostage. The Prime Minister, Mrs Thatcher, then called in the Special Air Services (the SAS). Members of the Service got into an adjoining building without being observed and placed listening devices on the internal walls. The devices enabled them to ascertain the location and number of the Embassy's occupants. Negotiators in Princess Gate 'explained' through loud-hailers that the scuffling noises the terrorists could hear from the neighbouring building were made by carpenters and other repair workers going about their normal work. Then the SAS men climbed onto the roof of the Embassy and abseiled down the rear wall, hacked their way in through the windows and the wall, threw in stun grenades and shot dead five of the six terrorists.

The Ayatollah Khomeini thanked Mrs Thatcher quite effusively.

There were allegations in Iran that the terrorists had been backed by Saddam Hussein, the dictator of Iraq. Later in the same year the Iraq-Iran war broke out. It lasted until 1988 and was won by Iraq, partly because several nations, including the United States of America, supplied Saddam with sophisticated weapons.

The Philosophy of War and Peace 115

Hostages in the Lebanon in the 1980s

The short term goals motivating the Lebanese guerilla group that held Brian Keenan hostage for several years during the 1980s were never made clear either to him or to its other victims. It is probable that the low-level uneducated men in direct charge of the prisoners were not capable of explaining or even really understanding the motives of their leaders.

It is thought that the group was funded by Iran. It operated only in the Lebanon and according to Keenan and others its seizure of Westerners might have been part of an attempt to negotiate the release of fourteen Muslim fighters (or rebels or insurgents) imprisoned in Kuwait. Keenan says, too, that the actions of his captors were also responses to American and British support for Iraq's war against Iran, and to the economic sanctions imposed on Iran by Britain and the United States before and after that war.

Brian Keenan is an Irishman from Ulster who in 1986 was employed as an English lecturer by the American University in Beirut. He was taking a walk in Beirut when he was seized by gunmen who threw him into an old car and held him for the next four and a half years in what he describes as 'the terrifying squalor of the secret underground prisons of Lebanon's militants'. For several months he was held in a rat- and cockroach-infested cell, alone, blindfolded, and naked except for a pair of shorts. His captors' immediate aim was to find out the names of the CIA operatives who they believed were attached to the American University in Beirut. They refused to believe the Irishman Keenan had no information about the CIA. After two years he was joined in his cell by another captive, a British journalist, John McCarthy. They and others held in nearby cells were from time to time moved around the country to different prisons, most of which were primitive rooms underground. The hostages were always chained at the wrists and legs and sometimes chained to walls as well. They were subjected to constant beatings.

Even though Keenan's guards knew no English and not much French his long captivity and his knowledge of French gave him some insight into their minds, minds which seem to have been very different from those of SOE operatives or the men who followed Castro.

Keenan writes that most of the guards were in their early 20s, had no education and no or little experience of life. They had a terrific longing to be heard and taken notice of. Temperamentally they were extremely volatile, so mercurial as to verge on the psychotic, a state which caused them to engage in senseless abuse and violence. He describes their opinions as 'myopic and absolutist' and says their furious rantings against the United States and Zionism, President Reagan and Prime Minister Margaret Thatcher, were made up of 'second-hand rhetoric they had been force-fed and then regurgitated'.

Keenan believes that fundamentalism in any guise is 'an expression of a terminal sickness'. It is not theologically liberating and not politically revolutionary, rather it is repressive, reactionary and prohibiting, a mind-set harking back to the middle ages (Keenan, 1991).

In October 2003 Brian Keenan gave a talk on BBC television which was beamed to listeners around the world. In it he said the pronouncements of George W. Bush about 'the axis of evil' will only rally more young men in the Middle East to the cause of Jihad. He said that *terrorism*, like *Jihad*, is a term bandied about for the gullible by the myopic. By calling young Muslims terrorists and threatening to attack Muslim countries the President and others only legitimise aggression as righteous.

These words caused offence to some listeners in the United States. One such listener said on the WWW that Keenan's opinions were 'sadly ridiculous'. Another announced, somewhat irrelevantly, that 'The White House does not engage in international terrorism.'

Negotiating with hostage takers

Is it unethical for governments or others to negotiate with hostage takers? Or is it is unethical not to do so? Margaret Thatcher and Ronald Reagan were both strongly opposed to such negotiations. For example, Mrs Thatcher refused to discuss the plight of John McCarthy, the British journalist incarcerated along with Brian Keenan in the Lebanon. I believe her attitude might have been different if the Irish Republican Army had held Airey Neave hostage instead of shooting him. Neave was her favourite minister.

More recently the current leaders of Britain and America appear to share Thatcher's opinion. But there is not much doubt, is there? that those leaders might well ransom important people if any such became hostages. It is almost impossible for the children of an American President or a British Prime Minister to be captured by fanatics because such offspring are always well protected and what is more they do not serve in the military, unlike the sons and daughters of royal families. However if such an extremely improbable event ever did occur it is not easy to believe, is it? that the captives, the children of politicians, would be left to linger for years in prison like Brian Keenan and Terry Waite. Can anyone really suppose they would end up being decapitated like some of the civilian contractors held hostage in Iraq?

The opinion that people taken hostage should not be ransomed is, and has been, a minority view both in history and today. In former centuries rich European travellers captured by pirates off the Barbary coast could expect to be ransomed by their rich friends. Other hostages too would sometimes be freed as a result of the efforts made by an order of nuns which had given itself the task of collecting money needed for ransoming poor people.

During the present war in Iraq, France and Italy have both been prepared to rescue their nationals from fanatical captors, sometimes, it seems, by paying ransoms. In the years following 1948 Israel's neighbours instigated a number of attacks on the new State and during those years the policy was to free several enemy prisoners of war in exchange for one or two Israeli captives. The policy sent a message to Israelis, and to everyone else too, the message that Israel valued the life of each one of its soldiers more than any leverage it might gain by refusing to negotiate. Such a policy must surely encourage members of the armed forces to fight bravely because it shows that every man is prized by the government as well as by his family. A soldier in Israel is not a disposable piece of cannon fodder.

The life and times of Terry Waite

When the Prime Minister of Britain and the President of the United States announced their policy of non-negotiation the Christian churches stepped into the breach. Thus the Englishman Terry Waite managed to persuade his employer, Robert Runcie, Archbishop of Canterbury, to send him as an envoy to the Middle East and North Africa. Waite hoped to enter into negotiations with the people who were holding hostages in Libya and the Lebanon. After the Archbishop had given his permission Envoy Waite travelled to North Africa where he managed to sweet-talk the Libyan ruler, Colonel Gaddafi, into freeing his prisoners. Several visits to Beirut followed. All in all the work on the hostages project lasted from 1982 to 1986, during which time Waite and the Archbishop received moral support from the Pope and from several members of the Episcopalian and Presbyterian churches in the United States. As it happens the first two Lebanese prisoners released as a result of Waite's activities were clergymen; the Reverend Ben Weir, an American, and Father

Lawrence Jenco, a Catholic priest. Weir had been held from 1984 to 1985 and Jenco for about a year and a half.

After securing the freedom of a surprising number of prisoners Waite himself was captured in Beirut in January 1987 and held hostage until November 1991. He spent almost all the time chained to a wall in solitary confinement. He does not know why he was eventually set free (Waite, 1991).

PART IV
THE PEOPLE IN ARMS

Chapter 13
Guerillas and Partisans

A little rebellion now and then is a good thing
(Thomas Jefferson, letter to James Madison, January 1787).

The just war re-visited

The classic account of justice in war includes the dictum that war can be carried out lawfully only by properly appointed rulers, a rigid notion which rules out any possibility of justifying rebellions and insurgencies, including, of course, the American rebellion of 1776 and the French revolution of 1789. Intuition tells us however that rebellions, revolutions and insurgencies in general can be just or unjust, and morally lawful or unlawful in direct or inverse proportion to the evil or illegality of an existing regime, elected or not as the case may be. Most European monarchs, and a regicidal English Lord Protector, and various elected and unelected Presidents all over the world, not to mention dictators like Franco, Mussolini, Stalin and Adolf Hitler, have all been recognised either in the short run or in the long run as 'properly appointed'. Leaders of guerilla bands, on the other hand, have not generally received international recognition, that is to say, not unless and until they have taken over the government of their respective countries. 'Marshal' Tito of Jugoslavia was eventually recognised by the United Nations Organisation. Cuba's Fidel Castro has been recognised by several countries including Russia, Canada and more recently Venezuela and Bolivia—though famously not by the United States of America. Ho Chi Minh of Vietnam was recognised even by the United States not so very long after his forces had driven the American army out of his country.

Guerillas, partisans, rebels

It is possible for Governments to be overturned by invaders or by guerilla forces or by rebellious elements in the army.

A war of resistance is not the same thing as a war of terror though it can be accompanied by terror. Guerilla fighters are often described as *terrorists*, a term loaded with infamy; the word *partisan* on the other hand, has no noticeable derogatory implications. Yet there is not much difference between a military partisan *per se* and a guerilla fighter *per se*. One practical difference is that partisans sometimes wear uniforms whereas guerillas are usually irregular volunteers wearing ordinary clothes. Whether a guerilla or partisan happens to behave well or badly has nothing to do with their military status.

The word *partisan* is or ought to be purely descriptive, nevertheless it has overtones which mean 'these men are on *our* side'. During the second world war and for a short time afterwards the resistance fighters in France and Norway, and Tito's forces in Yugoslavia, were all referred to by the Western Allies not as guerillas but as partisans. When fighting against 'us' resistance fighters and irregulars have more often been described as guerillas or insurgents or terrorists.

What is guerilla war? Why do men engage in such warfare, who do they fight, and how do they fight? Guerilla war ('little war') is waged by bands of people rebelling against a government or an occupying force. Guerilla fighters hide in forests and mountains or live hidden amongst ordinary civilians. The Vietnamese leader Ho Chi Minh described the Viet Cong as 'fish that swim in the sea of the people'–at which an American general famously riposted 'We will dry up that sea.'

The possible causes leading to guerilla war include political conviction, religious conviction, and hatred of occupying powers. The resistance movements in Western Europe in the 1940's were fuelled by a deep detestation of Nazi cruelties. Tito's forces in Yugoslavia were inspired by communism as well as by hatred of the German occupiers. Islamic Jihad is an outcome of a certain kind of religious teaching. The Italian group, the Red Brigades, who carried out kidnappings and the murder of politicians, developed their own extremely left-wing ideas. The German Red Army Faction, also known, after its leaders, as the Baader-Meinhof gang, was another group inspired by socialist ideas. Baader and Meinhof and their followers were also inspired, one suspects, by a sheer love of mayhem and excitement.

Andreas Baader and Ulricke Meinhof were captured in 1972 and later committed suicide in prison. Baader shot himself twice in the back of the head.

Not all rebels are guerillas. In Spain in 1936 General Franco led a successful rebellion against the elected government, the Popular Front, in which he was supported by a significant portion of the Spanish army (and also by virtually all the clergy and other religious). His soldiers wore distinctive uniforms and fought battles against their former comrades as well as against the local and international amateur soldiers who tried to support the elected government. The *casus belli* of the conflict were as follows: the Popular Front Government had removed some of the privileges of the Catholic church, secondly, it had granted a degree of independence to the Basque people in Northern Spain and thirdly it had socialist tendencies.

During the civil war Franco called in the German air force to bomb the Basque capital, Guernica, an undefended city. After his victory he restored the lost privileges of the church.

Guerilla war has been condemned both in legal documents and by moralists. Its original non-status in international law was apparent from the early Geneva protocols wherein it was either not mentioned at all or if mentioned then deemed unlawful. Thus no provisions were made in those early documents to extend the legal protections covering prisoners of war to guerilla fighters. The status (or rather the lack of status) of captured guerillas seemingly allowed for them to be secretly imprisoned with no access to relatives or the Red Cross and even to be executed without trial. However in the second part of the twentieth century, when several wars were being fought by and against guerillas, the older views were rejected, first by public opinion — at least in some countries — and then, in 1977, by additions to the Geneva documents.

Morality and resistance

The ethical standards found in guerilla wars, like those to be seen in conventional warfare, vary from case to case.

There are some good reasons for condemning guerilla war. Early rulings and protocols demanded that fighters identify themselves by wearing uniforms. Guerillas, however, usually wear ordinary clothes and so are able to launch surreptitious surprise attacks on uniformed soldiers and other targets. To make matters worse the 'other targets' might be civilians who have no personal complicity in the perceived bad behaviour of a government or an army. Not all the Westerners captured and held hostage by Lebanese guerillas in the 1980's were complicit in the actions of their governments and the same must be true of some of the civilian hostages taken and executed by guerillas in Iraq during the current war in that country. The absence of special clothing means a burden of guilt is placed on the uniformed soldiers on the other side who cannot easily distinguish hostile fighters from non-combatants and can therefore be lured into killing innocent people. Unfortunately military forces engaged in dealing with insurgencies rarely acknowledge guilt or even accidental wrong-doing when innocent bystanders are killed in those circumstances. However the British army in its dealings with the Irish Republican Army and the Ulster Volunteer Force during the latter part of the twentieth century was an exception. If one of its soldiers was under reasonable suspicion of having deliberately or recklessly fired on unarmed people he would be court-martialled.

When considering guerilla movements from an ethical point of view one can apply a number of criteria which enable one to classify their behaviour as better or worse, justifiable or not.

Guerilla warfare has been described by its supporters as the last resort of the weak against the strong, the last resort of ordinary people against vicious rulers. But—as already noted—several guerilla wars of the twentieth and twenty-first centuries have been identified with terrorism, in some cases when real terrorists have lived as guerillas, in others when propaganda took over because the hard facts were not known.

Guerilla activities have also been deemed insurgencies and Guerilla fighters as traitors. Yet the governments or occupying powers opposed by insurgents include a few whose own legitimacy is very dubious. Such dubious entities include some of the most evil dictatorships that have ever received international recognition.

Chapter 14

The SOE versus the Axis Powers

fortis fortuna adiuvat
(fortune favours the brave — Terence)

The resistance movements in occupied Europe, 1940-1946

In his book *The SOE/Special Operations Excecutive*, Professor M.R.D. Foot described the role of the organisation as follows:

> The SOE was a small tough British fighting service. It was formed in deadly secrecy in July 1940 to tackle one of the nastiest regimes even in this century, Hitler's German empire. It helped to bring down Hitler and Mussolini, fought against their ally, Imperial Japan, and was quietly wound up in 1946 when its work was done (Foot, 1999, p. 1).

M.R.D. Foot, *croix de guerre*, was himself a member of the SOE.

The aim of the fighting force was to wage subversive war behind enemy lines, making up its rules as it went along, learning the hard way by trial and error. Some of its agents were eccentric, perhaps even misfits, most were very courageous. Women as well as men served as agents and women as well as men died at the hands of the Gestapo.

The 'outfit' was in part a research organisation and in part a guerilla movement. Some of the research involved collecting information about the history of unofficial warfare, for instance the wars waged by the Boers in South Africa, by T.E. Lawrence and his Arabs, by the Irish during 'the troubles' and by anti-Franco forces in the Spanish civil war of 1936–1939.

In the beginning its attention was focussed on France and Austria. Leaflets such as 'The Partisans' Handbook' which explained the use of explosives and various other methods of sabotage were dropped over the occupied countries. It would seem that the SOE assumed the Nazi aggressors were hated all over Europe, a mistake, possibly, in the case of Austria but certainly not elsewhere on the continent.

In some cases the ultimate leaders of the resistance movements were Governments in Exile centred in London. When those governments were led by rulers accepted as legitimate before the onset of hostilities their activities, which consisted in the main of radio broadcasts, conformed to the conventional rules of justice in war insofar as those include an account of what counts as a proper authority.

The resistance movements and the SOE itself were undoubtedly guerilla fighters. Were they also terrorists? They attacked railroads and military installations and they killed Nazi soldiers and members of the Gestapo and ordinary citizens judged to be supporters of the occupying power or guilty of betraying secrets. According to modern rules of conventional warfare attacks on military personnel by uniformed soldiers do not count as terrorism, of course, unless prefixed by torture. Those rules also allow the execution of spies and traitors. The collaborators killed by the SOE were known or believed to be spies, which is to say, they were traitors in the eyes of the resistance. It has to be admitted, though, that until the formulation of the additions made to the Geneva Protocols in 1977 fighters not in uniform (including of course the British SOE agents and local anti-Nazi resistance groups) would all have counted as what the current administration in the United States once described as illegal combatants.

The activities of the SOE depended heavily on the use of aeroplanes and parachutes. Night flights over Europe dropped wirelesses, weapons, food, information and last but not least agents willing to join the local resistance forces for spells of duty, long term or short term as the case may be. Agents were either bi-lingual Englishmen and Englishwomen or native speakers of various European languages, often German or Dutch.

Certain important military men in Britain were wary of the SOE and some of them tried to block its efforts. Their attitudes probably derived from what they had been taught about the ethical and non-ethical conduct of war. M.R.D. Foot quotes from a memo by Sir S.C.F. Portal (later Lord Portal) who was one of the British Chiefs of Staff during the second world war:

> I think that the dropping of men dressed in civilian clothes for the purpose of attempting to kill members of the opposing forces is not an operation with which the Royal Air Force should be associated. I think ... there is a vast difference between the time-honoured operation of dropping a spy from the air and this entirely

new scheme for dropping what one can only call assassins (memo of February 1941; Foot, 1999, p. 131).

Professor Foot points out that the SOE had no aeroplanes of its own. Nevertheless the RAF did in fact drop 'assassins' into occupied Europe in spite of Portal's opposition. Portal's assistant, Arthur Harris, later Commander-in-Chief of Bomber Command, also put some brakes on the SOE, though not because he objected to the guerilla tactics of the resistance and its British helpers. He contrasted the work of the SOE with his bombing offensive, claiming that the former was nothing but a gamble whereas his own destruction of German cities was a gilt-edged investment. Foot says Harris opposed the activities of the SOE because he feared his own attempts to lay the area waste could possibly be hindered.

Foot's own judgement on the activities of the SOE is of considerable interest. He states that although it is obvious the SOE and its allies in the resistance movements could not have won the war by themselves, nevertheless their influence was critically important in a number of ways. Successful attacks on military facilities must have made a difference to Nazi capabilities — Foot mentions *inter alia* the destruction of the heavy water plant in Norway, thought to be the first stage in a German plan to manufacture an atomic bomb. He also believes that resistance movements diverted enemy attention away from the main fighting fronts. The tasks of guarding ammunition depots, railway junctions and bridges, which in the United Kingdom were left to elderly men, had to be watched over by German military units in the nations which had been over-run by the Nazis. Secondly, he says, the activities of the SOE and the resistance groups influenced the way people regarded the occupiers. The Axis powers had advanced into West Europe, East Europe, China, Indo-China, Singapore and Burma 'with almost contemptuous ease' so that in all those countries 'there was a sense of shame and desolation'. By supporting the fledgling resistance movements the SOE helped to replace shame and desolation with a degree of hope and a new self-respect, strengthened by a well justified detestation of the occupying powers. In 1942 the Czech resistance movement managed to assassinate Reinhard Heydrich, a deputy chief of the Gestapo charged with the task of subduing the countries occupied occupied by Germany. The retaliation was typical of the Nazi regime: two Czech villages, Lidice and Lezacky were destroyed, the ruins ploughed into the ground like Carthage of old and all the inhabitants except for nine children were killed.

Foot says some SOE agents were reckless, even trigger-happy, while others took advantage of the war to engage in adulterous affairs and general fornication. On the other hand there is no evidence that the agents engaged in torture or deliberately targetted unarmed civilians going about their ordinary business. Targetting civilians would have made the outfit very unpopular. It is clear the agents knew they were fighting against a monstrous tyranny and were inspired by that knowledge to avoid behaviour resembling that of their opponents. If you know or genuinely believe the enemy is wicked you don't imitate him unless you are ignorant and illogical and have been incessantly deluged by extremist propaganda.

The inspiration of leaders in exile

Queen Wilhemina of the Netherlands, who went to London when her country was over-run, was indubitably a proper authority before the outbreak of war and surely could be deemed as such after she arrived in England. From London she sent regular radio messages to her people. The same is true of King Haakon VII of Norway, who, after refusing a German demand to abdicate, was able to reach England from where he too contacted his people by wireless. The legal situation was somewhat different for France because General Charles de Gaulle (1890–1970) became the French leader in exile by a process of self-election. He left his country as soon as the Nazi armies moved in and after little more than a week had persuaded the authorities in Britain to give him air time on the BBC. Nine days after arriving in London he spoke as follows:

> Forced by the bewilderment of my countrymen, by the disintegration of a government in thrall to the enemy, by the fact that the institutions of my country are incapable, at the moment, of functioning, I, de Gaulle, a French soldier and military leader, realise that I must speak for France.

Just as memorable were the words he broadcast 3 weeks later:

> Since they whose duty it was to wield the sword of France have let it fall shattered to the ground I have taken up the broken blade ...

In occupied Europe listening to such broadcasts was liable to attract the attentions of the Gestapo, nevertheless resistance leaders took the risk and retailed the contents of the messages from the BBC in the form of news sheets. Radio equipment was hidden in all sorts of unlikely places: in logs in the forest, in stoves and inside chopping blocks.

The fates of Petain and Laval of Vichy France

Southern France was ruled by a government located in the town of Vichy and led by two men, one the ancient 'hero' of the first world war, Marshal Henri Philippe Omer Petain (1856–1951) and the other the Nazi collaborator Pierre Laval. The rest of the country was subjected to direct German rule.

When Petain decided to co-operate with the Nazis who had occupied his country older people in France recalled the words on a report made when the Marshal was a young soldier:

> If this officer rises above the rank of Major it will be a disaster for France.

After his German puppet-masters installed him in Vichy the French people began referring to Petain as 'Philippe le Ga-Ga'. Patriots were not pleased when puppet le Ga-Ga removed the historic words *Liberty, Equality, Fraternity* from documents issued by his government and replaced them with the slogan *Work, Family, Homeland*.

Petain and Laval were both sentenced to death for treason but because of his age Petain's sentence was commuted to life imprisonment. He died in prison in his ninety-fifth year.

Chapter 15

Resistance in Norway

The tree of liberty must be refreshed from time to time with the blood of patriots and tyrants

(Thomas Jefferson, letter to W.S. Smith 1787).

The German invasion and Quisling

In 1940 the population of Norway consisted of three million people scattered over what is a mostly mountainous territory. Germany invaded the country on April 9 1940, rapidly taking the capital Oslo and all the airfields, weapon depots and principal towns. Norwegian soldiers and sailors attempted to fight back — the sailors managed to sink a German cruiser — but to no avail. The southern areas of Norway had all capitulated by May 1940 though fighting continued for a while in the north.

Vidkun Quisling, leader of the Norwegian National-Socialist (Nazi) Unity Party, the NS, quickly declared himself Prime Minister. Hitler at first supported Quisling in this but soon appointed a Reichskommisar, Terboven, who had the job of telling Prime Minister Quisling what to do on important occasions such as the gagging of the press, the setting up of phoney trade unions and sports organisations, and the execution of resistance workers and strikers.

Because of the Nazi-Soviet Pact signed in August 1939 the Norwegian Communist Party supported the German invaders. The communists wanted the King, Haakon VII, to abdicate: he refused. On June 7 1940 a British cruiser collected the King and his ministers and took them to England.

The patriotic people in the Norwegian resistance movement were marked by courage and self-sacrifice, the far fewer Norwegian collaborators were presumably motivated by pro-Nazi beliefs or by fear or greed.

Resistance came from unexpected groups, unexpected, that is, to modern minds perhaps too influenced by ideas about the necessity of conflict between left and right. Some trade unionists, for example, became Quislingite informers whereas the members of the national ship-owners' organisation unanimously refused to instruct the captains of Norwegian vessels on the high seas to return home. Some of those ships were serving with the Allies. Two prominent ship-owners were arrested, sent to Germany and imprisoned there until 1945. All the judges of the Supreme Court resigned when ordered to add members of Quisling's party to their ranks. Bishop Berggrav organised a protest letter signed by the Norwegian bishops which reached London from where it was broadcast back to Norway. Berggrav was summoned to meet Himmler who let him go with a warning having perhaps decided that punishing a distinguished high-up clergyman might be a bit risky. Sports groups refused to co-operate with similar groups set up by the National Unity Party and would not accept Germans as members. When a number of skiers and skaters were arrested there was a sports strike of 300,000 people. There were also school strikes.

Quisling's political meetings were boycotted or attracted demonstrations singing *God Save the King* and the national anthem *Yes, we love with deep devotion ... this our land* . The singers and others wore H7 badges, on which H7 stood for King Haakon VII.

Resistance leaders knew that if Quisling was ever to set up a wholly independent Nazi government he would conscript young Norwegians to fight alongside the German army. So from May 1940 fishing boats and other small craft took batches of men to Britain, returning with military instructors and cargoes of arms and radio sets. In 1941 a representative of the resistance movement was sent to London to join the government in exile.

Anti-Nazi Norwegians also constructed their own radio sets. They listened to BBC broadcasts and thereby heard news of the war going on in other parts of Europe. Members of the resistance published and distributed clandestine news sheets and sent thousands of letters to individuals; all such activities would be heavily punished if detected. Workers engaged in 'silent espionage', in other words, the go-slow. There was also some early industrial espionage. Later the heavy water plant where German scientists were working on a Nazi atomic bomb was attacked. The resistance leader on that occasion was a scientist, Leif Tronstad, who was informed on and killed in March 1945.

In Stockholm the Norwegian Legation continued to represent King Haakon's government and was able to send money to the resistance movement. Sending money became easier after 1943 when the danger of having Germany violate Sweden's neutrality had receded.

Civil servants, teachers, professors and trade unionists were ordered to give 'positive and active support' to Quisling's Nazi Party. Those who openly refused were interned.

Gestapo Chief Reinhard Heydrich (later to be killed by the resistance in Czechoslovakia) arrived in Norway accompanied by many of his henchmen. His appearance in the country was followed, not co-incidentally, by the use of torture, carried out by German Nazis and Quisling-ite prison officials.

In February 1942 Terboven appointed Quisling President and head of the Norwegian Government. Quisling seems to have been a very untalented man, always making foolish decisions. Terboven frequently had to come to his rescue.

Quisling wanted to create a Fascist Corporate State like the one that Mussolini created in Italy. In such a State all organisations of citizens, including children's organisations, were supposed to be run by the government. Membership of the State organisations was to be compulsory and one duty of the teachers' union would be to instruct its members to indoctrinate children in Quisling's Nazi ideology. No-one knew when the war was going to end but the resistance knew that six years of indoctrination had already turned German children into horrible human beings, creatures unthinkingly obedient and utterly callous. So leaders of the resistance began to tour Norway secretly asking teachers not to join Quisling's new teachers' union. A letter was drafted for individuals to post to the Education Department, it said the signatory would not teach Nazi doctrines because to do so would be against his/her conscience. The Department was flooded with thousands of these letters. Over 100,000 parents also wrote to the Department complaining about the NS regulations. The Norwegian Bishops sent letters to the Education Department. They insisted that the new rules violated the right of parents to bring up their children in the way they believed best.

Quisling threatened to sack all the teachers and put them to forced labour but changed his mind and instead closed the schools for a month. However the Germans stepped in and arrested 10% of the teaching professions, sending many to concentration camps. About 500, though, were taken away to work in Kirkenes in the far North. They were housed there in stables and cardboard tents. Information was smuggled out of the Kirkenes camp and sent to Sweden.

On the other hand some 200 teachers agreed to work with Quisling's administration.

In Norway 86% of the people are baptised Lutherans. Their church has an Episcopal and Synodical structure, its services normally include the Eucharist and its Churchmen understand the Real Presence in Luther's own terms. One Sunday the Dean of Trondheim Cathedral was forcibly prevented from holding a service because Quisling wanted to celebrate 'The Act of State'. A pro-Nazi priest was happy and willing to officiate at the ceremony. After the Dean postponed his service to the afternoon huge crowds turned up. They were prevented from entering the building but collected at the gate, praying, singing and demonstrating. After those events Quisling wrote to all the Deans of the Norwegian church, saying he intended to sack the Bishops and promote the Deans into Bishoprics — provided the Deans agreed to sign up with the Norwegian Nazi organisation. They all refused. The Northern church's attitude to Quisling was rather different from the Vatican's attitude to Mussolini.

The Norwegian church is a State church. The clergy next decided to resign from their government posts while continuing with their pastoral duties, a situation which Quisling said was 'insurrection'.

Ninety percent of lawyers in Norway refused to join Quisling's NS organisation, 100% of ship-owners behaved likewise.

Nazi terror tactics

On April 9 1941, the anniversary of the German invasion, there were nation-wide silent demonstrations. On September 8 1941 there were strikes in Oslo. On September 10 1941 Reichskommisar Terboven declared a state of emergency, in other words, the implementation of terror tactics. There were two on-the-spot executions, then mass arrests followed by more executions. The German occupiers ordered that for every German soldier killed by the resistance 50–100 Norwegian hostages would be shot.

Quisling and his masters ordered that men engaged in non-essential trades such as hotel work were to be recruited under compulsion to work in heavy industry. A labour leader, Jonsson, resisted and was sent to Dachau where he died.

In 1942 the Gestapo started rounding up the Norwegian Jews. The resistance managed to smuggle about a thousand across the border into Sweden but the remaining 780 were captured and sent to the death camps in Germany. Twenty-four returned alive at the end of the war.

During 1943 a policeman was executed for refusing to obey a NS order.

Another 14 policemen disappeared, probably executed, and several more were interned. After that many members of the police force decided to obey the NS administration.

Quisling sentenced people to death under laws passed retrospectively.

When in the Autumn of 1943 students and professors at Oslo University refused to join NS organisations the SS invaded the campuses and made many arrests. Several hundred students were sent to 're-training camps' in Germany.

The collaborator Ninnan, executed in 1947 (see below), successfully infiltrated a number of resistance groups and as a result the inhabitants of a small village were confronted by a Gestapo group. Resistance men shot and killed two of the Germans. The Gestapo then destroyed every house in the village, also all the fishing boats, and interned every male between the ages of 16 and 75 in concentration camps in Germany. The remaining villagers, women, children and old men, were interned in Norway.

Captured resistance workers were routinely tortured.

In 1943 the NS administration announced that there would be mobilisation of workers to grow food in Norway for Norwegians. It later turned out that in a letter to the SS dated January 17 1944 one of Quisling's ministers, Riisnaes, promised to supply a total of 30,000 men to fight with the German army against the USSR even though Germany at that time was in full retreat after the battle of Stalingrad. Riisnaes told the SS that all Norwegian men of military age were going to be rounded up, sifted for communists (who would be interned) and trained in Norway for two weeks, but without weapons. No doubt he thought weapons could easily find a way into the hands of the resistance movement. After 14 days, he said, the conscripted men could be taken to Germany. He advised they be enrolled in the SS, given SS uniforms and weapons and posted to Russia via Finmark. They should be told, he said, that though not Germans they were 'Germanic soldiers' with a duty to fight for the Master Race (Gjelsvik, 1979).

None of this actually happened in the end.

The attacks on the heavy water plant

The Germans converted a hydro plant at Ryukan into a plant for manufacturing heavy water. Heavy water, of course, is used in the manufacture of atomic weapons. Norwegian commandos damaged the plant but it was repaired. Then they bombed it. At that point the Germans decided to convey the heavy water to Germany, first in a train from the plant to a lake, then on a ferry across the lake, then by sea.

By then there was only one trained commando left in the district, Knut Haukelind, and the task fell to him of destroying the heavy water, either by blowing up the train or sinking the train ferry. Both the train and the ferry would be carrying ordinary Norwegian civilians going about their ordinary business. There was a danger, too, that if the German guards were killed there would be reprisals. Knut Haukelind decided the operation should be carried out on a Sunday because on Sundays there were fewer passengers than on weekdays. A local man engaged in the transport business arranged for the heavy water to be taken onto the ferry and Haukelind managed to smuggle explosives on board. The ferry blew up and sank to the bottom of the lake. There were 53 passengers on board: 26 were killed.
These details about the ferry come from Jonathan Glover's book *Humanity* (Glover, 1999).

The end of the war

In 1944 Quisling ordered a general mobilisation of young men, allegedly for civilian or quasi-military tasks like guard duty. The resistance asked people to boycott the registration procedures and a majority did so. The police began rounding up young men in the streets, inadvertently bringing about the 'lads in the forest' movement. It was summer and the 'lads' were able to live in makeshift accommodation. Food was secretly brought to them by their womenfolk and sympathising shop-keepers. Food also arrived from sources in Sweden. The lads in the forests eventually numbered between 4 and 5 thousand.

In 1944 the Chief of Police was assassinated by the resistance at which Quisling and Terboven immediately ordered the execution of 27 prisoners and five hostages. The resistance sent a circular letter to every known Quisling supporter, warning them that unless they gave up their attacks on their fellow citizens they would be punished as soon as the war ended.

At some time during the last months of the conflict the Allied air forces began dropping weapons to the resistance.

In order to prevent the German army in Norway from joining the battles in the rest of Europe the railway lines were sabotaged and the railway administration office in Oslo blown up. The Gestapo executed 14 young men who had cut the lines — their last killings in Norway.

On April 20 1945 Hitler committed suicide after appointing Admiral Doenitz as his successor. Doenitz summoned the German leaders in Denmark and Norway and ordered them to capitulate. Allied forces arrived in Norway on May 8 and disarmed the Germans.

The fate of the traitors

Three traitors were executed in Norway in 1945, Quisling himself and two of his ministers, Skanke and Hoel. His 'minister for Justice', Riisnaes, was declared insane and another ex-minister committed suicide.

In 1947 the collaborator Rinnan was tried on a charge of murder and executed.

The moral power of resistance

Norway provides striking evidence of the moral power of resistance activities. The Norwegian navy never co-operated with Germany; local commandos carried out many 'hits' against the occupiers; and at the end of the war an army of 365,000 German soldiers surrendered to 60,000 Norwegian guerillas. A photograph of that moving event used to hang in all Norwegian schools. Perhaps it still does. The photo shows a senior German officer handing his sword to a member of the resistance. The German is wearing black military uniform, the young resistance fighter is clad in civilian clothes; a shirt and jacket, Norwegian knee breeches, and woollen stockings.

Chapter 16

Guerillas in Cuba

La historia me absolvera
(History will absolve me — Fidel Castro)

The character and aims of Fidel Castro and Ernesto ('Che') Guevara

Since governments in South America have often been very right-wing popular anti-government military activity there tends to be left-wing. Popular dissent, though, has rarely had any long-term results in that part of the world. Fidel Castro's guerilla movement of the 1950s and his subsequent lengthy period of rule are unique not only in Cuban history but in the history of the rest of Latin America.

It is almost certainly true that Castro and his comrade Ernesto 'Che' Guevara were not tempted to enrich themselves through corruption. Nevertheless Andrew Kenny, the same journalist who wanted to innoculate his readers against the idea that Hiroshima and Nagasaki were war crimes (see below, p. 214) asserted in *The Spectator* (February 4 2005) that Castro has made himself a billionaire by reducing the Cuban people to extreme poverty. The writer did not offer any references to back up his assertion and Cubans certainly don't *look* impoverished. Widespread poverty is not easy for rulers to hide, as anyone who visits India can testify. Moreover the island's dependence on its main crops, sugar and tobacco, has been reduced by a government decision to develop tourism, a decision taken at least ten years ago. The main towns now have large hotels built by capitalist firms located in capitalist Singapore. Cuba has become a popular holiday destination for Canadians, Germans and Spaniards.

Fidel Castro and Che Guevara thought to send agents into some of the dictatorships on the mainland of Latin America, a policy which eventually resulted in Guevara's death by torture in Bolivia in 1967.

A very short history of Cuba
(Drawn from Bourne, 1986 and Foner, 1963.)

When Christopher Columbus discovered the island he was being financed by the King of Spain, hence Cuba became a Spanish possession. Spain was looking for gold and silver and found plenty of both in the South American mainland whereas in Cuba they had to engage in farming, cultivating corn, sugar and tobacco. It turned out that the natives of the island could not be enslaved because they preferred suicide to captivity hence the Spanish colonisers had to import slaves from Africa. About half the present population of the island has African blood.

Cuba was governed by Spain and Spanish colonisers for about 400 years

The country has had several mostly unsuccessful revolutions including a number of slave revolts. During the 19th century there were uprisings in 1812, 1868, 1879, and 1895. The 1895 insurgency was led by Jose Marti (1853–1895), a man who in Cuba is revered much as George Washington is revered in the United States. Some Cuban dissidents and revolutionaries favoured annexation by the USA but Marti did not. He admired the freedom and idealism of the States north of the Mason-Dixie Line but believed that America was aggressive and expansionist and not unduly hostile to slavery as such.

Marti began his insurgency by issuing a manifesto listing the following points: the war against the Spaniards was to be conducted in a civilised fashion; the participation of the Negro people was essential; non-combatant Spaniards would not be the targets of revenge, persecution or extortion; private wealth would be respected unless it was used against the revolutionaries; the revolution would introduce a new regime in Cuba.

The campaign began in December 1894.

> On May 19 1895 Marti rode forth in his first encounter with the Spaniards. He was ambushed by a group of soldiers and shot dead (Foner, 1963, pp. 347f).

Cuba under Castro has no statues of its living leader (though a huge outdoor wall painting of his colleague Che Guevara was created after Guevara's death). In this respect Cuba is different from the former Soviet Union and Iraq before 2002, not to mention various dictatorships in Africa and elsewhere. Jose Marti, however, is remembered, and with reverence. The Museum of the Revolution in

Havana commemorates not Castro's revolution but Marti's and his impressive marble Mausoleum in Santiago da Cuba appears to be a place of pilgrimage. When the Mausoleum was urinated on by American Marines the then Ambassador of the United States was ordered to apologise, which he did. It turned out the aforesaid Ambassador had never heard of Marti until that occasion.

A number of America's presidents considered annexing Cuba. Thomas Jefferson thought annexation was inevitable. James Polk, a Democrat from North Carolina and presidential incumbent between 1844 and 1848, offered Spain $100,000 for Cuba but the offer was rejected. Polk was succeeded by Zachary Taylor, a Whig who as an army general had carried out Polk's project of annexing Spanish-held territories in the West, taking Texas, New Mexico, California and North Arizona into the United States. Taylor died in office and was succeeded by Franklin Pierce, a defender of slavery, who in 1853 offered Spain $150,000 for Cuba. That offer too was rejected.

After the American Civil War American investors began to buy Cuban land and businesses. By the 1920's two-thirds of the arable land in Cuba was owned by businesses in the United States. Most of the mines and smelting works also passed into the hands of American firms.

In 1897 President McKinley announced that God had favoured him with a Divine Revelation to take over the Philippines. Following the instructions from Heaven McKinley formed a plan to seize Cuba and the Philippines with the stated aim of ousting Spain while purporting to support local freedom fighters. Under McKinley America also invaded Hawaii and Samoa. Meanwhile Spain crushed Cuba's 1895 revolution and drove many of the rural people into the cities where they could be watched and where some, it is said, actually starved to death. On that occasion the United States offered to intervene on the side of the rebels but the offer was rejected: American troops were not wanted and American motives were not trusted.

On December 10 1898 the Treaty of Paris ceded Puerto Rica, Guam and the Philippines to the United States while Cuba was offered independence on condition it agreed to accept a constitution drawn up by America. It accepted the conditions and the constitution as proposed. The document included the Platt Amendment, a passage which gave the United States the right to intervene in the island's affairs at any time it saw fit. America was allowed to build and occupy naval bases on the island; it still holds one such base at

Guantanamo Bay. Finally, Cuba was banned from negotiating international loans.

American troops remained in the island between 1898-1902, then withdrew, then returned for three years between 1906 and 1909, returned again in 1912 and then again in 1917. No Cuban could become President of the country without the support of the United States; all Cuban Presidents, whether elected or not, were given shares in American firms and access to American luxury goods; most were corrupt or corrupted; all were in effect dictators during their periods of office; some were amazingly brutal.

In 1929 President Herbert Hoover supported the advent of the dictator Machado who remained in power until Franklin D. Roosevelt withdrew American support in 1933. Between 1942 and 1952 an African-Chinese NCO, Fulgencio Batista, ran the rigging of elections from behind the scenes and then seized power for himself.

What would annexation have been like for the inhabitants of Cuba in, say, 1898? A letter sent by the American war office to General Nelson Miles, Army chief of staff in that year, contained the following opinions and instructions:

> The inhabitants (of Cuba) are indolent and apathetic ... Immediate annexation to our federation of such elements would be folly ... We must clean the country, even though it be by applying the same means that were applied by Divine Providence to Sodom and Gomorrah (Bourne, 1986, pp. 7-8).

In the long run, however, the annexation of Cuba would perhaps have had similar results to the long-term outcome in Hawaii, assuming, that is, that the suggested Biblical cleansing was not carried out. It is true that after 1898, when Hawaii was ceded to the United States, the native population continued its long trend towards extinction, a trend partly caused by imported diseases — including leprosy from China — and partly by poverty. On the other hand when Hawaii became the 50th State of the USA after the second world war an American legal system was put into place so that Hawaiians today have the protection of laws similar to those in the rest of the country. Unfortunately pure-blood Hawaiians are now few and far between and in the larger islands the local culture has been squashed by the advent of tourist hotels and giant shopping malls. The City Fathers of Honolulu claim that their town has the largest shopping mall in the world.

Guerilla war in Cuba
(Drawn from Bourne, *ibid.*)

As mentioned above Cuba has had several unsuccessful revolutions. The 1959 rebellion, which was initially led by quite a small group, succeeded partly because of the hatred inspired by the dictator Batista, partly because of the unusual intelligence and charisma displayed by the guerilla leader, Fidel Castro, and partly (as von Clausewitz would have pointed out) because of the character of the Cuban people.

Castro was born in 1927. At the age of 6 he was sent to a Catholic boarding school run by the de la Salle brothers in Santiago de Cuba; then, at 11, to a Jesuit boarding school in Havana where he became a star pupil and a star athlete. He remained in some sense a 'son of the Church' and has encouraged it to continue its work in Cuba. Pope John Paul II visited the country in January 1998 and was welcomed by Fidel Castro and his Council of Ministers; photographs show that Castro was wearing a formal suit instead of his usual army gear when he respectfully bowed to the seated Pope.

While Castro was studying law at the University of Havana he became an admirer of Edward Chibas and his opposition party, the Orthodoxos. Chibas publicly named and denounced politicians, businessman and military officers, accusing them of plundering Cuba, fixing elections and keeping working people in conditions of near slavery. After Chibas's death in 1952 Fidel joined the Orthodoxos and ran for election to the Cuban Congress. But a few days before the election the strong man Fulgencio Batista seized power in a military coup. Castro, who had qualified as a lawyer, filed a criminal suit demanding Batista be gaoled for crimes against the 1940 Constitution which guaranteed elections. All the judges but one voted to throw out the suit. Batista immediately gaoled many of the people who had protested against his seizure of power.

Castro concluded that military dictators can only be removed by military means. For months he and his friends secretly trained like-minded young men in the use of guns. Their skills were put into operation in 1953 in an attack on the Moncado military barracks, an attack which failed. Most of fighters were captured in the barracks and tortured to death but Castro was seized by a sympathetic black army officer who drove him to a municipal prison and allowed him to show himself to the public before taking him in. Some time later a prison guard claimed that he had been ordered to poison Castro. He refused and was court-martialled for disobedience.

Castro was tried separately from his colleagues. In court he made an historic speech 'History will absolve me' which was surreptitiously copied by a girl journalist and reproduced and distributed as 10,000 mimeographed copies. The document did not mention Marxism or socialism but promised new laws, some of which were vaguely socialistic.

Castro was sentenced to serve a prison term of 13 years but a year later Batista declared an amnesty. Six weeks after being released Fidel went into exile in Mexico. Batista sent agents to Mexico to kill him but by then he was being protected by bodyguards.

Guevara, an Argentinian, had been living in Colombia, a country with an elected president, Arbenz, who had tried to expropriate land owned by American businessmen — with compensation. When Arbenz was overthrown by an army led by a Honduran general Che Guevara left for Mexico where he met Castro for the first time.

In 1956 Castro and Guevara and their guerilla band obtained a 58 ft. motor launch, *Granma,* and also purchased a remote house in Mexico. On November 24 1956 the armed guerillas, 82 in number, set off in *Granma* for the Oriente (Eastern) Province in Cuba. The boat went aground on the 2nd of December and all the heavier weapons were lost. Castro and his men set up camp but were trapped by Batista's army. Three guerillas were killed, others were captured and some of the remaining men abandoned the project in despair. Castro and 21 of his followers evaded capture and scattered into the woods. Of those 22 men fourteen reached a farm owned by a supporter and on Christmas day 1956 left for the mountains, the Sierra Maestre. Four of their former comrades found them there. The group was also joined by seven peasants. During January the guerillas obtained weapons, first when they attacked an army post and then when they surrounded an army patrol. Local men who wanted to join them were accepted if they could bring a gun. Some managed to steal weapons from Batista's soldiers.

In those early days many people in the United States and Canada admired Castro and his revolution (Canadians still do). On February 17 1957 Herbert Matthews, a senior editor at *The New York Times*, met Fidel at the foot of the mountains and wrote a glowing account of the guerillas for his newspaper. Two more American reporters visited the Sierra Maestre and took photos of themselves and Castro on top of the highest mountain in Cuba. On March 25 1957 fifty-two new recruits, including three from the United States, arrived in the mountains. In June 1957 a young Catholic priest joined Castro and more clergy, including some Protestants, arrived later. Castro asked them to give services for his men. At that time Cuba's regular army had no chaplains.

On July 12 1957 the guerillas published *The Sierra Maestre Manifesto*. It demanded a united front of all the anti-Batista opposition parties, free elections and press freedom, and asked that there be no interference from the United States of America.

In July 1957 Frank Pais, one of Castro's colleagues in Santiago, was captured and shot.

In Autumn there was a lull for the harvest.

In February 1958 the guerillas captured another army outpost. Shortly after that Castro named Judge Urrutia 'provisional governor of Cuba'. Urrutia was the judge who had issued a one-man minority report stating that Castro's criminal suit against Batista's *coup d'etat* should be upheld.

In May 1958 Batista placed a cordon of 10,000 soldiers around the Sierra Maestre. The cordon was supported by aeroplanes (bombers), fuel and spare parts sent from the United States. Fidel's brother Raul managed to capture 10 Americans who were carrying out the supply work and was consequently visited by the American consul. Raul said the prisoners would be released as soon as the United States stopped supplying fuel and spare parts to Batista's men and also forbade Batista to use American-made armaments against the rebels. The consul promised that Batista would halt the bombing but only for three weeks; Raul accepted the compromise. After the resumed bombings, which killed a number of peasants, Castro said: 'I am going to wage war against them' — meaning the United States.

In August 1958 Batista's army withdrew from the mountains and a number of its soldiers defected to the rebels.

In their final push in October 1958 the guerillas followed a three-point plan. A group led by Castro would remain in Oriente Province and encircle Santiago; a second group was to land at the Western end of Cuba; and Che Guevara and his men were to land on the Southern beaches in the middle part of the island, cutting off communications between Batista's men in the Eastern and Western provinces.

On New Year's Eve of 1958 one of Batista's men, General Cantillo, who was in charge of Oriente Province, decided to bring his army over to the rebels. He told Batista the move was merely a ruse. It seems the dictator did not believe the General because at 2 am on New Year's Day 1959 he fled to the Dominican Republic. Cantillo took power, then passed it to a younger officer, Barquin, who did not want it. Barquin ungratefully arrested the General and telephoned Castro urging him to arrange for Judge Urrutia to be made President. On the same day, January 1st, the commanding officer of Santiago met Castro and surrendered the city.

Fidel Castro, flanked by Judge Urrutia on one side and the Catholic Archbishop of Santiago on the other, spoke of the new era awaiting Cuba.

On January 2nd Che Guevara's forces arrived in Havana and according to a British journalist, a man called Tetlow : 'they behaved impeccably'.

Mexico recognised the new government of Judge Urrutia.

Castro took a long march through Cuba, which according to observers had a quite extraordinary emotional impact. Had he held elections during the first years of his rule he would have won overwhelmingly. His literacy programs and health care programs were, and are, immensely popular. The kind of health-care provisions installed in Cuba are not to be found anywhere else in the Hemisphere, though some of the Canadian Provinces have arrangements which resemble them to a certain extent. According to an item published in the British journal *The Lancet* on 14/8/2004 the Cuban government regards health care as a basic right rather than as a commodity. Health care is free for all citizens and there is one General Practitioner for every 650 people. Cuban doctors also help provide care in South America and Southern Africa while the Latin American School of Medicine, established in Havana in 1999, gives free medical training to persons from poor areas of South and Central America. The new doctors have to promise to return to their own countries and districts.

On 5 January 1959 in response, it is said, to public pressure Castro agreed to punish torturers and killers. There must have been a largish number of these men because under Batista 20,000 people were killed in 8 years, which is 2,500 per annum or about 7 every day. The killers and torturers were executed by firing squad after tribunals which Fidel Castro compared to those of Nuremberg. The press reaction in the United States was very hostile.

Castro took up residence in Havana and appointed a former prison guard as his security chief, the same man who had been court-martialled after disobeying an order to poison his prisoner.

Cuban exiles in Mexico began to return home.

The Prime Minister chosen by the rebels resigned in February 1959 asking Castro to take over.

In the same year the US ambassador resigned. His replacement from Washington was a career diplomat and was regarded by many of his countrymen as an apologist for the new regime.

Castro visited the United States at the invitation of newspaper editors and was welcomed by huge crowds in Boston, Princeton and New York City. But the people in the Southern States and the Mid-West detested him.

President Eisenhower absented himself on a golfing holiday during the visit, leaving Vice-President Nixon to meet the visitor.

Eisenhower then sent a memo to the State Department recommending an army of exiles be funded to overthrow the new regime.

When and why did Fidel Castro embrace Marxism?

The answer probably has something to do with the attitude of the United States and something to do with the influence of Che Guevara and Fidel's own brother Raul. Raul and Che were both Marxists.

Castro followed up his success against Batista with a not very drastic re-allocation of land, an action which was enough to convince the American government that he was a communist.

In August 1959 the United States launched a hemispheric strategy to mobilize South American nations against Cuba. The strategy included setting up groups of Cuban exiles with the aim of either overthrowing Castro or assassinating him. America and its allies also placed an embargo on trade with Cuba (the embargo was still in force in 1998 when it was criticised by Pope John Paul II during his visit to Havana). After the trade embargo Fidel turned to the Soviet Union to buy goods and arms, leading to a deal with Nikita Khrushchev under which Russia loaned Cuba $100,000,000 for 12 years at 2.5% interest and agreed to purchase one million tons of sugar per annum for four years in exchange for oil, steel and iron.

Ike's pointed snub in 1959 was in sharp contrast to the reception Castro received in Moscow two years later.

On July 17 1960 Castro resigned, probably as a ploy to prove to the United States that he had near-total support in Cuba.

A huge rally demanded that he take over again as Prime Minister. He responded with the battle cry 'Fatherland or Death!' Cuba's Institute of Agrarian Reform then seized 70 thousand acres of land owned by businesses in the United States, promising compensation.

In April 1961 boats carrying armed Cuban exiles landed in Cuba at the Bay of Pigs and were quickly overcome. Later hit and run attacks by exiles were a nuisance rather than a threat and as fear of an invasion diminished Castro sought rapprochement with the United States. Cuba's delegation at the United Nations was instructed to approach officials in the Kennedy administration. Kennedy himself spoke to a journalist saying he regretted his country's former support for dictators in Cuba, especially the support offered to Batista. Just as the journalist was reporting the President's remarks to Castro news came through that J.F. Kennedy had been assassinated.

At the time of writing this book (2006) Fidel Castro is still alive and still in charge of Cuba though there are reports that he is in poor health.

The local guides tell tourists that he dodges the people sent to assassinate him by sleeping in a different location every night.

When Pope John Paul II visited Cuba in January 1998 he said a mass every day. On the 22nd of January His Holiness met Castro and his ministers in the Palace of the Revolution at 6 pm; on the 23rd he visited the University of Havana which contains the remains of a martyred priest, Fr. Felix Verela; on the 24th he visited the Sanctuary of San Lazaro, a place for sick people which is called 'the world of sorrow'; on the 25th he met representatives of the Jewish Community at the Papal Nunciature. Also on the 25th Pope John Paul conducted a liturgical celebration with clergy and laymen at Havana Cathedral followed by a meeting with the Catholic Bishops of Cuba. During his stay he condemned the America-inspired economic embargo. He said it harmed the poor.

There are several similarities between the attitudes of Rome and Spain to Queen Elizabeth I (see p. 243 below) and the attitudes of the United States to Fidel Castro.

Carl von Clausewitz on guerilla war

Von Clausewitz describes the role of irregular soldiers in his celebrated book *On War* in a chapter entitled 'The People in Arms'. He is interested in situations in which governments place their populations on a war footing but his account of the reasons for the success or failure of such ventures also applies to revolutionary groups and to resistance fighters.

Clausewitz says that a 'people's war' works like 'smouldering embers, it spreads slowly and consumes the basic foundations of the enemy' (Clausewitz, 1993, chapter 26).

After such slow burning the war turns into a general conflagration which closes in on the opposing forces.

Von Clausewitz also compares a regular army to an automatic device and a people's army to a living man. And he says the conditions for success for the people in arms are as follows: First, the war must be fought in the interior of the country; it must not be such as could be decided by a single stroke; the forces of the people must range over a wide territory; the spheres of operation must be rough and inaccessible, which is to say, mountains and forests with scattered settlements and very few roads; most of the fighters should be poor men because poor men are used to hardship; and the national character must be suited to the method of warfare.

Those conditions were present in Norway and Yugoslavia during the second world war, in Cuba in the 1960s, and during the 1964–73 war in Vietnam.

PART V
AGAINST WAR

Chapter 17

Pacifism in the East

The eight-fold path: right view, right aim, right speech, right action, right living, right effort, right mindfulness, right contemplation.

(Gautama Siddhartha)

The Jains

The Jain religion, like Buddhism, resembles Hinduism in some respects but both teachings reject the Hindu caste system and both reject the doctrinal belief in a creator god. Although each system is often described as a religion Western Buddhists in particular reject that label. There are no substantial Jain communities in the West.

Jains believe that one must avoid harming living beings and it is said that some of the more devout carry brooms, sweeping the paths they walk on in order to protect the lives of insects who might otherwise be squashed by human feet. The religion has two orders of monks in one of which the members wear white habits and in the other no clothes at all; those are said to be sky-clad. In my experience one rarely sees people carrying insect brooms in India except for sky-clad Jains near holy places.

Mohandas Karamchand Gandhi acquired the concept of non-violence or non-harm (*ahimsa*) from the Jain communities living in Gujarat, his place of birth.

Buddhism and the Buddha

Gautama Siddhartha, always known as the Buddha, which is to say, the Awakened One, lived, it is believed, during the sixth and 5th centuries BC, possibly between 563 and 483 BC. He is sometimes said to be a younger contemporary of the 24th 'prophet' of Jainism from which it is inferred that Jain teachings are older than his. However the supposed earlier Jain prophets are not historical.

Buddhism lists the causes of war and violence as greed, hatred and delusion, the last item being the primary cause of the other two. Delusion generates strong attachments to religious, political and social opinions and creates false beliefs about the value of material goods. Greed shows itself in attachment to property, money, territory, and economic dominance over other people. Hatred and violence are the results of greed and delusional fear. In Buddhist iconography greed, hate and violence are sometimes represented by a pig vomiting a snake.

According to the Buddha the idea that one can reduce desires by giving way to them is seriously mistaken because giving way causes desires to increase and multiply. The growing pressure of greed generates envy and more delusion, followed by hatred and conflict.

Buddhist values include compassion, loving-kindness, empathy, patience, forbearance, equanimity, and readiness to admit a fault or a mistake. There are five central precepts:

- Abstain from killing or harming living creatures
- Abstain from taking what is not offered or given
- Abstain from misconduct in sensual pleasures
- Abstain from false speech
- Abstain from drugs and alcoholic drinks.

The five precepts are accepted by all Buddhists, lay people as well as monks, though monks have many other rules as well. For lay people there is an ideal of 'right livelihood' which includes the rule that one should not engage in arms traffic.

How would a serious Buddhist ruler respond to an aggressive attack on his country? Is defensive war permitted? The duty of Buddhist monks is clear, they must not engage in violence (and the same is true, in the main, of Christian monks and priests.)

The Buddha himself belonged to the princely ruling caste, a warrior caste, nevertheless he of course spoke against warfare. In the following lines he asserts that warfare always generates more of the same:

> The slayer gets his slayer in his turn
> The conqueror gets a conqueror
> The abuser gets abuse
> The wrathful gets one who harms
> Thus by the evolution of Karma
> He who plunders is plundered.

The word *Karma* means action (amongst other things). The original law of Karma teaches that human beings and animals are reborn after death in forms appropriate to the nature and quality of their previous actions so that a man who behaves like a beast will be reborn as a beast. In a more general and probably later form the Law of Karma is that actions always have results either on the character of the actor, or in the reactions of other people, or both. Good deeds improve the character and encourage others to respond in friendly and helpful ways, bad deeds have the opposite effect. If I am known to be too self-centred to answer the telephone other people might not answer my calls

Complete non-violence is best, followed by self-defensive actions which aim at peace. It is understood that those who have to rule are often tempted by greed and a desire for conquest.

Can one rule without using force? Some Buddhists hold that internal policing is needed to protect the weaker members of the community; most agree that the death penalty is neither good nor necessary.

Hindus believe or once believed that warriors who die in battle go straight to a special heaven. When the Buddha was asked if that story is true he at first remained silent but after being nagged for an answer he reluctantly replied that such a warrior would either be re-born as a lowly animal or would end up in hell.

The Emperor Asoka

Asoka (268–239 BC) inherited a large empire comprising most of India except for part of the south. Early in his reign he conquered the region of Kalinga but his horror at the carnage caused him to abandon war. After becoming a Buddhist he continued to maintain an army, explaining to neighbouring States that he was prepared to defend his realm against attacks and harassment but preferred not to fight and would never wage aggressive war.

Asoka sent emissaries abroad in order to bring about 'conquest by Dharma'. As a result a link with Sri Lanka was effected when his son Mahinda, a monk, took Buddhism to that country.

The term *Dharma* refers to the basic laws and patterns of the universe and also to the Buddha's teachings about those.

A Buddha-inspired text which became influential in Tibet is thought to reflect Asoka's teachings on war. It states that a good ruler always seeks to avoid war, either by negotiation, or by placation, or through strong alliances. If defensive war cannot be avoided a good ruler will do all he can to protect his people and will bear in mind the need to protect life. He will not burn cities and villages, nor will he destroy harvests, reservoirs or orchards, because those are the sources of life 'for gods and for men and for animals'.

There are similarities between Asokan ideas and some rules about justice in war propounded by Christian thinkers in the middle ages.

Authorities are not sure as to whether Asoka did or did not make Buddhism the State religion but they seem to agree that he supported Jain monks and Hindu priests as well as Buddhist monasteries and urged his subjects to tolerate and respect all religions. He instituted a 'Ministry for Dharma' which seems to have worked like a Ministry for Justice. He ordered that wells be dug wherever they were needed and that trees be planted at roadsides to provide shade for travellers. He also created an organisation resembling the RSPCA. After his conversion he gave up hunting and stopped eating meat.

According to at least one version of Buddhist teaching 'all is in flux', hence there is no such thing as an unchanging body or an unchanging mind. Some Buddhists consequently hold that most people have distorted perceptions of reality because they consciously or unconsciously believe in the existence of unchanging material or immaterial selves. The refusal to accept that bodies change and minds change, the refusal to accept that there is no such thing as an unchanging self, leads to, or allows, the idea that 'I' have a country, 'I' have interests, 'I' have important religious beliefs — and so on.

Buddhist thinkers remark that changes in national boundaries and international alliances are even more conspicuous than changes in the minds and bodies of human beings and the other animals. Alliances between different countries change more often, and much more abruptly, than human beings do. As noted earlier George Orwell also draws attention to that fact in *Nineteen Eighty-Four*.

Avoiding war

Buddhist teachings include creative suggestions about ways to avoid war. Governments should attempt to defuse potential conflict between nations in roughly the same ways in which conflict between smaller groups or between individuals can be defused.

When there is danger of war rulers should seek consensus by drawing attention to shared principles. If consensus cannot be achieved they should seek for a majority vote. Offences should be overlooked whenever a guilty party cannot remember them and acts of aggression should be overlooked if committed when the aggressive party was out of his mind. Offences which the guilty party acknowledges and repents should always be forgiven.

Representatives from each side should be appointed whose task it would be to apologize on behalf of those they represent. This is called 'covering over with grass.'

Some of these rules resemble the Quaker suggestions about how best to resolve the stupid, stubborn Cold War quarrels carried out in the United Nations Assembly during the Cold War (chapter 24, *ibid.*).

There is an Indian legend about a dispute caused when two tribes separated by a river both claimed all its water for their crops. The Buddha flew across the sky and settled the argument by pointing out that the loss of lives is worse than a shortage of water. In another legend the Buddha appears as a king whose city is surrounded by enemy soldiers. He opens the gates to the soldiers saying ' I want no territory that can only be kept by doing harm'. According to this story he is deposed and imprisoned until the conquering king undergoes Karmic suffering in the form of burning sensations and so releases him.

Peter Harway writes that Indian history mentions many occasions on which Hindu kings persecuted Buddhists but has no records of Buddhists persecuting Hindus. Buddhist monks were sometimes asked by kings to negotiate armistices and peace treaties.

According to a verse of the Pali canon all soldiers, including conscripts, are guilty, in other words, the rule against traffic in arms covers each and every warlike use of arms and not only buying and selling. On the other hand Buddhist rulers did repel aggression by force. Moreover repelling aggression has sometimes been replaced by the very different option of pre-emptive strikes.

Mahatma Gandhi

Mohandas Karamchand Gandhi (1863-1948) was of course a Hindu by birth but as noted above his doctrine of *ahimsa* came to him from the Jains.

He studied law in England, then spent 20 years in South Africa, returning to India in 1914. He supported Britain during the first world war but also became interested in the Home Rule movement. He joined the National Congress Organisation (founded in 1885) and began to urge what turned out to be a programme of satyagaha. The word *satyagaha* was invented by one of Gandhi's disciples, it is based on Sanskrit roots and means *the way of truth*, which is to say, the way of non-violent civil disobedience.

Gandhi advised his followers to become self-sufficient, for example by spinning and weaving their own clothes instead of selling cotton to manufacturers and then buying back ready-made garments. He himself obtained a spinning wheel, learnt to spin, and gave up wearing Western dress. In 1930 he led a march of 200 people to the sea where they collected salt in order to avoid paying salt tax to the British authorities. Various acts of civil disobedience led to prison where he would sometimes begin a 'fast unto death'. The authorities, fearing no doubt that his death in gaol could lead to violent civil strife, always freed him when he became too emaciated.

Gandhi was opposed to the caste system and taught his followers to call the non-caste Indians, the untouchables, 'the children of God'. In 1942 Sir Stafford Cripps visited India and offered the country full Dominion status within the British Commonwealth, including the right of secession. It was understood that steps in that direction would have to wait until the end of the war. Unfortunately Gandhi had a rush of blood to the head and told his colleagues in the Congress Party to reject the offer, which they did. He had decided India should not be asked to fight for Britain and the British rulers of India. A state of emergency was declared and a number of Congress Party members were imprisoned.

If Indian soldiers had followed Gandhi`s recommendation Japan would have conquered the country and ruled it in the way they ruled Korea and parts of China, i.e., with the utmost brutality. Anyone attempting *satyagaha* would have been used for bayonet practice.

In 1947 the post-war Labour Government finally fulfilled a number of earlier promises and announced India`s independence. Gandhi hoped and probably believed that the different religious believers in the sub-continent could live side by side without fighting but the Muslim leader Mohammed Ali Jinnah (1876–1948), who was opposed to Indian unity, had already left the Indian National Congress and founded the Muslim League. In 1947 Pakistan ('the land of the pure') came into being with Jinnah as Governor under the auspices of the United Kingdom.The resulting transfers of Muslims and Hindus across the new border led to the massacre of thousands of travellers in both directions.

Gandhi was assassinated by a fellow-Hindu in January 1948.

Gandhi is admired by Buddhists and other non-Hindus not least because he showed that non-violent resistance could sometimes be an efficacious method of dealing with injustice.

Ghosananda
(Taken from Harway, 2000.)

The tensions in the Far East left over from wars in Korea and Vietnam continued for many years. In 1992 a Cambodian monk, Ghosananda, composed the following prayer :

The suffering of Cambodia has been deep,
This suffering causes great compassion,
Great compassion makes a peaceful heart,
A peaceful heart makes a peaceful person,
A peaceful person makes a peaceful family,
A peaceful family makes a peaceful community,
A peaceful community makes a peaceful nation,
A peaceful nation makes a peaceful world.
May all beings live in happiness and peace.

In 1993 he and 69 others led a 19-day peace march from the border between Thailand and Cambodia to Phnom Penh passing unharmed through territory still harbouring remnants of the Khmer Rouge. The original 70 monks were eventually joined by 8,000 other people. Ghosananda later led more peace marches including one made up of 800 monks and nuns.

Buddhist violence and its supposed justifications

Buddhism lacks any plausible rationale for engaging in warfare and therefore tends to have an overall humanizing effect on its believers. Yet it has to be agreed that some who claim to follow Dharma have been extremely violent. Pol Pot, the ruler who instigated the mass-murders carried out in the terrible killing fields of Cambodia was a Buddhist, at least in his beginnings.

The Buddhist majority in Sri Lanka has for many years been engaged in a civil war with the 'Tamil Tigers'. Trickling immigration from Tamil Nadu to Sri Lanka has been going on for hundreds of years but the number of migrants was greatly boosted in the 19th century when British planters brought in Tamils to work as indentured labourers. The descendants of Hindu immigrants from South India now constitute 20% of the population of the island. Some contrive to live in peace with their neighbours, for example Hindus as well as Buddhists celebrate the Sri Lankan New Year in April. In 1983, however, a civil war broke out; it continues to this day in spite of the efforts of Norwegian peace negotiators. The latest truce was declared in 2005 but collapsed in 2006.

During the Vietnam war the United States held bases in Thailand from which bombing raids were carried out on Cambodian and Vietnamese targets. According to the author Peter Harway a well-known Buddhist monk once announced that killing communists and leftists is not demeritorious because such killings are not the killings of persons. Whoever destroys the nation and its religion is not a real person. The intention to kill communists is not to kill persons but to kill the Devil. Like some of the Westerners described in chapter 25 (below) the same monk played a numbers game, saying that killing 5,000 people in order to save 42,000,000 is a good thing to do. Harway reports that this uncharacteristically bloodthirsty Buddhist was denounced by a Supreme Patriarch but not punished because monks are allowed free speech.

Revolts against British rule in Burma occurred in 1839, 1855, 1858 1860, 1922 and 1930. The uprisings were led by charismatic leaders, laymen who the people identified as Bodhisattvas. A Bodhisattva is like the Buddha, he is an enlightened being, an awakened being. However monks did not take part in the violence.

In Tibet the followers of Tantric rites are taught that killing a very harmful person is allowed but only in extremely restricted circumstances.

According to a late text (circa 4th century AD) the Buddha himself in an earlier incarnation put to death a number of Brahmins (high-caste Hindus) in order to save them from their own bad Karma.

Japan and China have long histories as military nations. In both countries it was believed that Tantric rites ensured victory in battle.

Buddhism (Zen) arrived in Japan in 538 AD. There were clashes between different groups of Buddhists and by 1100 AD many of the larger monasteries had defensive armies made up of warrior monks. Temples were fortified and protected by armed priests. A dictatorship which lasted from 1603 to 1867 was inaugurated when Shoguns (knights) destroyed military monasteries and slaughtered thousands of monks. The knights preferred a more warlike religion. Shinto, still the official religion of Japan, originally taught that the Emperor is to be identified with the Deity and that his commands, issued through mainly military spokesmen, must be obeyed without question.

The survival of Buddhist traditions

Buddhism has often had to compete with nationalism, xenophobia, and militarism, most especially during the 20th century. Nevertheless its teachings like those of the Society of Friends have strong resources for conflict resolution which have never been completely forgotten. The need for compassion remains central to Buddhist teaching, of course, and prominent Buddhists — such as the Dalai Llama, Ghosananda of Cambodia and Aung San Suu Kyi of

Burma—have indeed expressed compassion for both sides during times of violent conflict.

Chapter 18

Pacifism in the West

There never was a good war or a bad peace
(Benjamin Franklin)

Pacifism and early Christianity

It would seem that the complete rejection of war did not appear in the West before the Christian era. Some of the early Fathers of the Church wrote against war and killing. Tertullian (160-220) for instance wrote:

> How will a Christian make war—nay, how will he serve a a soldier, even in time of peace, without the sword, which the Lord has taken away? (Tertullian, 1869, p. 171).

Origen (185–254) said that Christians should be exempted from military service. He compared them to the priests of other religions to whom the shedding of human blood was forbidden (Origen, 1953, p. 509).

According to Peter Brock (Brock, 1972) the early collections of legislation made in Christian communities in the first and second centuries ruled that after baptism soldiers had to leave the army which doubtless explains why some early saints refused to serve as soldiers. St. Maximilian of Numidia, the son of a soldier, was required to join the Roman army. When he refused the authorities pointed out that other Christians were serving and asked him 'What wrong do they do?' He replied 'Thou knowest what wrong they do.' Maximilian was executed in the year 295.

Brock also relates how in the year 356 St. Martin of Tours threw down his weapons on the eve of a battle; when accused of cowardice he said he would go into the field unarmed.

Under the Romans Christianity was for a time a religion for Jews and women, people not required to undertake military service, on the other hand those who converted to the new religion a bit later included men who were already soldiers. Peter Brock suggests that the fierce persecution of Christians which took place before the rule of the Emperor Constantine might have been a reaction to the fact that these increasingly numerous citizens were refusing to take part in the defence of Rome.

After early times the Christian Church adopted the teachings of Augustine on war and peace. As noted in chapter 3 (*ibid.*) Augustine held that war is akin to punishment and since punishment of citizens by the State—'the violence of the magistrate'—is not forbidden so war too must be permissible. Punishment, moreover, is not incompatible with love since parents lovingly chastise their children. According to Augustine a Christian Emperor has a duty to fight barbarians and God will support his cause if he does.

The creed nowadays called pacifism was condemned by the Church at the Synod of Arles in the 4th century which ruled that a soldier who laid down his arms in time of peace would be excommunicated. The decision is interpreted by pacifists as showing merely that police work was regarded as a legitimate form of violence and by anti-pacifists as a decision to recommend excommunication whenever a soldier laid down his arms, that is to say, in peace time as well as in times of war. The second interpretation seems likely to be correct yet hundreds of years later some clergy in some places were still imposing penalties on those who killed human beings—and they did not exempt soldiers who killed other soldiers in battle. Thus Norman bishops drew up a list of the various particular penances owed by those who had fought in the Battle of Hastings and in 1070 Bishop Ermenfried, the papal legate in England, confirmed their text.

The historian H.E.J. Cowdrey describes the document composed by Ermenfried as follows:

> The penances laid down by the bishops varied according to motivation and to the time of killing and to the number of killings. Some motives were more sinful than others, thus those who fought and killed for personal gain were supposed to do penance for seven years whereas those who killed in obedience to their rightful prince, King Harold or Duke William as the case may be, only did penance for three years. As to timing, it was less bad to kill during a battle than before or after . The more people one killed the heavier would be the penance. William himself claimed to have killed 2,000 men so his initial penance would have been pretty heavy. Sentences could be commuted by giving alms and some commentators believe that William's were commuted when he decided to pay for the construction of a new church, Battle Abbey (Cowdrey, 1969).

Cowdrey says that the Papal Legate's penitentiary is evidence for the continuance of an older Christian view that engaging in warfare, even at the command of a prince and in a just cause, involves grave sin.

It seems plain that the older view was adhered to by some clergy and rejected by others. Two hundred years before the Battle of Hastings Pope Leo IV (847–855) had already decreed that, although to kill a Christian is a sin, to kill an infidel is not. Pope Urban II (1088–1099) repeated that ruling when he launched the first Crusade. He also decreed that privately or publicly killing people who had been excommunicated is not murder.

Pacifist sects: Waldensians, Lollards, Mennonites

Anti-war-ism is a characteristic form of renewal for Christianity. Pacifism is not part and parcel of institutional Christianity, yet it is characteristic of Christianity in that until fairly recently nearly all Westerners who could be described as pacifists were in fact members of Christian sects. Only a minority of Christians have been pacifists but historically most Western pacifists have been Christians. Their anti-war-ism was, and still is, inspired, by certain passages in the Gospels, and by what has been taken to be the general tone of Christ's teachings, and by His non-resistance to the soldiers who came to arrest him.

Before the Reformation pacifism was adopted by a number of groups and sects, all of which were condemned for heresy by the Catholic church.

The Waldensians, followers of Peter Valdes of Lyons, who died in 1217, acquired vernacular versions of the Bible and lived lives of poverty and religious devotion. They were persecuted as heretics but survived in Piedmont until a massacre in 1655.

The Lollards in their petition to Parliament in 1395 said:

> Manslaughter by battle or by law ... is contrary to the New Testament unless it is justified by express revelation (Douglas, 1969, p. 849).

By *express revelation* the Lollards meant special revelations issued in particular circumstances and concerned only with those circumstances. The instruction given to Joshua by God — as recorded in the first chapter of the Book of Joshua — is an example.

The Lollards were followers of John Wycliffe (1330–1384), an Oxford theologian who translated the Bible into English. Lollardy was favoured by King Edward III and also to some extent by his successor Richard II. In 1382 it was declared a heresy by Pope Urban VI in spite of, or perhaps because of, its having found favour with two English Kings.

Mennonites are followers of Menno Simons (1496–1561), a Dutchman and an ex-priest. They were severely persecuted in Holland and Switzerland but managed to find a haven in North America in 1663.

The Society of Friends

In the Protestant England of the 17th century George Fox, who was born in 1624 and died in 1690, created the Society of Friends and preached 'the inner light' and peace, justice and tolerance. Fox, an apprentice shoemaker, left home at the age of 19 and began wandering around England, walking into churches in order to interrupt the services, refusing to take his hat off to any man, and expressing a quiet rejection of social conventions. As a result he was insulted, persecuted and imprisoned. In later life he worked as a missionary in Barbados, Jamaica, America, Holland and Germany.

Members of the Religious Society of Friends gather in silence until moved by the spirit to speak according to an inner light which is held to be a living contact with the Divine Spirit.

Quakers have always opposed slavery as well as war. In the 19th century they supported William Wilberforce (1759–1833), an independent Member of Parliament, in his long fight against the traffic in African human beings. Wilberforce's struggle against the British slave trade started in 1788 and finally succeeded in 1807. His supporters, who continued the campaign after he retired from Parliament in 1825, succeeded in abolishing the trans-Atlantic traffic in 1833, the year Wilberforce died. After that date all new slaves in America were born and bred on the plantations.

Quakers refuse to fight in wars. During the first world war the military profession tended to regard them as traitors but by the time of the second it was accepted, at least in Britain, that the Society of Friends and other pacifist sects should be exempted from military service.

Papal teaching during and after the Cold War

We have seen how the Catholic Church gradually developed the theory of the just war between the 9th and the 14th centuries and how pacifism was declared heretical. If we are to judge by the words of Pope Pius XII, anti-war-ism was still regarded as heretical in the middle of the 20th century. He said:

> A Catholic citizen may not appeal to his conscience as grounds for refusing to serve and fulfill duties fixed by law if the decision to undertake military operations is reached by freely elected leaders and there is express danger of unjust attack (*New Catholic Encyclopedia* vol. 14, 1967, p. 804).

The same encyclopaedia states elsewhere that conscientious objection to military service is 'morally indefensible'.

However there seems to have been a radical shift in Catholic teaching on conscientious objection. The decisions of the Second Vatican Council held between 1963 and 1965 included the following:

> It seems just that the law should make provision for the case of conscientious objectors who refuse to carry arms provided they accept some other form of community service

and:

> We cannot but express our admiration for all who forgo the use of violence to vindicate their rights and resort to those means of defence which are available to weaker parties (Flannery, 1974, pp. 987–988).

Pacifism not a unitary thesis

The word *pacifism* was not invented by Fox or any other Quaker but dates from the beginning of the 20th century. The 1984 *Supplement to the Oxford English Dictionary* states that it first appeared in 1902 when it was used, and defined, by a Frenchman attending an international peace conference. Pacifism, he said, is anti-war-ism. In *The Times* of July 30 1906 the word appeared again, this time in inverted commas, and in 1915 *The National Review* claimed that 'the greatest war in history is now being fought in the cause of pacifism', meaning anti-war-ism in the sense of lasting peace. The *OED* also quotes from a 1930 issue of the *Baltimore Sun* which castigated 'pacifists and defeatists'.

It is possible to think of pacifism not as a unitary thesis but as a collection of closely linked theories. Some 'ism' words name a type of action, for example baptism; some a kind of trait, for example alcoholism; some a state of affairs, for example barbarism; some a practice, for example vegetarianism. Then again an 'ism' word can be the name of a single theory, as it might be Calvinism or monetarism or positivism. Finally it can refer to a set of related theories such as realism or paganism or polytheism. Pacifism falls into this last class since it has been predicated of a number of different movements having somewhat different ideas. Quakers and Mennonites, for example, are pacifists for religious reasons; on the other hand some non-religious and anti-religious Anarchists are pacifists too (albeit of a different type) because they believe that States have no right to conscript men into armies.

Let us take *pacifism* to be the name of a theory with several branches or varieties all of which share as a common feature a principled opposition to war. Pacifism is indeed anti-war-ism.

Anti-war-ism must be distinguished from love of peace pure and simple since many soldiers profess a love of peace, no doubt with good reason. It is different, too, from pragmatic attempts to abolish war. It does not necessarily involve opposition to all forms of physical violence since integrational pacifism accepts 'the violence of the magistrate'.

A rational preference for peace is compatible with the view that war is a necessary evil, hence such a preference is not necessarily pacifistic.

Some love of peace or attachment to peace is vocational. Thus Buddhist monks are forbidden to shed blood and are not allowed to watch battles or even mock battles. On the other hand Buddhist laymen are permitted to serve as soldiers, at least according to some opinions. Christian priests must not shed human blood but they teach that laymen may and in some cases must go to war. It follows that vocational attachment to peace need not entail anti-war-ism and so is not the same thing as pacifism.

Pragmatic attempts to abolish war or reduce its impact do not necessarily stem from pacifism. Such attempts might be the result of a belief that war is bad for trade (though of course it isn't!) or wasteful.

Some pacifists hold the view that all violence whatsoever is wrong, others accept the 'lesser violence' of police forces and schoolmasters.

Some Christian pacifists believe that one must always turn the other cheek, in other words they hold that evil must not be resisted but others allow non-violent resistence and acts of passive resistance of the kind advocated by Gandhi.

It follows from the above that there are two reasons to reject the conflation of anti-war-ism with opposition to all violence as such. The first reason is that the term *pacifism* was coined to refer specifically to anti-war-ism and only anti-war-ism. The second reason is that people who have been retrospectively described as pacifists or who nowadays describe themselves as such, are not by any means invariably opposed to the physical force used by policemen or parents or schoolmasters. Some are but their opposition is not of the essence of pacifism. Many pacifists are vegetarians but opposition to eating animal flesh is not the same thing as pacifism nor is it logically entailed by it.

Although the common core of pacifism is a principled opposition to warfare the moral or religious principles which dictate a refusal to shed human blood in war are various.

To begin with anti-war-ism may be conditional or unconditional. Thus some Christians have believed that war was permissible in Old Testament times but ceased to be allowable after the new teaching of Jesus after He put away Peter's sword.

Again some people who call themselves pacifists argue that war might have been all right when only soldiers were involved but ceased to be so when the weapons used kill civilians and indeed are intended to do that. War has ceased to be what it used to be, it is a different kind of activity altogether.

Thirdly there are those who believe that war might be permissible if all those who engage in it are volunteers but ceases to be so when impressment or conscription are involved. These are perhaps borderline pacifists.

The last two varieties of conditional pacifism could be dubbed *just war pacifism* since they exemplify the idea that most war or most modern war cannot fulfil the canons of justice which make the activity all right. For thinkers of this variety the supposition that a typical modern war could be just in its methods somewhat resembles a supposition that an ordinary adult human being could be completely without sin. Conditional pacifists of this kind believe the rules of justice in warfare are coherent and that no wars fought with modern weapons can follow those rules.

Possible classifications

It would not do to discuss the nature of pacifism without taking into account at least some of the things its supporters and its historians have had to say. Let us now consider the views of Peter Brock (Brock,1968, 1972, 1973) and John Yoder (Yoder, 1971).

Peter Brock is an historian who has traced the development of pacifism in the United States, England and Europe. He treats pacifism as much the same thing as resistance to war in all its forms but at the same time holds that there are different ways of resistance and different reasons for resistance.

- Vocational pacifism, he says, is the pacifism of men in holy orders. It can though it need not go with anti-war-ism or opposition to all forms of violence.
- Eschatological pacifism is an interim ethic which teaches that on the last day when the world ends there will be an apocalyptic battle between the forces of good and evil but until then war is completely forbidden.
- Separational pacifism is the view that the redeemed or favoured of God must separate themselves from the rest of mankind because ordinary humanity is irredeemably wicked. The New Testament is taken as a divine Law which replaces the teachings of the Old. War is condemned absolutely but the violence of the magistrate is accepted conditionally even though that violence too belongs to the realm of evil.
- Integrational pacifism is the title Brock gives to groups who combine an ethic of peace and peace-seeking with the setting up of reform movements the platforms of which include opposition to war but other items as well, the abolition of racial segregation for example. These pacifists are not opposed to government nor to the internal, i.e., local use of force by government. Brock says that most modern Quakers are integrational pacifisms.
- Goal-directed pacifism pursues specific aims using non-violent techniques. Gandhi's fasting is of course a famous example.

Another historian, John Yoder, is a Mennonite professor of theology. He divides pacifism according to its different motivations, as follows:

- The Christian claim to be a universal church entails that no Christian has a special loyalty to any one nation or race. Christianity has adherents in all the nations of the earth and cannot take sides between nations.
- Just war pacifism entails the view that because of the destructiveness of warfare there exists a rational presumption against any war's being just rather than unjust. It follows that no government has a right to force its citizens to fight, the citizens themselves must weigh up the evidence for and against the justice of each war.

- Absolute pacifism teaches that all deliberate killing of human beings is intrinsically evil.
- Political pacifism or pragmatic pacifism teaches that refusal to fight is the only way to stop governments from ordering wars. Gandhi's use of non-violent action aimed at specific ends is a form of pragmatic pacifism.
- One variety of Christian pacifism demands a new standard of righteousness based on the New Testament.
- 'Kantian' pacifism teaches that pacifism can be willed to be a universal law of nature and is therefore the subject of a categorical imperative.

Yoder's classification like Brock's contains some overlapping strands but like Brock's it is important because it reminds us of the different kinds of moral and religious reasons that lie behind characteristic pacifist teachings and behaviour.

Just war pacifism arose after the invention and deployment of atomic weapons. It allows that some wars might be justified even now or might have been justified in the past. After the second world war stricter pacifists, Quakers for example, sometimes worked alongside just war pacifists in organisations such as the Campaign for Nuclear Disarmament, Bertrand Russell's so-called Committee of 100, and the Women's Peace Camp at Greenham Common in Britain (see chapters 20 and 21 below).

Chapter 19

Conscription and Conscience

Conscription is the tap-root of militarism
(General Jan Smuts — att.)

Conscription

Conscription is by no means a new phenomenon. In the Greek city states all free citizens were expected to give military service. The Roman polity expected all fit men to serve when necessary though it is said conscription of Roman citizens was only nominal. For it would appear that conquered barbarians were very willing to become soldiers in return for some of the privileges Rome could give them.

Oliver Cromwell relied on impressment, that is, seizure, to make up his armies, so too did the English navy during the Napoleonic wars.

The little German Dukedom of Hesse conscripted men into its army and then sold them in batches to other nations. For example in the 18th century Hessians fought alongside French soldiers against an English army in what is now Canada.

Standing professional armies had appeared in Europe in about 1450 but only became really important after 1798. France introduced conscription during the revolution and Napoleon, of course, needed conscripted men in order to carry out his expansionist adventurism. But many men in France were exempt, farmers being an important example. In the 20th century the mechanisation of farming and industry meant fewer men were excused military service in time of war.

The armies of Tsarist Russia relied on a particularly horrible kind of conscription. Military officers were professionals but could buy themselves out but ordinary men, serfs and such, in other words those destined for the other ranks, were seized by the authorities, or sold by their owners, and could be conscripted *for life*.

In the 19th and 20th centuries compulsory military service became the rule all over continental Europe. Britain, however, did not introduce it until 1916, abolished it in 1919, and re-introduced it in the second world war. National Service, as it was called in Britain, continued for some years after that war.

In 1910 Lord Haldane created the British territorial army which was made up of volunteers and still is.

The United States introduced conscription when it entered the first world war in 1917 and again during WWII. It raised an army to fight in Vietnam by a system using compulsory registration followed by selective conscription (the draft). College students were exempt during their years of study which probably led to an increase in the number of Americans with Ph.Ds.

The draft produced an army with a high proportion of poorly educated working class men and many blacks. Some have argued that the draft was a fairer system than one relying on volunteers driven by poverty and unemployment.

Quakers during the Boer war and the first world war

During the Boer War the prominent Quaker Joshua Rowntree visited South Africa and on his return reported to the Society of Friends that the British army was burning farms and had set up concentration camps for women and children. The Society objected to the war itself, of course, but also to the methods used. Its stance was publicly known and Friends' meetings in Britain were attacked by mobs accusing the Friends of being pro-Boer.

At the outbreak of war in August 1914 the Society of Friends began to organise volunteer work for its members. Quakers worked in hospitals and canteens, took care of destitute Belgian refugees, and drove ambulances in France and Flanders. The British Friends' Ambulance Service began in 1914 with 43 volunteers, all unpaid. By the end of the war the number of Friends working in the ambulances had grown to 600 men, twenty of whom were killed by enemy fire. Many more were wounded. Ninety-six received medals for bravery, including some who were awarded the Croix de Guerre.

In 1916 the first British Military Service Act came into force. The Act made provision for conscientious objectors who could prove they already belonged to a pacifist sect, typically the Society of Friends. Local tribunals were organised whose task was to establish the facts regarding claims to membership of such sects. The tribunals, usually made up of relatively prominent members of the community, were issued with a government list of the national contributions conscientious objectors could be asked to perform in place of military service. The approved alternatives included work in hospitals and in prisons, poor relief, work with the Red Cross and on the land, and help in caring for disabled soldiers. Some of the tribunals swept the list aside and ordered conscientious objectors to report to munitions factories. Some sent conscientious objectors to prison or directly to the front. There were tribunals which ruled that local units of the existing Friends' Ambulance Service could not remain independent but were to be placed under military command as soon as they left for France. In the first six months after the passing of the Military Service Act the tribunals assigned more than 2,500 conscientious objectors to combatant or non-combatant duties in the army. Those who refused to comply would be arrested and handed over to the military authorities. Parliament repeatedly assured the country that conscientious objectors were not to be punished by the death penalty but on June 15 1916 four were court-martialled and shot. Others were imprisoned, sometimes in chains, and/or put onto bread and water diets in solitary confinement. The objectors held in civilian gaols included a number who were not released until the middle of 1919 (Hirst, 1923). The behaviour of several tribunals became an open scandal.

The Defence of the Realm Act made it illegal to print, publish or distribute any leaflet relating to war and peace without the approval of the official Press Bureau. The Society of Friends decided to ignore the Act and did not seek approval from the bureau for its publications. Three men were gaoled for this offence in 1918.

After the United States joined in the war in April 1917 its government exempted Mennonites and Quakers from combat duty. Exempted men were called up for tasks defined as 'work the President declares to be non-combatant'; such tasks included medical services, engineering and serving as quarter-masters. Over 200 American conscientious objectors joined the Red Cross in France but were promptly drafted into the American army. Soon afterwards their names appeared on a list of deserters. By the end of the war about 500 American conscientious objectors had been imprisoned in military gaols.

It appears to be the case that the Western Allies treated conscientious objectors during the second world war in a more civilised fashion than they had in the first.

The Vietnam war

Vietnam became French Indo-China in the 19th century after France helped General Nguyen Anh unite Annam and Tonkin and subsequently allowed him to make himself Emperor. Japan occupied Indo-China in WWII but as allies of Germany and honorary Aryans they invited Vichy France to administer the area.

In September 1945 the Vietnamese communist, Ho Chi Minh, declared independence. The declaration was soon followed by French re-occupation, leading to a conflict which lasted for nine years in its first phase and eventually for a total of thirty years.

In 1954 a conference in Geneva partitioned Vietnam at the 17th parallel with a communist capital at Hanoi in the North and a non-communist capital at Saigon in the South. The communist forces included the Viet Minh, which had been founded by exiles in South China in 1941. It began operations in 1943, its aim being to expel the Japanese and the French from Vietnam. At that point it received assistance from the United States. The Viet Cong was set up after the 1954 Geneva conference with the intention of uniting the two halves of Vietnam under communist rule.

The Viet Cong's attempt to bring about the so-called liberation of South Vietnam was bitterly opposed by America which began sending help to the South in 1964. President Johnson authorised military assistance after receiving intelligence about an attack on an American gunboat in the Gulf of Tonkin in August. The information was later shown to be mistaken.

In America and elsewhere in the West 'the Vietnam war' is generally taken to refer to the years between 1965 and 1973. Substantial American military contribution began in 1965, rising to 125,000 men in that year and to 400,000 men in 1967. The war ended in January 1973 when American army leaders and political advisors flew out of Saigon amid scenes of chaos, leaving their local allies to face the music. The Viet Cong took Saigon on April 30 1975 and, fortunately for its inhabitants, Ho Chi Minh did not choose to engage in large-scale revenge.

Ho Chi Minh was very different from his neighbour Pol Pot of Cambodia. Pol Pot, leader of the communist Khmer Rouge (Red Cambodia), thought the best way to introduce a new regime was to systematically put to death all members of the Cambodian upper and middle classes—men, women and children. It is thought that 2,000,000 people were killed in three years. When Ho Chi Minh's army invaded Cambodia in 1978 and put an end to the dreadful slaughter Pol Pot disappeared into the forests. Tourists in Cambodia are sometimes shown one of the tyrant's killing fields. It contains a grove of trees on which infants' brains were dashed out after their parents had been shot. Watery indentations in the soil mark the location of what used to be mass graves. Nearby there is a large tower containing dozens of crowded shelves holding human skulls. Phnom Penh, the capital city has a museum or gallery displaying hundreds of photos of desperately unhappy people taken by their killers shortly before they were shot. When I was visiting Cambodia in April 1998 the death of Pol Pot was announced on the radio. The reports stated that the monster had been found dead in his bed in a hideout in the forests. Local people believed the dead body was a decoy, they said the corpse depicted in the photographs had the wrong colour hair.

'Heck, no, we won't go!'

The Vietnam war eventually became unpopular at home in the United States and was also condemned by certain friends of America. Student dislike of President Johnson's policies became tumultuous after American newspapers published a photograph of a child covered with burning Napalm, also pictures of deformed babies. The deformities were said to have been caused Agent Orange, a defoliant sprayed on Vietnamese crops and forests.

The United States' army in Vietnam was by and large made up of conscripts but, as mentioned above, men were exempted temporarily if they were full-time students. Also exempt were those who already belonged to named pacifist sects: the Quakers, the Mennonites and the Plymouth Brethren. Christians, Jews and agnostics who simply believed the war was unjust in its aims or its methods or both were not officially exempt and at times were accused of cowardice or treasonable pro-communism. Yet some of these 'just war pacifists' occasionally managed to convince draft boards that their opinions were genuine and should be respected.

Non-exempted young men aged 18 + were ordered to register for national service and were sent numbered draft cards. A high number on the card meant it could be some time before the draftee was called on to serve his country. The service would either be in an important occupation at home or in the armed forces in Vietnam but the decision was not up to the drafted person.

There was considerable resistance to the draft (Rorabaugh, 1989) especially among radical students whose ideas were shared by or perhaps borrowed from certain idols in the world of pop music. There were student sit-ins and protest meetings in the Universities and 'protest concerts' given by popular bands and singers. In the University of California many such events were arranged by the Freedom of Speech Movement (the FSM), created in response to new rules banning students from publishing leaflets about war and peace. Young people chanted chants aimed at President Lyndon B. Johnson:

> Hey, hey, LBJ, how many kids have you killed today?

The student Freedom of Speech Movement printed and sang new songs, including the following:

> Jingle bells, jingle bells,
> Jingle all the day,
> Oh what fun
> It is to have
> Your mind reduced to clay!
> Civil rights and politics
> Just get in the way
> Questioning authority
> When you should obey ... (Rorabaugh *op.cit.*)

Some young men ostentatiously burnt their draft cards in public, a risky action because destroying a draft card had been ruled a felony. Students distributed news sheets condemning the war and accusing the President's business friends of making big profits from military contracts. The Dow Chemical Company was picketed by students because it manufactured Napalm.

Not all the resistance came from the liberal left. There was an organisation called Conservatives for Political Action, one of whose members went on a 10-day hunger strike outside the offices of his local draft board.

A number of men took drastic action and left the country. Most fled to Canada where they were treated sympathetically by anti-draft programmes set up in Toronto, Montreal, Vancouver and elsewhere. The programmes supplied absconders with food and clothing and helped them find work and accommodation.

The war in Iraq is being fought by volunteer soldiers and it is interesting to note that certain vaguely leftish news reporters who might well have opposed the draft for Vietnam had they been writing in those days, have recently suggested that those who volunteer for Iraq have been put under pressure both by their personal circumstances (in other words their poverty) and by the aggressive military recruitments carried out in towns where many young people are out of work. Journalists of that interesting ilk say a draft would be a better way to raise an army for Iraq. In June 2005 an op-ed article in *The New York Times* supported a military draft as follows:

> (Headline: Let Someone Else's Child Fight.)
>
> ... It is easy to be tough when you have nothing at risk. The hawks want the war [in Iraq] to be fought with other peoples' children, while their own children go safely off to college or to the mall. The number of influential American officials who have children in uniform is miniscule ... the vast majority of parents who support the war do not want their children to fight it ... (One mother said) 'I would not want my children to go ... I support the war and I think we need to be there ... it's not going well ... But we can't leave.' ... How do you justify sending other peoples' children off to fight while keeping a cloak of protection around your own kids? If the United States had a draft ... its warriors would be drawn from a much wider swath of the population and political leaders would think much longer and harder before committing the country to war.

Chapter 20
Campaigns (Law-abiding)

Mankind must put an end to war or war will put an end to mankind
(John F. Kennedy)

The Campaign for Nuclear Disarmament

The aim of the British Campaign for Nuclear Disarmament (CND), set up in 1958, was to persuade the British people and British politicians that their country should give up building and stockpiling nuclear weapons whether or not the United States and the Soviet Union did so as well.

The first chairman of CND was John Collins, a Canon of St Paul's Cathedral (Collins, 1966). Collins went up to Cambridge, to Sidney Sussex College, to read mathematics, with what success he does not divulge, then spent another two years at Westcott House studying theology and other elements of priestcraft. As it turned out he spent little more than a year as a curate in an ordinary parish and the rest of his working life as a teacher (Kings College London, Westcott House Cambridge), as a College Chaplain (Sidney Sussex Cambridge), a College Dean (Oriel College Oxford), a Chaplain in the Royal Air Force, a priest-in-ordinary at the Chapel Royal, a Canon of St Paul's Cathedral, and a political campaigner.

After a visit to Wales during the Great Depression of the 1930's Collins became a (democratic) socialist. In Wales he saw people of both sexes and all ages suffering from near starvation and a complete lack of hope. In the 1940s a newspaper accused him of being a communist. He sued for libel and won. Marxism, said Collins, must be rejected firstly because it denies the spiritual side of life and secondly because communist regimes in Soviet Russia and Eastern Europe and China actively persecute Christian priests and Christian believers.

Collins joined the Royal Air Force in 1940 and in 1941 was appointed Chaplain to a station associated with Bomber Command. In 1944 he was transferred to the Bomber Command Headquarters at High Wycombe. During his time in the RAF he was four times threatened with courts martial: in each case the threat was withdrawn, usually (he said) after he had suggested to his Commanding Officer that he check King's Regulations.

Collins wrote about the British 'Establishment' and its threats as follows:

> I found how vulnerable it is when once you cease to be afraid of it ... Provided you stand on principle, avoid getting personally involved, seek no preferment and remain unconcerned about its rewards or its punishments, you can always resist the pretensions of the Establishment, expose its weaknesses, and, if you are patient, persistent and lucky, sometimes defeat it (Collins, 1966, p. 82).

One of the abortive threats of court martial was made shortly after Collins invited the Minister for Aircraft Production, his friend Stafford Cripps, to give a talk to the airmen at High Wycombe without bothering to ask permission from his Commanding Officer. The title of the talk was: 'Is God my Co-Pilot?'

Stafford Cripps argued that officers should only send men on bombing raids if they believed in good conscience that the raids were morally right as well as justified from a military point of view. Attendance at the lecture was voluntary but according to Collins the topic attracted a large audience. Some officers complained that the advice given by Cripps might threaten discipline and hinder the war effort. Collins later reported that 'Cripps replied with great courtesy and wit and by routing the opposition (i.e., the officers) gave great pleasure to the other ranks'.

Arthur 'Bomber' Harris, the Air Chief Marshal, responded by asking his personal staff officer, the so-called philosopher T.D. Weldon, to give a lecture on 'The Ethics of Bombing'. Attendance this time was compulsory. It seems Weldon must have argued in favour of area bombing because Collins responded to the talk by asking:

> Was I correct in supposing that the lecturer had mistakenly taken his topic to be 'The Bombing of Ethics'? (Collins, 1966, p. 89).

He reported that after a pause 'the press-ganged audience relaxed tension with a roar of laughter'.

After the war Collins sought concord with the defeated enemy. He and others organised a trip to England by the Berlin Symphony Orchestra, with its conductor Furtwangler. The visit took place in October in Earls Court and the programme included a performance of Beethoven's fourth piano concerto, with Myra Hess as soloist.

(Myra Hess had stayed in London during the war giving many concerts in the middle of the blitz.) Collins, Victor Gollancz and Yehudi Menuhin all argued against taking revenge on Germany, Collins and Gollancz even opposed the Nuremberg trials. Because of their interpretation of Jewish and Christian religious teachings they wanted the war criminals to get off scot-free or perhaps with a reprimand. To my mind that view ignores an important aspect of judicial punishment which among other things is a way of drawing lines between different kinds of behaviour. Personal forgiveness is fine but no individual has a right to forgive crimes committed against other people. The State and its judiciary do have the right to judge and if need be punish those who perpetrate evil deeds against members of the community. It can be argued that in the absence of an international convention a State might well have a moral right to judge and punish those who perpetrate crimes against members of other communities. The Nazi destruction of the Jews of Europe was such a crime. There is more to punishment than revenge though some form of revenge must be part of punishment. In the absence of retaliation the evil-doer could fail to understand or perceive the nature of his actions and others too might fail to see or understand his crimes.

In 1939 Canon Collins believed in the possibility of a just war conducted for ethical reasons and in morally acceptable ways. After all, if there has ever been such a thing as a righteous war surely the defensive war against Hitler was exactly that.

In August 1945, however, Collins became a Christian Pacifist. On hearing the news of Hiroshima he had telephoned Stafford Cripps, a member of the wartime cabinet, and expressed his horror at the event. Cripps told him that the British cabinet had not been told of the decision to bomb Hiroshima. This was almost certainly the truth of the matter because according to Collins every one of Stafford Cripps's contemporaries described the man as completely honourable and truthful.

Whether Collins came to believe that modern war does not and cannot conform to ethical principles or rather decided that all war whatsoever is wrong in principle is not at all clear. Like Bishop Bell, however, he certainly realised that in warfare the combatants' choice of weapons has ethical and political significance and moreover will always have after-effects on later thinking. Collins himself described his pacifist stance as equivocal. He said that in the world as it is Christians cannot rule out the use of force to restrain evildoing and asked himself whether pacifism is a vocation or a categorical imperative. On the other hand his attitude to nuclear weapons was quite unequivocal. He said that he had never doubted that the manufacture, let alone the threat to use them or their actual use, is not only wholly contrary to the Christian Gospel, but ought to be wholly repugnant to Christian conscience.

In 1954 Collins at first supported the war against Korea because he thought the United Nations Organisation was carrying out the important duty of preventing aggression. Then he changed his mind, partly because the United Nations' forces were using napalm and partly because it seemed likely that General Douglas MacArthur (1880–1964), having crossed the Yalu river into North Korea without waiting for orders, was capable of dropping atomic bombs on the enemy's ally, China, if only he could get hold of some. In the event President Truman found MacArthur too hard to handle and gave him the sack.

Not all military officers are belligerent all the time. General Dwight Eisenhower (1890–1969), President of the United States from 1952 to 1960 made an unusual statement when he left the White House at the end of his second term. As mentioned earlier, he warned that America was in danger of being manipulated by a powerful internal entity which he referred to as 'the military-industrial complex' — a shorthand label which has passed into the English language on both sides of the Atlantic.

Canon Collins' different statements about Korea led first to his being pelted with rotten eggs and tomatoes by communists and then attacked in the same way by anti-communists.

Collins believed those responsible for waging war will stop at nothing when victory or defeat is at stake. Yet the issue of victory versus defeat was not the only excuse given for stopping at nothing. The bombs dropped on Hiroshima and Nagasaki were explained and justified by political leaders who expected their side to win anyway. The choice was not between victory and defeat but between the number of Allied casualties that would follow an invasion of Japan versus the lives saved by the enemy's almost instant surrender after Hiroshima and Nagasaki. Post-war justifications and excuses invariably take that form.

A year or two after the British Labour Party had been voted into power in the post-war general election the Prime Minister, Mr Attlee, announced that Britain would be manufacturing its own stockpile of atomic bombs. A non-military reason for manufacturing

The Philosophy of War and Peace   185

and stockpiling such weapons was expressed at a Labour Party conference in 1957 when Earnest Bevin, who had been the Foreign Secretary in the 1945-51 Labour governments (and who Collins in his book unfortunately confuses with CND supporter Aneurin Bevan), said that if Britain did not have nuclear weapons of its own the country would be 'sent naked into the international conference chamber'. The Tory Harold Macmillan must have agreed with Bevin; in 1962 he said: 'It (the British atom bomb) puts us where we belong, among the great powers'.

Why did governments and peoples fail for such a long time to respond to the horrible prospect of an atomic or nuclear war? Collins suggested the following reasons:

- Habits of thought are not easily changed: conservatism is the natural condition of society.

- Most governments needing information on military matters are at the mercy of defence establishments and security advisors, both of which are usually very conservative.

- Some members of the military profession have a natural itch to try out bigger and better weapons.

- Vested interests, in this case the manufacturers of military equipment for example, can influence government decisions. (Should we add scientists to the list of those with vested interests?)

- The main reason or cause of silence is the secrecy surrounding defence matters and especially anything to do with nuclear weapons.

Collins was certainly right about secrecy. Civil servants' love of keeping people in the dark caused some utterly preposterous decisions during the Cold War, decisions which must have been based either on culpable ignorance or seriously delusional states of mind. According to files in the national archives opened for the first time in August 2005 the men responsible for planning Britains's recovery from a possible nuclear attack thought they would be able to hush up the location of any such attack. A legal advisor to the Home Office said that in the event of a third world war members of the public should not be told where in Britain atomic weapons had fallen. Seven years after Hiroshima and Nagasaki senior Home Office mandarins were under the impression that a nuclear strike on Britain would not be much worse than a blitz by conventional weapons. They imagined a situation in which survivors could easily identify the dead and banks would be open and happy to loan money to families who had lost their breadwinners (*Daily Telegraph*, August 2005).

The mandarins later realised that the public would probably notice the mushroom clouds caused by nuclear bombs.

All the calculations made by these geniuses were based on the assumption that a nuclear weapon dropped on a large British city would kill 2,000 people; yet the two atom bombs dropped on Japan had killed more than 100,000 people.

Did the British and American people, did the mandarins, know about the dangers of radioactive fallout? Or was the information suppressed? In 1962 Harold Macmillan, the Conservative Prime Minister, was asked in the House of Commons about the effects of nuclear fall-out from bomb tests in the Pacific. He replied that according to the advice given him by defence experts there was no evidence of any ill effects outside the prohibited zone. It is not clear whether Macmillan himself had been misinformed: Collins says the advice was in any case 'a silly and shabby deception' by someone or other. When a nuclear bomb was tested on Bikini Island the atoll was declared a prohibited zone and the people living there were evacuated. People living in the rest of the Marshall Islands group were not evacuated and as it turned out were indeed damaged by fall-out. So too were the sailors on a Japanese boat 'The Lucky Dragon' which had been fishing well away from the prohibited zone.

Collins contrasts the strict either-or church rulings on sexual matters with the clerics' silence or equivocation in regard to war, attitudes which he suggested showed the churches were prepared to abandon ethics. He notes that when Mussolini decided to wage aggressive war against Ethiopia, in the course of which the Italian army used mustard gas, Cardinal Pacelli, later Pius XII, blessed the troops on their departure. Pacelli did not enquire about the weaponry to be used — why should he? Then again, why should he not? He was surely educated enough, and indeed as one born in 1876 old enough, to have known about the use of mustard gas in the first world war.

Collins was a canon of St Paul's Cathedral from 1949 until he retired. He says he felt guilty about accepting the post and as a result gave a number of rather naughty sermons. Some included unfriendly references to the cathedral and its architecture, in others he lectured the congregation about nuclear disarmament. He says that both kinds of sermon were occasionally interrupted by loud hostile comments from his listeners.

The Campaign for Nuclear Disarmament was formally constituted in January 1958. It took over the role of the National Campaign Against Nuclear Weapons Tests which was led by a Quaker, Arthur Goss. Goss's campaign body organised the first (1958) Aldermaston March in which several thousand people marched at Easter from London to the Aldermaston nuclear weapons establishment, a distance of about 50 miles. In the following years the Easter marches reversed direction and went from Aldermaston to London, ending instead of beginning with speeches in Trafalgar Square. On each occasion thousands of people marched and thousands of citizens lined the streets to welcome them.

Bertrand Russell's tergiversations

Bertrand Russell was gaoled during the first world war on account of his anti-conscription activities. Still a pacifist of sorts in 1939, he congratulated the Prime Minister, Neville Chamberlain, for appeasing Hitler. Between 1945 and 1948 Russell changed his mind again and publicly advocated threatening the Soviet Union with atomic war. Russia, he said, should be invited to join an international confederation led by the United States which would agree to allow an American monopoly of atomic weapons. If the Russians refused to join then, he said, the conditions for a justifiable war be fulfilled and a *casus bello* would not be hard to find.

In a private letter Russell surmised that the Soviet Union would probably not yield and would have to be attacked before it got the bomb. His letter listed three options:

(1) The best option: to go to war before the Soviet Union got the bomb

(2) The second best option: to go to war after the Soviet Union got the bomb

(3) The worst option: submission to the Soviet Union.

Russell denied having ever said these things until the private letter was made public in 1954.

Russell's biographer, Ray Monk believes Russell lied about many things. When Monk began his research he did so in the expectation that his admiration of Russell would grow, instead he came to dislike the man. In 1948 in a talk to a public school (Westminster) Russell said that the West must have a war with Russia before she gets atomic weapons. Without such a war Britain would end up being governed by Russian communists. Ten years later he accepted an invitation to become the first President of the Campaign for Nuclear Disarmament (Monk, 2000).

The theory of deterrence must have worked in Stalin's favour, at least in Russell's mind, after 1949. That was the year when the Soviet Union manufactured and tested an atomic bomb. Stalin's possession of the weapon might also have dissuaded politicians from making a pre-emptive strike.

In October 1949 Mao Tse Tung declared China a communist state.

In February 1950 Senator Joseph McCarthy alleged that there was a large number of card carrying communists in the American State Department.

In June 1950 North Korea invaded South Korea. General Douglas MacArthur was sent to South Korea with American and allied forces and the backing of the United Nations. (The Soviet Union was boycotting the UNO at the time.)

In November 1950 Mao Tse Tung sent troops into Korea. Prime Minister Attlee flew to Washington and got an assurance from President Truman that he would not order the use of atom bombs in the Korean conflict. Attlee also tried to persuade Truman to recognise communist China and allow it to join the United Nations organisation. But the President refused to do that.

The war ended in a stalemate.

Bertrand Russell was terrified by the war in Korea and still very hostile to the Soviet Union. However in 1954, after the first American hydrogen bomb (600 times more powerful than the Hiroshima bomb) was tested at Bikini Atoll Russell stopped advocating nuclear war and instead proposed a commission of experts from neutral nations who would estimate the probable effects of such a war on belligerents and neutrals. Their report, he said, would be sent to the rulers of the Great Powers. Then Bertie changed his mind again, he decided the commission should not consist of scientists from neutral countries but should include some from belligerent communist and anti-communist countries. In pursuit of this goal Russell wrote to Einstein and to Joseph Rotblat in 1955. Both responded favourably. When Einstein died shortly afterwards there were newspaper headlines: 'Einstein's Last Warning' referring to his statement that nuclear war could extinguish life on Earth.

Russell next advocated a meeting between scientists of all nations to discuss ways of convincing world leaders of the dangers of nuclear tests and the possibility that a nuclear war would end the human race. A wealthy Canadian, Cyrus Eaton, offered his home in Pugwash, Nova Scotia, as a venue for the meetings (chapter 22, *ibid.*).

At one point Russell announced that it was futile to ask the United States and Soviet Russia to give up nuclear weapons. They would not do so until war itself was abolished by a world government. However he decided that the proliferation of such weapons could be prevented and had come to believe that Britain should disarm unilaterally.

In 1957 Russell wrote an open letter in *The New Statesman* addressing it to Khrushchev and Eisenhower. This communication began with the words 'Most Potent Sirs ...' and went on to argue that their two nations both had an interest in four things: the survival of the human race, the international control of nuclear weapons, lower military expenditure, and the dispersal of world-wide fear.

Khrushchev, the intelligent peasant parvenu, replied in a letter, also published by *The New Statesman,* in which he said that nuclear stockpiles ought to be destroyed. President Eisenhower did not himself reply to Russell's missive, instead he asked his Secretary of State for Defense, John Foster Dulles (1888–1959), to set out the American position on nuclear weapons. Dulles wrote that the Soviet commitment to class war is inherently violent whereas the American stance 'is based on the moral law'. He declared that the United States would not give up nuclear weapons unless Russia gave up its commitment to class war. On hearing Dulles' view Khrushchev wrote again, and at length, insisting there was no need for either country to renounce its ideology.

Russell did not approve of Aldermaston marches — they were not his own idea. His biographer, Ray Monk, thinks Bertrand Russell was always motivated by tremendous vanity.

In 1960, an American, Ralph Schoenman, then aged 26 and soon to be dubbed 'Russell's Viper', offered to act as the old man's secretary.

Chapter 21
Campaigns (Non-law-abiding)

*We all inhabit this small planet. We all breathe the same air.
We all cherish our children's future.*

(John F. Kennedy)

The Committee of 100

The non-law-abiding versions of British anti-nuclear campaigning were mild and non-violent, consisting mainly in minor acts of obstruction and trespass.

Bertrand Russell's American secretary, Ralph Schoenman, claimed to be devoted to the cause of nuclear disarmament. He persuaded Russell that direct action was needed. The idea was that 100 famous people should form a Committee whose members would be willing to take direct action against the British government. Behind the first 100 there would have to be another 100 willing to take their place, then another, and another, and another, as the first and each successive 100 were gaoled. A total of several thousand famous people would be needed.

According to Ray Monk Russell was at first opposed to the idea of direct action but eventually adopted Schoenman's suggestion because of what he saw as its sensational news value (Monk, 2000).

There never was a Committee of 100. But a handful of relatively well-known people agreed to take part in sit-ins: they included Augustus John, Vanessa Redgrave and Herbert Read. Russell, of course, became President of the Committee.

When in 1960 the Labour Party conference narrowly voted to adopt a policy of unilateral nuclear disarmament the party leader, Hugh Gaitskell, swore 'to fight, fight and fight again' to overturn the decision.

The Committee of 100 organised mass rallies in London. At one of those two thousand people marched to the Ministry of Defence and sat down in the street for two or three hours The police ignored them but at a later rally, held in Trafalgar Square, the police are said to have behaved rather badly. On that occasion Russell and others were arrested and gaoled, which was supposedly what they wanted to happen; Russell himself, however, obtained a medical report causing his sentence to be reduced from two months to seven days (Monk, 2000).

Schoenman began travelling the world as Russell's secretary and as his emissary to various heads of State. He wrote violently anti-American letters to politicians and to newspapers dictated and signed (allegedly) by Russell. The letters compared President Johnson to Hitler and the American people to Nazi war criminals. Many of the letters to newspapers were written in a markedly American and un-Russellian style but the old man always insisted that though Schoenman may have composed them he, Russell, always read them before signing.

Schoenman also created 'The Russell Peace Foundation'. It was funded from various sources including Russell's private fortune. Russell made Schoenman one of his executors under his Will with the power to direct money to various organisations.

A 'War Crimes Tribunal' was set up in Scandinavia by Russell and Schoenman at which America was found guilty. Russell did not attend it but sent (or at least signed) a violently anti-American message.

Some people, possibly conspiracy theorists, suspected that Schoenman was an *agent provocateur* working for the American Central Intelligence Agency. It was alleged that the Agency's aim, and Schoenman's aim, was to discredit the Campaign for Nuclear Disarmament. Possible reasons for suspecting Schoenman of duplicity were roughly as follows:

Details of a secret plan to form a direct action committee became public as the result of a 'misdirected' invitation sent to possible sympathisers by Schoenman or one of his colleagues. The leak occurred just before a Labour Party conference which was to vote on unilateral nuclear disarmament. Members of the CND feared the leak would affect the outcome of the vote (it didn't).

Canon Collins and Bertrand Russell signed a joint statement affirming their amity and stating that all members of the Campaign for Nuclear Disarmament were free to work for nuclear disarmament in any way they saw fit. Two weeks later Russell repudiated the agreement and sent a letter in which he resigned from the CND and viciously attacked Collins. Was that Schoenman's work?

In 1967 Schoenman travelled to Bolivia in search of Che Guevara, supposedly in order to take him supplies. After discovering Guevara's address Schoenman was arrested by the Bolivian police, then rescued by the United States' Consul and returned to the United States. Che Guevara was captured soon afterwards.

During the Vietnam War Schoenman and/or Russell sent a telegram to the Soviet leader, Kosygin, urging him to place the Russian air force at the disposal of the North Vietnamese. Schoenman was summoned to the Russian Embassy in London where the Consul told him such an action would lead to war between America and the Soviet Union, adding:

> Mr Schoenman, people who advocate World War III are either crazy or are working for the Central Intelligence Agency (Monk, 2000, p. 469).

Was Ralph Schoenman working for the CIA? Was he behaving as outrageously as possible, with the aim of discrediting anti-Americanism? Or was he simply somewhat demented? Bertrand Russell's descriptions of his self-selected secretary were highly laudatory, indeed they were sugary, ridiculous and surely somewhat deluded. Nevertheless it is possible that Schoenman's motives might have been just what Russell thought they were.

Nowadays Ralph Schoenman has a website or possibly more than one website — there might be more than one person with his name. The website with photos of Bertrand Russell must surely stem from the philosopher's Viper. The messages on it keep changing, all but a few are very hostile to America and those which are not are hostile to Israel. In December 2005 Schoenman's website advertised a book written by himself. It accuses 'Zionists' of conspiracy, a suggestion somewhat reminiscent of the so-called *Protocols of the Elders of Zion*.

The huge public party organised for Lord Russell's 90th birthday was attended by excellent people who listened to excellent music and to speeches by the famous. It included, also, a disquisition by the egregious Viper absurdly entitled 'The Beauty of Bertie'.

Why did Russell allow such a vulgar speech, why did he attend such a vulgar, boastful display?

Canon Collins thought Russell was usually motivated by vanity. He is reported by Ray Monk as having said:

> Russell was a very vain old man, a great man, a very great man, but a very, *very* vain old man (Collins, quoted by Monk, 2000, p. 413).

Russell sacked Schoenman in 1969.

Greenham Common

The Women's Peace Camp set up outside an American air base on Greenham Common (near Newbury in Berkshire) conducted a more dogged and more inventive campaign.

During the second world war the Royal Air Force had taken over part of Greenham Common as a base for its fighter planes and bombers. The base fell into disuse not long after the Allied forces landed in Normandy. However the Ministry of Defence retained control of the area and it was re-opened in 1950. After a NATO decision of 1979 the base was leased to the United States Strategic Air Arm and re-named USAF Greenham Common. A little later, however, it was re-named RAF Greenham Common, possibly as a way of damping down anxieties and resentments felt by some of the people living nearby. The perimeter was guarded by British troops but the military personnel inside were Americans.

The base was re-vamped by the United States Air Force. It acquired new layers of fencing and a number of watch towers. As in other US bases around the world it was inhabited by whole families and equipped for their sake with American-style schools, shops, cafes, and entertainment facilities. There was no need, and perhaps not much opportunity, for air force wives and children to leave the base or meet any local people. The American air force began to install the silos needed to house the B47 bombers carrying Cruise Missiles armed with nuclear warheads.

On September 4 1981 a group called Women for Life on Earth marched from Cardiff to Newbury and set up camp on the common next to the base. There were 36 women and 4 men on the march but the women, the majority, decided it would be best for the camp itself to be for women only. One or two men were said to be rather cross about that.

The Campaign for Nuclear Disarmament was asked to join in but its officials said it was too busy. However it sent the campers £250, worth about £1,250 in today's currency.

The marchers arrived at Greenham on September 8 1981. Soon afterwards four marchers, following the practice of the suffragettes, chained themselves to the fence around the base. They were removed by guards carrying metal-cutting implements.

The Peace Camp women sent a letter to the American Commander of the base explaining to him that while the 96 Cruise missiles made Britain a target for a Soviet pre-emptive strike the British government had no control over the base and the policy had never been put to the people in an election, had never been so much as mentioned in election speeches from either of the two main parties. The Commander did not reply in writing but came out and said he did not mind how long they stayed. It seems he may have changed his mind later because according to the Peace Campers he said on a subsequent occasion that he would like to pour gasoline over the camp and set it on fire.

The camp received support from many individuals who donated food, tents, bedding, chemical toilets, tarpaulins and plastic sheeting to cover communal areas, material for making banners, and a caravan for use as a kitchen. Many more people started to arrive. By November 1981 the camp had turned into a small 'village' near the main gate into the base.

At the 1981 CND annual conference the chairwoman described the peace camp in complimentary terms. This led to a standing ovation for the Greenham women.

On one early occasion the women tricked a sentry into leaving his box, at which they rushed into it. Installation of new sewers at the base was blocked by women sitting down in the road leading to the gate. Other blockades prevented workers' cars getting to the base. The blockaders spoke to the drivers who said they agreed with the women but needed the work to support their families.

Newbury District Council decided to evict the campers. In September 1982 bailiffs arrived and destroyed the camping equipment. The women moved back, sleeping in the open or under plastic sheets rigged up on the branches of trees. About a dozen were taken to court for breach of the peace. Their defence lawyer called a woman doctor who described the effect of radiation fall-out and another defence witness who referred to the Geneva accords governing warfare. The women themselves scoffed at the court's understanding of what constituted a breach of the peace.

After they were gaoled (for 14 days) they refused to work in prison and refused to wear prison garb and as a result were sent to the punishment block, which meant there was no room in that block for ordinary criminals to be punished. The Home Office described their presence in the punishment block as 'a disruptive influence'.

Vigils were held outside the prison.

In December 1982 the women purchased a large number of ladders and hid them in the shrubs surrounding the base perimeter. At 6 am on New Year's Day 1983 they began climbing over the three fences and up on to the silos which held the nuclear missiles.

Forty-four women danced on the silos as the sun came up. They were arrested and bailed and 42 went to trial in February — the other two skipped bail.

At their trial the women said their actions proved *inter alia* that the base was vulnerable to incursions by terrorists. Fourteen refused to be bound over to keep the peace and went to gaol. After their release 25 Peace Camp women climbed *into* Holloway prison and up onto the roof as a protest at the maltreatment of women prisoners. They too were tried. In their defence they described the way in which they and all the ordinary prisoners were treated in Holloway. They were found Not Guilty.

On January 17 1983 72 women occupied the lobby of the House of Commons in order to protest at the fact that the lease of the base to the United States Air Force, armed as it was with nuclear weapons, had never been debated in Parliament.

On January 27 1983 the Newbury District Council revoked the bye-laws which allowed free access to its common lands.

On April 27 1983 the women padlocked all the gates into base.

On July 7 they cut a hole in the fence.

On October 30 they destroyed 4 miles of fencing.

On November 1 Michael Heseltine MP told the House of Commons that the women were running the risk of being shot since in America itself the men guarding military establishments are authorised to shoot to kill.

On November 14 the cruise missiles arrived.

On November 15 all the gates were blockaded by women and 143 arrests were made.

In yet another piece of inventiveness it was decided to surround the base with thousands of people. Advertising the plan caused large numbers of women to arrive at Greenham, more than enough, they said, to cover the complete perimeter of the base. On December 11 the base was surrounded by women — and there were hundreds of arrests. Some women claimed they had been beaten up by the police.

On December 27 1983 three women got into the control tower and were not detected for three hours.

The Peace Campers began to give the Press last-minute notification of their plans and thereby started to get quite a lot of publicity. Much of the publicity was frivolous or anti-feminist — surprise, surprise.

It is possible that some of the claims made by the Greenham Women contained an element of exaggeration. Even if exaggeration is allowed for it looks as if Greenham at that time was the least secure military base in the world (Harford and Hopkins, 1984, *passim.*).

By the end of 1983 102 peace camps had been set up in Britain, a few in Central Australia (where weapons were tested), and a couple in New York State.

In 1990, the year following the fall of the Berlin Wall, the missiles were removed and the Greenham air base was closed down. It was kept 'on standby' until 1992 and then declared redundant.

Chapter 22

Pugwash and the Test Ban Treaty

> *But I have promises to keep*
> *And miles to go before I sleep.*
>
> (Robert Frost)

The American nuclear bomb tested in 1954 over Bikini atoll in the Marshall Islands released twice as much radioactivity as scientists had predicted. People in other Islands in the Marshall group suffered from, and in some cases died from, radiation sickness. In the following 12 months the fish stocks in Japanese markets were found to have been contaminated by the Bikini test.

The Pugwash conferences

A rich man, Cyrus Eaton, whose name deserves to be better known, offered his home at Pugwash in Nova Scotia as a venue for Bertrand Russell's proposed Conference on Science and World Affairs. The first Conference was held there in 1955; twenty-one scientists attended including seven from the United States and three from the Soviet Union.

The Conference was immediately accused of being a Communist Front; the after-effects of Joseph McCarthy's campaigns were still being felt after McCarthy himself had been discredited.

The Pugwash agenda comprised the following items:

1. The hazards of atomic energy
2. The control of nuclear weapons
3. The responsibilities of scientists.

There were many more 'Pugwash' meetings, including those in Canada in 1957 and 1958, in Moscow in 1960, in London in 1962 and in Melbourne in 1967. The total number up until the year 2000 was 250 meetings.

In 1995 the Pugwash Conference and its then president Joseph Rotblat were jointly awarded the Nobel Peace prize.

John F. Kennedy and Nikita Khrushchev

Were the science conferences partly responsible for the Test Ban Treaty of 1964? It seems likely that they might have made a contribution to the changes in political thinking that brought about the ban. There were other pressures as well however, including demands from terrified non-aligned nations, majority votes in the United Nations Organisation, protest marches in the West and elsewhere, and evidence, from Gallup polls, of the fears felt by the American public.

It is surely the case that politicians, once they have been given power, or have taken it, rarely listen to those whose opinions they do not share. But by great good luck for the human race it so happened that for two years in the 1960s both the United States and Soviet Russia had leaders who were more imaginative, more intelligent, and more willing to listen to others, than many of their predecessors.

Nikita Khrushchev, the intelligent peasant parvenu who ruled Soviet Russia from 1953 to 1964, and John F. Kennedy, the first Catholic President of the United States) and the youngest man ever elected to that office) were both willing to listen to the warnings of scientists in spite of the immense pressure placed on them by their scientific, military and intelligence establishments.

Averell Harriman on the Test Ban Treaty

In a Foreword to Glenn Seaborg's book *Kennedy, Khrushchev and the Test Ban Treaty* the American diplomat Averell Harriman (1891–1986) wrote as follows:

> As I write early in 1981 the political climate seems unfavourable to major progress in nuclear arms control ... the conclusion I and others have reached (is) that there must be such progress before very long if there is to be assurance of continued meaningful human life on earth ... the political climate in the world can change rapidly; no alliances or antagonism between nations should be assumed to be permanent ... Under these (present) circumstances it is a great challenge to statesmanship to be able to perceive genuine opportunities, often fleeting, when such opportunities arise. This is what President Kennedy did in 1963 in negotiating the Limited Test Ban Treaty with the Soviet Union (Harriman, in Seaborg, 1981, p. xi).

It takes two to tango and it took two to be statesmanlike during the Cold War. Nikita Khrushchev as well as President Kennedy must be given some of the credit. Khrushchev was not interested in being dignified. On two or three occasions at international conferences he astonished the news media by clownish acts that in some mysterious way drew attention to the lack of goodwill and genuine seriousness displayed by representatives of the countries of the West, representatives who, unlike him, tended to rely on evasiveness and pomposity.

As to John Kennedy, here is George Kennan's judgement, reported in Seaborg's book:

> Kennedy was the best listener I have ever seen in a high position anywhere ... he resisted the temptation, to which many other great men have yielded, to sound off himself and be admired ... he asked questions modestly and politely and and listened very patiently to what you had to say ... that is a very rare thing among men who have risen to exalted positions (Seaborg, 1981, p. 31).

It should be noted that to the warnings of scientists was added the fact that Kennedy and Khrushchev had given each other a terrible fright during the 1962 Cuban missile crisis.

All President Eisenhower's advisors had been in favour of continued testing. During the 1940s and 1950s America attended 70 international meetings devoted to the question of arms control. John F. Kennedy when still a Senator claimed that the American delegates to the arms control conferences were ill-informed and ill-prepared. He proposed that an independent research establishment be set up to investigate the possibility of arms control and also proposed that a new post be created: 'The President's special advisor for disarmament and arms control.' Howard Stassen, who favoured negotiating with Russia, was appointed to the post in 1955 but only lasted there for two years.

The Test Ban negotiations

In mid-1960, not long before he took office as President, J.F. Kennedy, then a Senator, complained that America never made any proposals about disarmament but left the initiative to Russia. On becoming President he complained that the entire government apparatus of the United States had fewer than 100 men whose work was concerned with disarmament.

In 1961 at the United Nations Organisation India proposed a complete test ban. A majority of the General Assembly supported India but America and Russia both vetoed the proposal. In September 1961 the Secretary General of the United Nations Organisation, the

Swede Dag Hammarskjold, was killed in an air crash over Africa. Some people suspect he was assassinated by villains hostile to the UNO. Not long after this event Kennedy addressed the Organisation. One of the things he said was:

> For fifteen years this organisation has sought the reduction and destruction of arms. Now that goal is no longer a dream — it is a practical matter of life and death. The risks inherent in disarmament pale in comparison to the risks inherent in an unlimited arms race (Seaborg, 1981, p. 81).

According to Glenn Seaborg, who was for a time the Chairman of the American Atomic Energy Commission, Kennedy was very worried about the possibility that the human race faced either rapid destruction by nuclear war or slower destruction by nuclear radiation. The President cannot have been happy about the opinions of his Defense Secretary, Robert McNamara.

After Kennedy was assassinated in November 1963 McNamara continued as Defense Secretary under President L.B. Johnson. As mentioned earlier in this book he subsequently reported to Congressional Committees with comments (cited by Finnis) which included the following:

> We have to have such power that the Soviets will understand that they will be literally destroyed ... the destruction of between one quarter and one-third of the total population and up to two-thirds of the industrial capacity ... We need to retain the capability, at all times and in all circumstances, of destroying the aggressor to the point at which his society is simply no longer viable in any meaningful 20th century sense ... (Finnis *et. al.*, 1987, p. 15)

By the end of 1955 Prime Minister Nehru of India, Albert Einstein, Albert Schweitzer and Pope Pius XII had already called for an end to bomb tests, so too had Otto Hahn and the members of the first Pugwash conference. The bio-chemist and Nobel Laureate Linus Pauling collected 9,000 signatures from scientists opposed to nuclear tests. After the Bikini Atoll test of 1954 63% of Americans polled by Gallup wanted tests to stop. (Before Bikini only 20% wanted the tests to stop.) In 1957 protests by ordinary people in the Western world reached unprecedented levels. In 1960 the British Labour Party voted in favour of unilateral nuclear disarmament.

In spite of all that Edward Teller and two other nuclear physicists visited the White House and urged President Eisenhower to continue testing the weapons. On the other hand Allen Dulles

(1888–1959), Secretary of State for Defense under Eisenhower, worried about the bad image America was presenting to the rest of the world.

Various disarmament proposals were mooted by the Soviet Union in the 1950s and 1960s but no agreement could be reached. The cruces of the difficulty were:

(1) Russia's belief that the American negotiators were deliberately dragging their feet, and

(2) America's belief that Russia was conducting secret underground weapons tests in spite of the fact that its leaders had at one point declared a unilateral moratorium.

On that second matter the opinions of scientists were divided, as were the opinions of the intelligence agencies. McNamara later said that Soviet Russia did not cheat but the United States did (chapter 26, *ibid*.)

Nikita Khrushchev, representing the weaker nation, wrote directly to President Eisenhower and Prime Minister Harold Macmillan suggesting a three-power conference. They agreed but asked for a delay of 12 months. Everyone then concluded that all three powers could, and would, spend the 12 months carrying out as many nuclear tests as possible. The proposed talks were abandoned when on the first of May 1960 Russia shot down an American U2 spy plane over the Soviet Union in the so-called Gary Powers incident — Powers was piloting the plane.

After Kennedy won the Presidential election in 1960 Eisenhower advised him to continue testing nuclear weapons. Or so he said in his book *Waging Peace 1956-1961*.

In August 1961 the Soviet Union announced that it would resume tests. In Seaborg's judgement the Russian tests were intended either as a way of bringing America to the conference table, or as a way for Russia to catch up on America's lead in weaponry, or both. Khrushchev himself stated that the reason for the Soviet tests was political. It seems he hoped to persuade the United States to negotiate on the status of Berlin, a city which according to Soviet thinking ought to have been made into a neutral international enclave. He said, too, that he wanted to begin negotiations on general disarmament. There is no reason to disbelieve him, after all, America was stronger than Russia.

Twenty-four non-aligned nations issued an anti-testing document in which they refused to blame the Soviet Union alone. They demanded that the leaders of America and Russia meet to discuss a ban.

From the Autumn of 1961 until September 1963 American diplomats and the American military were somewhat at cross purposes. The diplomats were worried about the effects of renewed testing on the voting patterns in the United Nations Organisation.

In September 1961 there was a top-level meeting in Belgrade at which President Kennedy proposed a ban on atmospheric testing. Such a ban would not need inspection teams to enter the United States and the Soviet Union because atmospheric tests could be detected from afar.

In October 1961 Defense Secretary McNamara urged the President to test items in the existing stockpile of weapons 'within three weeks'. He seems to have been an impetuous creature, and in any case only new weapons had been tested up till then. McNamara agreed that the point of such tests would be political not military. There was a fear, not substantiated by intelligence at that point, that the Soviet Union might be developing an anti-missile missile system.

Kennedy continued to resist testing and directly ordered Glenn Seaborg *not* to say in a television talk scheduled for October 29 1961 that the United States intended to conduct new tests. It seems though that someone or something (perhaps the Zeitgeist …) was too strong for the President. In November 1961 *Time* magazine published a six-page article by Seaborg in which he falsely claimed that Kennedy had decided to renew weapons tests and claimed too that the radioactive fall-out from such tests would not be serious.

Seaborg says in his book that Kennedy was always opposed to new American tests, adding that the American general, Curtis Le May, was surprised and worried when it suddenly occurred to him that Kennedy actually *meant what he said* about wanting a test ban. According to Seaborg Kennedy's main problem was that the Atomic Energy Commission had taken a stand against him. Moreover the members of Commission felt sure that he would have to agree with them in the end. At the time it was not understood in the West that Chairman Khrushchev labored under similar constraints; Kennedy and Khrushchev both had to placate their conservative advisors.

Because of public worries about fall-out it would not have been possible to carry out tests in Nevada in 1961–62. The Marshall Islands, where the Bikini test had taken place, was no longer available because the islands were administered by America on behalf of the United Nations Organisation and in the 1960s the United Nations would surely have refused permission to conduct new tests there. So Prime Minister Macmillan was asked for the use of a Britain colonial possession, Christmas Island in the Pacific. He was told the tests could be kept secret. Macmillan, though, believed it was impossible to conduct secret tests, and he knew the British public was far more hostile to testing than people in America. In spite of these considerations he finally offered the island to America provided Britain would be allowed to test some its own weapons in Nevada. One can't help suspecting that Macmillan's offer was inspired by the national tradition of diplomatic deviousness.

France got wind of the negotiations and asked to test French nuclear weapons in Nevada too. The United States said *Non* to France just as Russia had said *Nyet* to Communist China on a similar occasion.

On October 31 1961 Khrushchev announced Russia's intention to test a fifty megaton bomb, adding that his country possessed a 100 megaton device as well. He told the Soviet Communist Party Congress: 'God grant we never have to explode such a bomb.' Kennedy addressed the United Nations, saying that all the peoples of the world would unite in asking the Soviet Union not to explode such a terrible weapon. Testing it would add a great mass of radioactive fallout to that which had already been unleashed.

In December 1961 there was a summit meeting in Bermuda between President Kennedy and the British Prime Minister, Harold Macmillan. Macmillan urged Kennedy to make a major effort towards a disarmament agreement. Seaborg says the British Prime Minister enlisted 'all his persuasive eloquence' in an effort to prevent the test. In spite of Macmillan's eloquence the Christmas Island nuclear weapon tests went ahead. Preparations on the island began in February 1962 and tests were scheduled for April.

In March 1962 the Geneva meetings, which had been abandoned, were re-convened. The number of nations represented was enlarged to 18, as follows: there were five members of NATO (America, Britain, Canada, France and Italy), five members of the Warsaw Pact (Russia, Bulgaria, Czechoslovakia, Poland and Romania), and eight non-aligned countries (Brazil, Burma, Ethiopia, Mexico, Nigeria, Sweden and the United Arab Republic: the UAR was a union between Egypt and Syria, since dissolved.)

France did not attend the Geneva meetings because General de Gaulle wanted a decision to destroy all existing launch sites for nuclear weapons and that item was not on the agenda. America and the Soviet Union could not agree about weapons inspections. Russia believed that America wanted on-site inspections because it intended to attack the rest of the Soviet Union after bombing the sites. The non-aligned nations in Geneva tried to break the deadlock: they produced an alternative to the American proposal regarding inspections. Any such inspections, they suggested, could be made by groups of scientists from neutral countries. The United States asked for further clarification which it seems was not forthcoming.

The Christmas Island tests began in April 1962 as planned. There was a world-wide adverse reaction. Thousands of Japanese protestors marched through Tokyo and two thousand people stormed the United States Embassy in London. Some groups of American citizens made three attempts, all unsuccessful, to sail into the prohibited zone. The White House was picketed by a large crowd which included the scientist Linus Pauling.

Kennedy was next told by pro-test scientists that it would be feasible, and desirable, to test nuclear weapons in outer space. Such weapons could then be located in space as a deterrent, or, if deterrence failed, as a means of retaliation against a first strike by Soviet Russia. His scientific advisors, who possibly included the physicist James van Allen, told him that exploding such weapons in outer space would not affect the Van Allen Belts. The Van Allen Belts are layers of charged particles trapped by the Earth's magnetic field. Their existence was confirmed in 1958 after the first American space craft, Explorer I, associated with Professor van Allen, reached the outer atmosphere.

The United States made three attempts to launch nuclear weapons into space. The first attempt had to be aborted and another failed when its carrier rocket blew up on the ground. The successful launch was followed by an immediate increase in the radiation emitted by the Van Allen Belts, proving that the confidence scientists have in their own judgements can be sadly misplaced.

The American position on inspection was weakened when a new invention proved able to detect underground nuclear explosions and to distinguish them from earthquakes. America's Ambassador to Moscow announced the existence of the invention at an airport, behaviour which Seaborg describes as 'injudicious'. It is possible, though, that the Ambassador, like the unaligned nations, was doing his best to break the deadlock in Geneva.

The Cuban Missile Crisis

In 1962 America discovered that the USSR might be planning to instal nuclear weapons in Cuba. President Kennedy had a choice between attacking the installations or reinforcing the American naval base at Guantanamo Bay. He was urged to attack by his advisors but instead ordered a naval blockade of Cuba. Russian merchant ships believed to be carrying missiles set off across the Atlantic and there seemed a real danger that a nuclear war was about to break out.

The leaders of Guinea and Senegal announced that they would not allow the Russian ships to re-fuel in their ports. One of the Soviet ships was boarded and searched and allowed to proceed when no missiles were found on board. The United Nations met and asked the Russians to turn back and the Americans to end the blockade.

Khrushchev sent two letters direct to Kennedy, one of which offered to remove the bases if America removed its bases from Turkey. Senator Robert Kennedy advised his brother to reply to that letter. Then an American spy plane was shot down over Cuba and the American military urged the President to authorise an attack on the island. He refused.

The Test Ban Treaty is signed

The American Atomic Energy Commission continued to oppose a test ban treaty. Many Senators were also opposed to a ban and it is in the power of the Senate to cancel treaties signed by the President — President Woodrow Wilson, who set up the League of Nations after the first world war and naturally wanted America to join it, was stymied when the Senate cancelled his treaty with the League. Kennedy knew that if he signed a test ban treaty with Soviet Russia the Senate could have it cancelled.

In February 1963 the Atomic Energy Commission asked the President to authorise a new series of nuclear tests. He stalled.

In July 1963 Khrushchev invited the United States and Britain to send negotiators to Moscow in order that a test ban might be discussed. Prime Minister Macmillan sent Lord Hailsham (Quinton Hogg) and President Kennedy sent Averell Harriman. As a result of their meetings a limited test ban treaty was signed on 5/8/63, Gromyko signing for the Soviet Union and Dean Rusk for America.

Kennedy then had to persuade the Senate to endorse the decision. After weeks of intensive discussions, during which he managed to get the backing of certain members of the military (including Curtis Le May), more than two-thirds of the Senators voted in favour of the President's proposal. Kennedy signed the Treaty on October 7th 1963, seven weeks before his assassination. He had covered many miles before he finally slept.

Detente and SALT

The relatively friendly relations between Khrushchev and Kennedy had some good long term effects. The Russian leader introduced the idea that 'detente', or relaxation, should be brought into East-West discussions and some degree of 'detente' between the big powers did in fact come about. The immediate trigger for detente was a European Conference for Security and Co-operation convened by President Nixon and his Secretary of State for Defense, Henry Kissinger, in Helsinki. The Conference, which began in 1972 and went on for three years, was followed by talks on arms limitation which were followed in turn by further talks between the Russia and the United States which led to SALT I, the first Strategic Arms Limitation Treaty. Under the treaty America and the Soviet Union agreed to limit the production and deployment of intercontinental nuclear missiles.

SALT II (1979), set up during the presidency of Jimmy Carter, aimed to limit the testing of new intercontinental missiles. It was not ratified by the American Senate. After the fall of the Berlin Wall in 1989 the two Great Powers appeared to lose interest in testing weapons — they became more concerned with preventing proliferation.

China, India and Pakistan have already acquired the capacity to build weapons of mass destruction, so too have some smaller countries including North Korea, Israel, possibly Iran and maybe one or two States in central Asia, former members of the Soviet Union.

PART VI
PATRIOTISM,
PHILOSOPHY, RELIGION

Chapter 23

Patriotism and Solidarity

*The English, the English, the English are the best
I wouldn't give tuppence for all of the rest ...*

(Michael Flanders and Donald Swann)

The comic song, above, pokes fun at local patriotism insofar as it goes on to explain that 'all the rest' refers to the Welsh, the Scots and the Irish, in other words to all the non-English citizens of the United Kingdom. Patriotism has serious critics too of course.

Patriotism and treason

During the trials of Roger Casement during the first world war and that of John Amery after the second the prosecutors described treason as the greatest crime on the Statute books. Casement and Amery were both hanged even though Casement's attempts to bring German arms into Ireland failed miserably and Amery's treason did little damage since although he was a collaborator he was neither a gun-runner nor a spy. He was indeed a friend of Germany but all he did to help the Nazis was to make infrequent and not very successful broadcasts.

If the trials were to be held today it is not unlikely, other things being equal, that the English judiciary would regard Casement as a patriot. Even 90 years ago he might have escaped the death penalty if he not become the target of an appalling judicial and political campaign (Hyde, 1964). As to Amery, although not exactly stupid, and not clinically insane, he was clearly mentally abnormal in some way and would be recognised as such in this, the 21st century.

Adrian Weale, author of a book about traitors, suggests that since the very few men hanged for treason in Britain during the first part of the 20th century were not spies and did not harm Britain in any serious way the reasons or motives for executing them must have been political (Weale, 2001). The men who really did spy for Germany during the first world war were punished but not condemned to death. During the second war about 200 British citizens spied for the Nazis but only two were hanged, John Amery, as mentioned above, and William Joyce—who was probably not even a British citizen (Hall, 1954). Joyce and Amery were propagandists who seemingly held the foolish belief that Germany was in the right. It rather looks as if they were punished for what George Orwell called *thoughtcrime*.

In Britain the death penalty for high treason remained in force until near the end of the 20th century, long after it had been abolished for murder.

Can high treason only occur during a real war? That is a view supported by the following consideration: the pro-Soviet Cold War spies in Britain who were caught and punished were accused, not of treason, but of violating the Official Secrets Act. On the other hand spying for enemies in peace time has certainly counted as high treason in the past, for example during the reigns of Queen Mary and Queen Elizabeth I.

Is treason the worst possible crime? Many might feel that that torture and genocide are much worse. But those are practices which it is not always easy to punish because they are mostly carried out by armies or police forces at the behest of governments. Governments *per se* cannot be prosecuted, it is not possible to prosecute an institution, only the people who run it. Moreover punishing the individual rulers of defeated nations has been contemptuously described as 'victors' justice'. In an essay entitled 'Integrational Pacifism' Philip Smith of George Fox University in the United States remarks that in civilised countries the three internal functions of the capture, the sentencing and the punishing of criminals are carried out by separate agencies, namely the police, the courts and the prison services (or the hangman). He argues that when dealing with men accused of treason or war crimes a similar functional division would be the only way of ensuring justice (Smith, in Strub and Bleist, 2006).

If treason is the worst crime, or even just a very serious crime, then patriotism, it would seem, must be a virtue, perhaps even an absolute value. Certainly there are many who regard patriotism as an important virtue. Patriotism is usually defined as love of country but there is also such a thing as racial patriotism. Racial patriotism was exhibited by all those Austrians who welcomed Hitler's march into their country and the following Anschluss. To some Westerners the kind of patriotism displayed by the Austrian Nazis was not a virtue but as a pollution.

Love of homeland can also be polluted by leader-worship. Adoring a good man like the Emperor Asoka is all right but worshipping Hitler or Stalin is all wrong. During the 1960s and 1970s some young people in the West rejected patriotic attitudes altogether. They described themselves as 'internationalists'. Do internationalists have any special ideological reasons for committing treason? Perhaps not, on the other hand we might also ask whether they have any reasons *against* playing the traitor ...

Patriotic veterans

Some of the military veterans who fought in the Pacific during the second world war were prone to defend the bombing of Hiroshima by mentioning either an obvious personal reason or a slightly more impersonal one. Some veterans say: 'I am glad the atom bomb was dropped, it saved my life ' others say: 'I am glad about the bomb, it saved me and my friends and companions from death in the islands'.

It would be unseemly and indeed ungrateful to argue face to face with such men. Arguing in print though is not quite the same thing. The reasoning of the veterans appeals to utility but is not classically utilitarian. A classical utilitarian defence would necessarily refer to the happiness of the greatest number of people, including the residents of Hiroshima and Nagasaki as well as *our* people. No attempts to weigh up the total numbers of the happy and the unhappy have ever been made in this case. Nor are the conclusions drawn and the predictions made anywhere near 100% accurate. That Captain Jones's death in the Pacific was averted by the atom bomb attacks on Japanese cities is a might-have-been. His death in conventional warfare was not inevitable because not all the British, American and Australian soldiers fighting in the Pacific war zone were killed.

Veterans tend not to mention the bombing of Nagasaki. Moreover the argument looks rather different when it is realised that Hitler, instead of ranting about punishment and revenge, might instead have defended the bombing of London civilians on the grounds that it would obviate the need to invade England and would thus save the lives of thousands or 'millions' of German soldiers.

Patriotic journalists

It cannot be said that all journalists are utilitarians, on the other hand arguments from vaguely described good outcomes are very common in the op-ed items sprinkled among ordinary news reports. An essay by journalist Andrew Kenny in *The Spectator* of July 29 2005 is fairly typical. Its title is 'Giving Thanks for Hiroshima' and in it the author reasons as follows: We must be thankful that the atom bombs fell on Japan because the bombs which targetted Hiroshima and Nagasaki saved 'millions of lives'. The author supports his opinion by claiming that all the former second war combatants he has ever met and all the people who remember the war ('including my own parents') were, and are, quite sure it was the right thing to do. It is a pity he allowed himself to engage in Orwellian *groupthink*.

Journalist Kenny also goes in for guesswork; thus he believes that since the military casualty rate in the Pacific was 'frighteningly high', the American public might have become 'impatient'. Impatient how and for what? Surely the American public would not have wanted their country to surrender at that point? He claims, thirdly, that the number of civilians killed by the Hiroshima bomb was only 60,000 plus only 120,000 who died of radiation poisoning during the next five months and finally states that the Nagasaki bomb was necessary because there was 'dithering and defiance' from the Japanese High Command.

Another reporter, Frank Johnson, who usually writes 'funny chap' stuff, came over all serious in his *Daily Telegraph* column of July 30 2005. He stated there that 'the use of the bomb saved many lives' and urged all his own readers to peruse his colleague's article because reading it would 'protect' them from the idea that the allies committed war crimes against Japan.

It would be wrong, of course, to suppose that the consequences of actions must always be ignored, being a non-utilitarian doesn't commit one to that thesis. On the other hand arguments from utility can be unimpressive in quite ordinary ways, ways which even utilitarian philosophers would have to condemn. Poor arguments from utility, like any other poor arguments, can start from premises which are vague, or which do not refer to evidence, or which are made up of false assumptions or guesswork. Our first journalist did not tell readers where the imprecise figure of 'millions of lives' comes from nor did he say which lives he meant. Was he speaking of military casualties or of military plus civilian casualties, or of longer term casualties of either sort, or what? Was he just guessing? Why didn't he provide some evidence? A vague and seemingly unsupported guess of 'millions' of unidentified potential victims cannot be weighed against the probable or possible figures of 60,000 plus 120,000. (He didn't add in the death toll at Nagasaki.)

The Japanese Emperor was traditionally regarded as semi-divine. The only condition laid down by Tokyo after the first bomb was dropped was that the Emperor's life be spared. It is ridiculous to describe the request as 'dithering and defiance'. What is more there is no evidence that President Truman and the leaders of the other allied nations wanted to execute the Emperor. The Emperor of Japan was never tried for war crimes and in fact lived into old age.

The second part of the *Spectator* article is more interesting and somewhat more intelligent than the first part. The writer was rightly concerned at the prospect of a terrorist State or a terrorist organisation obtaining nuclear arms. He argued that the only way of preventing such a thing happening is, or would be, a total ban on the manufacture of such weapons. But that, he said, cannot happen. It would be rejected by the United States and by all the other countries in possession of nuclear stockpiles. On the other hand he hinted at a faint ray of hope: years ago one statesman *did* order the unilateral dismantling of his country's bombs. The apartheid regime in South Africa built six atomic weapons of the same type as the Hiroshima bomb. F.W. de Klerk, the last white president of that country, ordered that they be destroyed and that the plant which manufactured them be dismantled. Critics might well suggest de Klerk had a sneaky reason, perhaps he thought the likely new president, Nelson Mandela, could not be trusted with such weapons. The journalist regarded De Klerk's action as praiseworthy all the same.

Solidarity

It is natural to love the landscapes and townscapes of one's homeland, especially, perhaps, as they are recollected in memories of one's childhood. It is natural, too, other things being equal, for members of the gregarious human species to feel solidarity with family and neighbors. When (if) all the citizens of a country come to feel solidarity to one another their feelings constitute a variety of patriotism. The journal of the Catholic Worker Movement opposes the conventional form of patriotism as displayed in time of war and cold war but sometimes carries stories about the human solidarity to be seen between people living under tyranny in the Catholic countries of South America — in Argentina in the 1970s for example.

Solidarity is a vital ingredient in any internal opposition to tyrannical regimes. It was a conspicuous element of the Norwegian anti-Nazi resistance in the 1940's when ship-owners, clergy, teachers, sportsmen and many others secretly or openly opposed the government of Vidkun Quisling. Forty years later Polish workers belonging to the illegal but aptly named Solidarity Movement succeeded in toppling the Communist regime imposed on Poland by the Soviet Union.

The Polish Solidarity Movement grew out of a series of running strikes at the Lenin Shipyard in 1970. Because strikes are illegal in communist countries the striking workers were immediately sacked. In 1973 Lech Walensa, an engineer in the shipyard, was arrested and imprisoned. In 1980, after his fellow-workers had named him as their leader, Lech Walensa called for an Inter-Factory Strike Committee and also for a nation-wide policy of solidarity. The watchword 'Solidarity' became the name of the movement which eventually brought down the Polish communist government.

During the first world war German, French and British soldiers agreed to call an unofficial 'Christmas truce', an occasion which is now famous in history. The soldiers on the different sides laid down their arms and sang carols together across the muddy battlefield. No doubt the feelings of solidarity manifested on that occasion must have stemmed from a mutual realisation that all the men in the trenches were suffering the same pains, the same terrors and the same appalling conditions. Moreover most of them would have been born into Christian families, hence the carols.

Patriotism proper is a love of country which is necessarily confined to one country (or at any rate to one country at a time). It does not presuppose that other countries are enemies — some might be wartime allies for example — but other things being equal patriotism allows that the citizens of other countries are not necessarily entitled to the concern one might have for one's fellow-citizens. Nor are foreigners invariably regarded as entitled to the benefits to which citizens of one's own country are or might be entitled. (This aspect of patriotism is not inconsistent with the doctrine of the Master Race.)

Solidarity on the other hand is elastic, it is in principle extendable to outsiders and in theory could be extended to the whole human race. If it could be extended in practice as well as in theory we might see the end of war ...

Solidarity has many enemies: greedy people, cowards, deluded rulers, (Joseph) McCarthyism, ordinary criminals, religious bigotry, and State terrorism.

Human solidarity in Russia was badly damaged by V.I. Lenin, Felix Dzerzhinsky and Josef Stalin. As rulers of a nation of many millions these men and their followers managed to turn each man's hand against every man. People were terrified of the secret police (the OGPU and the KGB) and could easily be persuaded to betray their neighbours by giving false evidence against them. In the first volume of *The Gulag Archipelago* Alexander Solzhenitsyn begins by describing his own arrest and goes on to give chilling details of the way ordinary neighbourly people were persuaded to accuse each other of treason and *thoughtcrime* . Children subjected to evil propaganda could be talked into betraying their own parents (Solzhenitsyn, 1974).

Apart from its futile invasion of Afghanistan communist Russia did not launch any aggressive wars, it was too busy waging war on its own citizens.

Solidarity is also threatened by sheer size: speaking generally, the citizens of smaller countries seem to get on rather better with each other than citizens of large ones.

A certain kind of gun law is another threat because it creates fear. Fear of strangers is natural when householders and burglars alike can easily buy rifles and handguns and are allowed to carry them about whenever and wherever they want to.

Racial and religious differences don't invariably damage solidarity though they do so pretty often.

Violent television as peddled by Hollywood and other sources teach children and adults to perceive the world as full of dangerous enemies. The Kingdom of Bhutan provides a sad piece of evidence. It has been reported that until a few years ago the murder rate in that country was zero but then the King, probably under pressure from Western tour companies, rather unwillingly decided to allow the importation of television sets and DVDs. Soon afterwards the Bhutanese started sticking knives into each other just like everyone else.

Chapter 24
Catholics and Quakers

> *Blessed are the peacemakers*
> *for they shall be called the children of God*
>
> (Gospel according to Matthew, chapter 5)

Quakers and the Cold War

In 1949 the American Friends Service Committee began to issue a continuing series of intelligently creative statements about international relations and the Cold War. In one such statement the Friends noted that a twenty year hostility (1919–1939) between America and the Soviet Union had disappeared during their 1941–1945 alliance with Britain against Germany, Italy and Japan but re-appeared immediately the hostilities came to an end. After the war the United States continued to develop its military power, including researches into atomic and nuclear weapons, and since the Soviet Union suspected America of harbouring hostile intentions it continued to maintain a large army and began to develop atomic and nuclear weapons of its own. Idealistic economic plans heralded when the war ended were replaced to some extent by military programmes, leading to the creation of the North Atlantic Treaty Organisation (NATO) in 1949, the Australia-New Zealand-United States pact (ANZUS) in 1952, the South-East Asia Treaty Organisation (SEATO) in 1954 and the Warsaw Pact in 1955. West Germany began to re-arm in the 1950s and a new Cold War theory of massive retaliation was propounded by Dean Rusk, a civil servant and member of the Democratic party.

The American Friends Service Committee judged that there was little to be gained by trying to decide which side first showed ill will. Trying to find who to blame could not help matters. According to the AFSC the underlying causes were materialism and secularism, the lust for power, the inability of power to set limits on itself, and the 'poisonous' doctrine that one's own side is justified in using any means whatsoever to obtain its ends.

The American Quakers also argued that resistance to evil, when evil is attributed exclusively to the occupants of this or that geographical or ideological area, is futile. It is wrong to make judgments between groups of people defined by the area they occupy. Criticisms if any should be directed at political organisations not at peoples.

The AFSC remarked that Western nations have inherited some of the ideological benefits of the Judeo-Christian tradition even though they have also become somewhat secular and materialistic. The Soviet Union on the other hand was founded on atheism and Marxist materialism yet it is important to understand that there are, or were, some ethical ideas behind Marxist teachings. The Quaker organisation no doubt had in mind the Marxist-Leninist promises of social and material equality, ideals to which the Society of Friends itself is not necessarily hostile.

The AFSC noted that the Judeo-Christian ethic had existed side by side with an ethic of violence for many centuries. Pacifist teaching, however, has always been that the co-existence of Christianity and the violence of war involves a self-contradictory ideological dualism. It was once possible for non-Quaker Christians to ignore the dualism because in past times war, and preparation for war, were both only partial. But modern war, and modern preparations for war require an almost total effort, leading to the destruction of spiritual integrity and, it might be, to the eventual destruction of life on Planet Earth. The Committee concluded that it is absolutely imperative that conflicts be resolved in some way other than through warfare. An armed truce can only be a temporary expedient because each new crisis is a new temptation to violence.

An AFSC proposal from the 1970s argued that the United States and the Soviet Union would do well to accept the following facts and suggestions:

- First, the two super-powers should recognise that there is a world-wide longing for peace.

- Next, they should give up the idea that militarism brings security. Both sides are overlooking or forgetting that the third world war, if it occurs, will be overwhelmingly disastrous.

- The two sides should recognise that there are some basic similarities between the citizens of the United States and the people of the Soviet Union. Personal contacts between individuals from different countries should be encouraged. Quaker experience shows that such contacts can be beneficial.

- America and Russia should recognise that most of the rest of the world fears them — either one of them or both. Millions of people are terrified at the prospect of a nuclear war between America and its allies versus Russia and its allies.
- There are pragmatic reasons as well as moral and religious reasons for rejecting the idea that military means can bring security. America in particular should realise that military development increases secrecy, espionage and witch-hunting and therefore weakens democracy and civil liberties, the very things the country values and thinks should be defended by violence.
- The super powers should recognise that in a climate of intense suspicion nuclear war could break out by accident.
- Past cases of supposedly irresolvable conflicts disappearing should be borne in mind. For example, the centuries-long conflict between the Moslem world and Christian civilisation disappeared without either being destroyed. The wars between Roman Catholic and Protestant States also petered out without either being destroyed.

(The Quakers were not quite accurate in saying the long-running conflict between Christians and Muslims 'petered out'. In the 16th century the warfare between Muslims and Christians did indeed come to an end but largely as the result of battles — the Muslims, were driven out of Granada by Don John of Austria (1547–78), defeated by him again at the sea-battle of Lepanto and yet again at Tunis in North Africa. On the other hand the Catholic versus Protestant conflicts do seem to have simply petered out.)

Further suggestions from the American Friends Service Committee were intended mainly for its own country and were as follows:

- The United States should affirm its loyalty to the United Nations Organisation.
- It should strengthen the mediation and conciliation functions of the UNO.
- It should agree to allow third parties to mediate when there are diplomatic disputes between the super powers.
- At the United Nations Organisation it should vote *with* the Soviet Union whenever possible.
- It should not propose divisive motions at the UNO.
- When impasses occur the United States and the Soviet Union should both replace their UN delegations. Perhaps that would

give existing delegations a motive to seek agreement instead of wasting time in scoring points.
- America should work for the long-term elimination of national armaments and assist its own and other economies to change from manufacturing arms to other kinds of production.
- America should seek an agreement with Russia for a system of arms control and arms limitation, to include the outlawing of atomic weapons and the destruction of existing stockpiles.
- Negotiations on arms control and similar delicate matters should be conducted in secret, only the outcomes should be made public; otherwise public opinion becomes prematurely crystallized.

In an earlier statement, issued after its world conference held in Oxford in 1951, the Society of Friends said that the atmosphere of conflict had arisen between the super powers because they allowed national honour and vital interests to predominate. Both powers were also ruled by fear. The 1951 conference concluded that Russia and America were making no genuine efforts to reach agreement or establish peace.

In 1967 another world conference of Quakers insisted that non-violent solutions to conflict are an absolute necessity in the nuclear age. Non-violent action against nuclear armaments must become an organised mass movement. Quakers should join non-violent mass actions against war and also organise their own (Orr, 1974).

Quakers and terrorism

After the suicide bomb attacks in New York and Washington in September 2001 some journalists said 'everything is different now'. The world-wide Society of Friends, however, refused to accept that things were so different that the Society's teachings were no longer relevant. Quaker committees supported prosecution of any terrorists who could be caught without a war (which means, in effect, any terrorists living in the United States or in countries allied to the United States). The Society of Friends urged America to seek prosecution with the help of the whole international community, pointing out that prosecution involves the rule of law but war does not. They also remarked that no amount of force or threatened force can intimidate an enemy who has no regard for any human life including his own. Moreover killing terrorists creates more terrorists because it reinforces the myth of America as the Great Satan. Instead of reinforcing that myth the United States should do all it can to show it is false. America should honour the self-determination of other nations and the cultures of other nations and abandon any current tendencies to cultural imperialism.

The Society of Friends also argued that the seeds of violence on both sides lie in *possessions,* especially in the vast possessions owned by America and Americans. To overcome that problem the United States should try to find socially responsible foreign firms, even socially responsible enemy firms, to invest in and buy from.

Particularly stinging comments on American policies — stinging, that is, by Quaker standards — came from the Friends in New Zealand. The Wellington Quakers condemned the first American war in Iraq, the attack on Afghanistan and the fruitless attempts to capture Osama bin Laden. They rejected the assumption that the American army could and should act as an international police force, a role that would be best carried out by the United Nations Organisation (www: fcnl.org/).

Antipodeans are known for frankness, not to say bluntness.

The Catholic Worker Movement

The Catholic Worker movement was set up in America in 1933 by two Christian pacifists, Peter Maurin, a born Catholic and Dorothy Day, a convert (Day, 1952). Most current members are practising Catholics, worshipping regularly either in churches or at services conducted at the CWM address in New York. Catholic Workers commit themselves to prayer, to voluntary poverty, and to hospitality for those who are homeless, hungry, exiled or forsaken. They are committed to non-violence and continue to engage in non-violent protests against war and injustice. The movement is quasi-socialist in character insofar as it holds to the idea that working people will be happier (though certainly not wealthy) if they can live in small self-sustaining communities in which decisions are taken by the community rather than by big farmers or factory owners or overseers. In such communities people can work all the year round if need be without any fear of being laid off. According to the thinking of the Catholic Worker Movement it would be good if small communities, small groups of friends and families, could produce all their own food and clothing and furniture. By not taking jobs outside the community itself such people would not need wages and would not spend money. They would free themselves from the control of employers and overseers and also from income tax and sales tax and thereby avoid the need to make involuntary contributions to the upkeep of armies and prisons.

In 2004 there were 185 Catholic Worker communities in the United States running farms, farm shops, bookshops, and shops selling craft items of a religious nature. The movement owns or leases a property in New York where homeless people can get meals and in some cases rooms to sleep in. Its newspaper *The Catholic Worker* is published from that building, it appears ten to 12 times a year and sells for 1 cent per copy. On Sundays and holy days sympathetic priests hold religious services in the city establishment and also sometimes on the farms.

Members of the CWM demonstrate outside gaols when they consider that some prisoner or prisoners have been unjustly treated, including of course members of the movement itself gaoled for holding unauthorized marches and vigils. During the second world war and the Vietnam war Catholic workers were gaoled for refusing to register for the draft.

When a protest was organized in New York at the time of the 2004 Republican National Convention members of the Catholic Worker Movement joined up with several thousand other non-violent opponents of the war in Iraq. Protesters held authorized and unauthorized marches, some people lay down on the roads in front of the traffic and there were many arrests (*The Catholic Worker*, various dates).

Members of the CWM also take part in protests organized by the School of Americas Watch (see below).

Two priests

Several countries in Latin America have been plagued by unelected dictators who wage continuous undeclared war on their own people. Papa Doc Duvalier of Haiti and General Pinochet of Chile are just two examples. Priests and nuns have been among those tortured and killed by the dictators' policemen and soldiers.

In El Salvador Oscar Romero, a bookish and supposedly timid man, was elected by his fellow bishops to be the country's Archbishop. Three weeks after his election one of his priests was killed by government assassins, an event which seems to have galvanised Romero into following the example of the victim, a man who was murdered while trying to protect some impoverished peasants against State terrorism and the depredations of greedy unscrupulous employers. The Archbishop began, in effect, to preach against the government and army of El Salvador. He addressed soldiers, most of whom were peasants, telling them they had no obligation to obey wicked un-Christian orders and urging them to stop killing their fellow countrymen. His sermons put him into danger, as he well knew. He chose to ignore the danger though perhaps he had a premonition of his end; in March 1979 he said:

> A church that suffers no persecution, but enjoys the privileges and support of the things of the earth — beware! — is not the true church of Jesus Christ (*Catholic Worker*, 2004).

One day in March 1980 Romero was in his church delivering a homily. He had just finished speaking when he was shot dead by a sharp-shooter. Sharp-shooters also fired at the people who later attended his funeral.

In 1983 a missionary priest, Father Roy Bourgeois, set up the School of the Americas Watch, an organisation that holds annual vigils outside Fort Benning in Georgia (www: SOAW.org). The School of Americas was renamed Fort Benning after it wittingly or unwittingly confirmed that the students there, mostly from Latin America, were being trained in torture techniques under the direction of members of the United States military affiliated to the CIA. Some of the annual vigils organised by Fr. Bourgeois commemorate Latin Americans who had been murdered by government agents. In 2001 for example the vigil was dedicated to the memory of six Jesuit priests who along with their housekeeper and her daughter were assassinated in El Salvador, a deed attributed to graduates of the school at Fort Benning. Sombre marchers carried white crosses commemorating the eight victims and many others.

Father Bourgeois spent five years working with poor people in Bolivia before being thrown out of the country. It was his knowledge of South American political styles that led him to set up the SOA Watch. A statement issued by the SOAW in 2004 ran as follows:

> Ten Thousand non-violent anti-terrorists from all over the United States converged on Fort Benning, home of the terrorist Western Hemispheric Institute for Security Co-operation (formerly School of the Americas, but known throughout Latin America as the School of Assassins.) The message was clear. We do not fight terrorism with terrorism. We follow in the tradition of Jesus of Nazareth, Mohandas Gandhi and Martin Luther King Jr. We understand that terrorism breeds terrorism in a never-ending escalating cycle. We will stay here in solidarity with our brothers and sisters in Latin America ... We will stay the course, as long as it takes to close down this school whose gradu-

ates have committed again and again unspeakable crimes: murder, torture, rape, kidnapping and all forms of intimidation directed against the poor and oppressed, their leaders, and the religious who work in solidarity with them. We will close down this institution which shamelessly admitted that it used a manual describing torture techniques to train officers of some of the most abusive regimes in Latin America (www: SOAW.org).

That such statements can be broadcast all over the world says a great deal for the (North) American tradition of freedom of speech. So too does the fact that Mrs Cindy Sheehan, whose soldier son was killed in Iraq, and who has been picketing the White House ever since, is allowed to speak out against the President of the USA within sight of his dwelling place.

Chapter 25
Utility, Positivism, Error, Amoralism

Beyond Good and Evil
(book title — Friedrich Nietzsche)

Consequentialist nonsense

Classical utilitarianism as expounded by Jeremy Bentham and John Stuart Mill is subject to many objections most of which are quite well known. A rather compelling way of expressing one of those objections was made by Elizabeth Anscombe in conversation. She said that trying to discover the greatest happiness of the greatest number of people is a nonsense because it resembles trying to discover the greatest quantity of beer that can be drunk in the shortest period of time. She also said that when Mill put forward the idea of pursuing the greatest happiness of the greatest number of people he spoke as if advising us to measure two pieces of elastic against each other.

That Mill's utilitarianism is a nonsense does not mean that other forms of consequentialism have to be rejected out of hand. Perhaps one piece of elastic could be removed by considering only particular places or particular times when weighing up the possible consequences of an action or policy. On the other hand the policies dictated by consequentialist reasonings can hardly be permanent because each change of circumstances means new calculations will be needed. It requires a certain degree of intelligence to see that and not all politicians are intelligent. Bertrand Russell, however, who was an intelligent man, and also of course a utilitarian, made a great fool of himself when he kept changing his mind on matters of war and peace.

War and utility

A common defence of all-out war rests on an unstated assumption that 'our' lives are worth more than 'theirs'. Patriotism is thereby seen as an ultimate value not to be questioned but at the same time games are played with numbers rather in the style of utilitarian reasonings. In these games genuine and guessed-at statistics get mixed up. Reference has already been made to the statements of journalists; thus Andrew Kenny: 'by killing 60,000 Japanese civilians we saved *millions* of lives'.

Utilitarian reasonings of this ilk rely to some extent on slippery slope arguments as well as half-unconsciously assuming the only consequences that matter are those relating to one's own countrymen. It can happen that war is perceived as a good way or the only way to make sure of maximising the welfare or happiness of the greatest possible number of the citizens of one's nation and its friends. Professor Alan Dershovitz's proposal to legalise torture rests on similar semi-conscious assumptions.

When Amnesty International described the prison camp at Guantanamo Bay as 'America's Gulag' Professor Dershowitz probably became quite cross. Yet he—and other consequentialists—should not ignore the possibility that the end-results of one's deliberate actions on one's self are not always going to be benign. Widespread distrust of one's country and its policies is not a benign outcome and public revelations about torture are certain to spread distrust.

The guerilla movements of the second world war provide some examples characteristic of the questions which plague utilitarianism and utilitarians.

In 1942 the Czech resistance movement managed to assassinate Reinhard Heydrich, then a deputy chief of the Gestapo charged with the task of subduing the countries occupied by Germany. (Heydrich is described in some biographical dictionaries as a terrorist; he surely counts as an instrument of State terror.) The Nazi retaliation was typical of the regime: two Czech villages, Lidice and Lezacky were destroyed, the ruins ploughed into the ground like Carthage of old and all the inhabitants except for 9 children were killed. On the face of it the death of one man, albeit a very evil man, does not seem to be worth the deaths of all those who died in Lidice and Lezacky. But suppose Heydrich's death contributed to the downfall of German Nazism? Would it not then be justified? Utilitarians have to engage in a lot of guesswork so cannot easily answer questions of that kind.

There are always at least two answers: 'On the one hand ...' and 'On the other hand ...'.

Utilitarian *philosophers* do not usually work with real life examples. Their imaginary scenarios become famous, they are referred to as the creations of this or that professor and are endlessly chewed over. Most of the examples are fairly simple so that it *seems* possible to calculate the ratios between the happiness and unhappiness produced by different decisions. In real life calculations of utility are implausible because the chain of causes and effects between decisions, actions and outcomes is such that every action has outcomes which have outcomes and every outcome follows upon a long train of actions and events reaching back into the past. There is no way of deciding between short-term and long-term consequences. How far into the future are the calculations of utility supposed to reach?

'Anything goes'

Relaxed forms of utilitarianism have been used to defend violations of international protocols and the customary rules of war. The underlying idea is that in war 'anything goes'. Those who accept the thesis that anything goes seem to forget the probable results, including a backlash amongst allies, of adopting unethical policies.

The principle 'anything goes' is sometimes expressed in the form of an appeal to precedents. Air Marshal Arthur 'Bomber' Harris thought it was all right to attack civilian populations with bombs because the enemy nation had done so first. Defending quasi-utilitarian principles can also involve a refusal to distinguish between easily distinguishable cases. Harris, for example, appeared to be almost constitutionally incapable of distinguishing between the deaths of civilians who for non-military reasons happen to be in the line of fire when military establishments are attacked and the deaths of civilians caused by their being deliberately targetted when asleep in their homes.

Carrying out a policy of 'anything goes' causes men to lie to others and to themselves. It was noted earlier in this book that on August 9th 1945 President Truman described Hiroshima as a military base and as a target chosen to avoid, as far as possible, the killing of civilians. It would appear that he was lying, perhaps to himself, perhaps to others, perhaps to both. Another possibility is that he did not know anything about Japanese cities, did not know for instance that Hiroshima was a city of several million people. Ignorance is not always culpable, but it can be. As to lying, well, political lies create precedents and influence policies.

Logical Positivism

Logical Positivism is a creed invented in the 1920's by a group of scientists and philosophers calling itself the Vienna Circle. Their discussions were supplemented by activities resembling those of a political party, thus in 1929 the group issued a preposterously pompous Manifesto, *The Vienna Circle; its Scientific Outlook*, composed by Rudolf Carnap, Otto Neurath and Otto Hahn (Ayer, 1959). The description of the 'outlook' included boastful claims on behalf of the practitioners of science and 'scientific philosophy', scornful rejection of the idea of morality as rational and objective and condemnation of all religion. The document listed 'precursors', living and dead, approved of by the Circle: David Hume, Auguste Comte, the philosophers of the Enlightenment, John Stuart Mill, Ernst Mach, Albert Einstein, Jules Henri Poincare, Ludwig Boltzmann, Leibniz, Bertrand Russell, Helmholtz, Riemann, Duhem and Enriques were all given the supposedly honourable status of proto-positivists.

After graduating from Oxford A.J. Ayer visited Vienna and sat in on meetings of the Circle. When he returned to England he wrote *Language, Truth and Logic*, a glowing account of the new creed. In this work he announces that all propositions about good and bad, right and wrong express purely subjective states of mind, 'feelings' of approval or disapproval (Ayer, 1936). To logical positivists and its admirers the theory is known as *emotivism*, others labelled it the *Boo-Hurrah thesis*.

The error theory and quasi-realism

In 1977 John Mackie published a work in which he describes and defends what he calls an *error theory* of ethics. His book is broken-backed since in its later chapters the author unconsciously contradicts what he had said in the earlier ones.

The supposed error which Mackie discusses in his early chapters is ontological. It consists, he says, in the ordinary man's belief that right and wrong, good and bad, are objective properties like mass and motion (Mackie, 1977).

He begins his assault on the supposed error by repeating Hume's ban on inferring Ought from Is. He accepts the ban with no questions asked and goes on to say that many such inferences occur both in philosophy and in real life. However when the inferences propose rules of conduct resting on real needs or when actions rest on real desires Mackie concludes that the 'Ought' cannot be a *Moral* Ought. His reasoning here seems circular.

Mackie next produces what he calls the 'argument from queerness'. If rightness and wrongness were objective realities they would be very queer entities, 'utterly different from anything else in the Universe'. But aren't there lots of things in the Universe which are 'utterly different' from anything else? Are there not classes of things which *qua* classes are unique? Black holes are unique, utterly different from other things in the universe, brains are unique, utterly different from other things.

In her book *Natural Goodness* Phillipa Foot remarks that statements of the form 'such-and-such is good' are 'void for uncertainty' since people and things, actions, events and states of affairs, can be good or bad in different ways (Foot, 2001, p. 2). (Consider for example what it means to say someone has a good head: is it a good head for drink, a good head for heights, a good head for thinking with or just well-shaped?)

Good and bad are located in the real world but we don't know how or when until the kinds of goodness or badness in question have been specified. The terms *good* and *bad* have to be disambiguated if context alone fails to make the matter clear. 'Ordinary' words sometimes have to be disambiguated too, for example the order 'fetch the lamb' might have to do with the woolly quadruped in the garden, the meat in the larder or the baby in the nursery.

Mackie mistook the uncertainty pertaining to ambiguity for 'queerness'.

If good and bad really were imaginary properties, what could we say about their varieties? If good and bad are very queer entities what can be said about boorishness and politesse, punctuality and lateness, stinginess and generosity, courage and cowardice? Are these too all imaginary? Perhaps Mackie would reply with the circular reasoning he employed earlier, insisting, perhaps, that generosity and meanness, courage and cowardice, must be *either* imaginary *or* are not moral qualities. His conclusion, namely 'moral qualities are imaginary ', is also his premise.

The sub-title of Mackie's book is 'Inventing Right and Wrong.' In its later chapters he sets out to explain the processes of invention which he thinks we mistake for processes of discovery. Mackie asserts that virtually everyone has a sense of justice and virtually everyone has moral feelings and to ignore those feelings or fail to act on them causes psychological discomfort. On the other hand, he says, people, have to *decide* what moral views to invent or adopt because moral feelings and moral views do not originate in a perception of independently existing ethical properties. The origins of moral feeling and moral opinions are sociological, biological and Darwinian.

Against Mackie one can point out that evolutionary developments, biological processes and facts about human social life are not inventions but objective realities. Such realities can cause inventions but can also create other realities. Biology and evolution and the natural group life of human beings explain features of the universe which Mackie himself would agree belong to the realm of objectivity, for instance the existence of language, the capacity to estimate distances, the ability to understand complex causes. Indeed one can argue that *all* human capacities are the result of evolution and biology.

Hobbes said the origin of government, and also its point, lay in the fact that men need to be protected from one another. They seek this protection by promising to live in conformity with certain laws of nature; the third law of nature, for instance, is that men must abide by their covenants. Although Mackie puts the words 'laws of nature' into scare quotes he agrees that such laws are essential for human well-being. Moreover, he says, there are prudential reasons for wanting to be the sort of person who is virtuous and whose dispositions harmonize with some conception of the good and with some respect for the way life of the society in which one lives. Being that sort of person chimes with one's human nature and one's human needs.

Mackie eventually decides that although contract is important the true foundations of morality are human well-being and human flourishing. But well-being and flourishing and their opposites are *facts about the world.* It is not clear why Mackie thinks these true factual foundations can cause error.

Simon Blackburn defends a theory which he calls *quasi-realism.* Although his ontology is more sparse than Mackie's (like Hume he believes that causality as well as ethics is mind-created) he explicitly states that he agrees with Mackie's metaphysic of morals, his ontology of good and bad (Blackburn, 1984).

The Oxford English Dictionary's definition of the prefix *quasi-* yields the following results: a quasi-X is an X which either

(i) seems to be a real X, or

(ii) is not a real X, or

(iii) is almost an X, or

(iv) is a half-X

'Quasi-realism seems to be a realism' is *inexplicit*. 'Quasi-realism is not a realism' is presumably *false*, at least according to Blackburn. 'Quasi-realism is almost a realism' and 'Quasi-realism is a half-realism' can be interpreted to mean that the theory *resembles realism in part*, that it has elements both of anti-realism and of realism.

If that is something like what Blackburn intended then the label *quasi-anti-realism* would have done just as well. A mule is the offspring of a horse father and a donkey mother and since each parent contributes 50% to the creature's DNA the labels *quasi-horse* and *quasi-donkey* are both accurate if *quasi-* means *half-*. The DNA of quasi-realism is not so easy to establish, it all depends on whether Blackburn thinks of his theory as *almost anti-realism* or as *almost realism* or as *half-realism and half-anti-realism*.

To sum up: error theory/quasi-realism is the view that ordinary people believe, wrongly, that the words good and evil, right and wrong, describe reality. It is the view that people have certain natural sentiments which are caused by features of the real world and those sentiments produce the false belief that the universe as well as containing galaxies and viruses and heat and cold and clocks and the time of day also contains goodness and badness. That a man has ethical beliefs is a fact about *him* and points to no facts outside his head.

Simon Blackburn says we gild or stain the world by describing it *as if* it contained real features answering to our moral sentiments. He seems not to believe the gildings and stainings are optional because he adds that we *have to* cultivate our gilding and staining to the *right* degree, otherwise we will fail to avoid *the moral defect* of indifference to things that *merit* passion. But where does this 'have to' come from? Does it signify an obligation? How can there be real obligation if goodness and badness are not real? It doesn't make sense. And who is this 'we'? Why should this or that particular person cultivate what 'we' regard as 'right' or avoid what 'we' say is a moral defect? Blackburn first denies the reality of objective good and evil, then unwittingly allows the reality back in again — for what are *right* gilding, and *moral defect,* and *meriting,* if they are not varieties of good and evil? Binding the contradictory elements together with appeals to *groupthink* cannot remove the self-cancelling character of quasi-realism.

Amoralism

If right and wrong do not refer to realities there can be no objectively valid reasonings to show that Harry Truman or J.F. Kennedy or Josef Stalin or Mao Tse Tung ever acted well or badly, no objectively valid reasonings for or against killing people, for or against instigating the third world war, for or against harbouring delusions and suicidal policies. That being so there is some reason to regard the moral philosophies of Mackie and Blackburn on the one hand and A.J. Ayer on the other as different species of amoralism. After all *amoral* does not mean *immoral* — no-one is being accused of personal depravity.

Teachings such as those of Nietzsche and Freud and Marx and Ayer and Mackie and Blackburn eventually filter down to nonphilosophers. Their teachings have added to and reinforced the currently widespread egalitarian belief that ethical judgments have to do only with personal preferences. These long-term effects of philosophy can be observed in individuals who have never studied the subject. Consider for example a soldierly opinion: the American General, Curtis Le May, who was in charge of the bombing raids on Japan during the second world war, is quoted by Finnis *et al.* as follows:

> ... actually we in the bombardment business were not at all concerned about which weapon was used. We just weren't bothered about the morality of the question ... I used to be tormented in losing my airmen ... but to worry about the *morality* of what we were doing — Nuts (Finnis, 1987, p. 195; the italics are General Le May's).

Le May's attitudes have been held by individuals who lived in earlier times but nowadays those attitudes belong to a whole *climate* of belief. If the climate was not created by the mainstream moral philosophies of the twentieth century it was surely reinforced by them.

A Zeitgeist resting on amoralism produces soldiers like Lieutenant Calley and also poor unhappy men like Varnardo Simpson. Utilitarianism and error theory/quasi-realism share two delusions. One is the delusion that there is nothing which is categorically bad, bad in all circumstances. The other is that human beings and human societies have no need for categorical rules.

The Philosophy of War and Peace

About a hundred years ago Aleister Crowley, a diabolist, expressed an individualistic form of amoralism in the motto:

'Do what you will' is the only law.

If Crowley and/or the philosophers were right there would be no reason why lawyers should not openly take bribes. It would be quite all right for a judge to take a money bribe after pleading terrible or relative poverty. If he wanted to cut short a lot of unsettling philosophical and financial argumentation he could abandon utilitarianism and either plead the error theory/quasi-realism or announce his adherence to diabolism:

'Do what I will' is the only law.

Chapter 26

The Resources of Philosophy and Religion

The world is sustained by three things: truth, justice, peace

(Talmud)

Religion, science, politics

Can the sciences help the human race rid itself of war? Or can scientists discover ways of reducing the cruelty of modern warfare?

Certain practitioners of the sciences who nowadays explain and publicise their calling—on television for example—like to attack religion in ways that involve boasting about their own supposedly superior rationality, their own intelligence and devotion to truth and truthfulness. The publicity encourages the publicisers themselves and citizens in general to regard religion as the source of war and to think of the search for scientific truths as an inherently rational and even (in a way) an inherently ethical pursuit which must not be hampered. Yet the campaign, if it can be called that, ignores the ambiguous record of science.

In the first place the scientists of the past were not often atheists. Consider Newton: 'God in the beginning formed matter …' and Einstein: 'The Lord God is subtle …' Moreover today's scientists include a number of believing Christians and Jews. Jocelyn Bell-Burnell, for example, the astronomer who discovered pulsars, is a Quaker (www.bath.ac.uk [for Jocelyn Bell-Burnell]). The physicist Sir John Polkinghorne F.R.S., who resigned his Professorial Chair in Cambridge in order to study theology, is now a priest in the Church of England. Polkinghorne is also the founder of the Society for Ordained Scientists, a body which presumably has some members (www.polkinghorne.org). Secondly, and more importantly, the untrammelled search for scientific truth has helped many a world ruler wage war on his neighbours. Kings, and presidents, and prime ministers, and tyrants (sane or mad as the case may be), always rely on scientists and technicians to supply them with weaponry. It is true that during the Cold War several scientists in the West and even some in Soviet Russia eventually came to support nuclear disarmament; but who knows whether people like Linus Pauling and Andrei Sakharov outnumber all the Doctor Strangeloves? Although politicians sometimes express anxiety about the adverse perceptions of voters they never worry about a possible shortage of weapons scientists, they assume those will always be available. Finally, it is possible that today's atheistical scientists share the views of the Vienna Circle as to the nature of ethical statements.

Will there always be war? One reason to suppose so is that it is not easy for politicians to be good people. To begin with, the trade attracts a certain number of scoundrels, men who will try to subvert the decisions of their more well-intentioned colleagues. It is known or anyway believed that John F. Kennedy and Nikita Khrushchev were sometimes over-ruled by their supposed subordinates. Then again, good nature and sound education are not enough to make politicians in office think clearly and well. John F. Kennedy, less belligerent and more intelligent than some of his predecessors and successors, began a detailed analysis of the strengths and weaknesses of the nuclear policy hoping to substitute the idea of 'flexible response' — not excluding conventional weapons — in place of 'massive retaliation'. As is now known from White House tapes recently unearthed by American reporters all Kennedy's advisors, including Robert McNamara, urged him to agree to massive nuclear retaliation if the Soviet Union were to launch a conventional attack on a nation friendly to the Western powers (London *Daily Telegraph* August 2005). McNamara and his colleagues were very persistent and more or less refused to leave until the president agreed to accept their advice. If a concerned intelligent man could not in the end stand up to his advisors what hope would there be for an illiterate king (say) or a dyslexic president? Each would be at the mercy of the spoken word and therefore unable to check the advice given by their subordinates.

In any case princes and presidents have to protect their peoples, those who govern us cannot completely renounce warfare. The Emperor Asoka renounced aggressive war and modern rulers could think about following his lead, agreeing to fight only in self-defence and with the minimum force required. They could renounce cruel weapons like napalm and phosphorus bombs and mustard gas and the personnel bombs scattered over fields where children will later work or play.

Realism versus anti-realism in ethics

Anti-realists in ethics sometimes quote David Hume:

> In every system of morality, that I have hitherto met with, ... the author proceeds for some time in the ordinary way of reasoning, and establishes the being of a God, or makes observations concerning human affairs; when of a sudden I am surpriz'd to find, that instead of the ordinary copulations of propositions, *is*, and *is not*, I meet with no proposition that is not connected with an *ought*, or an *ought not*. This change is imperceptible; but is, however, of the last consequence. For as this ought, or ought not, expresses some new relation or affirmation, 'tis necessary that ... a reason should be given, for what seems altogether inconceivable, how this new relation can be a deduction from others, which are entirely different from it (Hume, 1968, p. 469).

Hume is credited with having discovered, or displayed, a distinction, a gulf, between fact and value, and the famous passage, above, has been regarded by many later philosophers as a *proof* that no propositions about moral matters can be derived from propositions about matters of fact. As stated earlier, the slogan 'No Ought From Is' underpins A.J. Ayer's 'Boo-Hurrah' theory, John Mackie's error theory and Simon Blackburn's quasi-realism, and has indirectly influenced school teachers and journalists and politicians and military men and ordinary citizens in general, encouraging them to think of moral judgements as the expression of mere personal opinions.

Hume's law, if we can call it that, rests on a *general* rule which few have questioned. The general rule is that *no* new relation can be validly deduced from 'others which are entirely different from it'.

If a general rule purporting to be true is actually false it can be overturned by counter-examples. In 1958 G.E.M. Anscombe published a three-page article, 'On Brute Facts', which over-turned Hume's generalisation with a counter-example (Anscombe, 1981, pp. 22–25).

Anscombe imagined having an argument with her grocer in the course of which the grocer claimed, and she denied, that she owed him money for a sack of potatoes. Both agreed that she had ordered the potatoes, and that he had delivered the potatoes, and that he had sent her a bill. But ordering potatoes and delivering potatoes and sending bills belong to the world of *Is*, the world of *facts*.

In the imaginary argument Professor Anscombe says to the grocer:

> You really must not jump from an is ... to an owes.

After ruling out certain possibilities, such as that her household had not really received any potatoes because she and the grocer were engaged in making an amateur film she concludes that given certain human institutions, in this case the institutions of buying and selling and sending bills, the deduction to a new relation ('owes') from another ('is') which is 'entirely different' is not 'inconceivable' but is valid (and indeed commonplace). It is true that the events as described require the existence of human institutions, in other words events only count as ordering, supplying, delivering and billing in a society which has the institutions of buying and selling and so on. Given the institutions the deduction from the facts, as 'She asked for some potatoes, the grocer delivered potatoes and then sent a bill' to 'She owes the grocer money' is not inconceivable at all.

In the paper just described Anscombe went on to develop the idea that certain facts are 'brute' relatively to others and also hinted that no facts are absolutely brute (as it were) but the hint need not concern us here.

Anscombe's counter-example shows that Hume's generalisation is false. It does not show that the special case, the case of deriving an Ought from an Is, can be valid. That question, however, was raised in 1960 by Arthur Prior,

> Even in a quite narrow sense of 'deduce' it is possible to deduce ethical conclusions from non-ethical premises ... using the principles of deduction of the ordinary propositional calculus and quantification (Prior, 1960).

He went on to give examples:

> Anyone who does what is not common in England ought to be shot
> All new Zealanders drink tea
> Therefore either tea-drinking is common in England or all New Zealanders ought to be shot.

> Either grass is blue or smoking is wrong
> Grass is not blue
> Therefore smoking is wrong.

> Undertakers are Church officers
> Therefore undertakers ought to do-whatever-all-church-officials-ought-to-do.

The onus of proof now fell on Hume's followers, obliging them to show that Prior was mistaken. The Neo-Humeans however do not accept the obligation, instead they tend to engage in dogmatic harrumphings:

> We can find no authoritative ethical prescriptions built into the order of things. No god wrote the laws of good behaviour into the cosmos. Nature has no concern for good or bad, right or wrong (Blackburn, 2001, p. 133).

The author of the above passage, who is an atheist, ought to have added that no god wrote the laws of physics into the universe either.

Between the 1950s and the 1990s the professional philosophers who displayed hostility to religion have usually been moral subjectivists or amoralists. But is it truly the case that Nature has no concern for good or bad? Nietzsche and Dostoevsky between them created or reinforced the illusion that if God does not exist there can be no difference between good and evil. The idea that good and evil depend entirely on the direct will of God might have influenced the thinking of the Vienna Circle and seems too to have affected Simon Blackburn. Blackburn takes up an oscillatory stance: *if no god then no objective good and evil* and also *if no objective good and evil then no god*. Unlike some other non-believers John Mackie makes no agitated references to the Deity. His atheism or agnosticism is *calme et profond*.

Socrates in *Euthyphro* made a suggestion that might counter the influence of Nietzsche and Dostoevsky. He suggested that what is pious is loved (by the gods) because it is pious and not pious because it is loved; and the same applies to other varieties of moral rectitude (Plato, *Euthyphro*, 1980).

More recently philosophical thinkers, agnostics as well as believers, have defended ethical objectivism, often relying on Aristotle. At the turn of the millennium two distinguished authors, Alasdair MacIntyre and Philippa Foot, published their separate powerful defences of objectivism. MacIntyre, who has always supported objectivism, took up the cudgels for the third or fourth time in his *Dependent Rational Animals* (1999); Philippa Foot in *Natural Goodness* (2001) argues for the reality of natural good and evil in a highly original way.

MacIntyre points out that various features of the physical environment are objectively good or bad for these or those species. It is good for wolves to be able to hunt, and to eat fresh meat, and to live in a pack. It is good for dolphins to live in clean water, and to eat fish, and for the young ones to have a close family life with their mothers and aunts. If there are any facts at all in the world then which animals need what conditions are genuine matters of fact.

The sub-title of *Dependent Rational Animals* is *Why Human Beings Need the Virtues*. Human beings, like other gregarious creatures, are dependent on one another, and as rational beings they have to take account of their dependence when deciding how to act. MacIntyre describes the physical (factual) dependence of infants on adults, the aged on the young and the sick on the well.

Rationality (and irrationality), virtue (and vice) really *are* written into the cosmos.

Philippa Foot argues that natural goodness belongs to whatever is needed to allow the existence and the flourishing of a human or non-human animal. As an example she mentions the capacity for self defence, a *natural fact* which is *naturally good* for any creature to have. Readers will surely agree with her, at least to some extent, since most of us know, either from becoming acquainted with scientific studies about animal behaviour or from our ordinary amateur observations, that a healthy adult creature of any species can defend itself by fight or flight or camouflage. Animals also defend their young, birds for instance defend their nestlings by drawing the attention of predators to themselves, thus risking personal destruction. (Birds are quite chivalrous.) Intelligent creatures like dolphins and elephants and human beings not only protect their own young, they help other members of the herd or school or society to protect theirs.

Philippa Foot argues that the self-regarding virtues, such as temperance, and the other-regarding virtues, such as justice, are not essentially different, they are on a par, they are alike. The reason is that both kinds of virtue are needed by the individual, both kinds go toward making a human being a good specimen of the species, both are involved in rational decisions about how to act and how to live.

Natural goodness really *is* written into the cosmos.

Militant atheists who think only a god could insert good and bad and virtue and vice into the universe unconsciously give the Deity rather more clout than they (presumably) think he deserves.

The common morality

In their book *Nuclear Deterrence* John Finnis and his colleagues say that after the second world war the Nuremberg judgements reflected the common morality's view of responsibility. By the common morality they mean the Jewish and Christian ethical codes which, though often violated, provide the standards of moral assessment which formed our civilisation. Even after those standards had been ignored, for example by war-time attacks on centres of civilian population, they were implicitly honoured in the public statements made by the winners after the war had ended (Finnis *et al.*, 1987).

There are different ways of interpreting the common morality. Punishment, retaliation and revenge are *loci* of some such differences. Those topics came to the fore in 1945–6, when (as noted earlier in this book) Canon Collins and Yehudi Menuhin suggested war criminals should not be punished however bestially they had behaved.

Contra Finnis *et al.* it seems that Christian teaching on war has often been somewhat equivocal. The Catholic authorities of the 16th century did not accept the common morality attributed by Finnis to Jewish and Christian teachings; thus after Gregory XIII was elected Pope in 1572 one of his first acts was to order the singing of a *Te Deum* to celebrate the news of the massacre of Huguenots on Saint Bartholomew's Day, August 23 and 24. Early Christian teaching did not hold that civilians should be killed purely and simply on account of their religious beliefs and not many Christians today think there is any need for such killings. Pope Gregory also fervently hoped that Catholic Ireland or the Catholic Netherlands would attack Protestant England but when they failed to do so he gave his personal support to plots to have Queen Elizabeth I assassinated (Kelly, 1986).

Roman Catholics today do not regard Protestant monarchs as legitimate targets for murder purely and simply because of their Protestantism.

Pope Gregory died in 1585. Since that time Papal attitudes to massacres and to war itself have certainly changed, especially during the second half of the 20th century. It is impossible to imagine John XXIII or John Paul II ordering a *Te Deum* to celebrate a massacre of Protestant civilians. It is even quite difficult to imagine either of them following the example of Cardinal Pacelli, later Pius XII, by blessing Italian troops – or any other troops – marching off to attack a relatively helpless foreign country.

Recent Popes have condemned the nuclear threats of the Cold War. John Paul II even suggested that such threats were unnecessary. He said it would be a mistake to say that divine Providence caused the fall of communism; it fell, he said, as a consequence of its own mistakes and abuses, its own inherent weaknesses.

War and delusion

What objective moral facts are specially significant in relation to war and peace? Buddhism teaches that delusion is the ultimate cause, the first cause, of war and violence and as noted earlier its iconography depicts greed and delusion as a pig which vomits a snake. The pig, I suppose, represents greed and delusion, the vomit—the snake—represents hatred and violence.

Although quite a few contemporary policy makers and politicians believe that greed is good and that hate is allowable if rightly directed, surely no-one seriously and consciously wants to be the victim of a delusion. But unfortunately delusions are not always easy to escape. Some men suffer from self-induced errors of thought, many more are influenced by the toxic combination of propaganda, *groupthink* and fear of *thoughtcrime*.

It is comparatively rare for a deluded person to recover spontaneously, as it were, from his delusions, or to cure himself, but it does happen now and then. It is possible, even for military men, to abandon delusional fears. General Curtis Le May (see chapter 25, *ibid.*), who for some years after the second world war was in favour of testing nuclear weapons *ad. inf.*, accepted a 1963 recommendation—or was it an order?—from John F. Kennedy who asked him to advise the American Senate that it should vote to support a proposed Test Ban Treaty. When colleagues asked Le May to explain his changed attitude he mentioned a new idea which had suddenly struck him, namely, that political as well as military considerations had to have a place in deliberations about defence. Did 'political' include 'moral' in the thoughts of the General? Probably not, but it surely did in President Kennedy's thinking.

Were the suspicions of Russian and American politicians self-induced during the Cold War? Were those men influenced by their own propaganda? Were they and their peoples engaging in Orwellian *groupthink*? Were they deluded? Robert McNamara, who made outlandishly belligerent remarks during the Cold War, later changed his mind about a number of matters. In short he *recanted*—and is perhaps unique among politicians on that account.

McNamara joined the government in 1960 as John F. Kennedy's Secretary of State for Defense, continued in the same role under L.B. Johnson and left government after the 1968 presidential election won by Richard Nixon, a Republican. In 1987 he published a book, *Blundering into Disaster*, in which he said that his former opinions and decisions had nearly all been mistaken. He had come to believe that the underlying causes of the Cold War were ignorance and 'insitutionalised hostility' and that its more immediate causes were incremental decisions, each one of which, taken alone, seemed 'rational or inescapable'. By 1987 he had decided that the Soviet Union did not want war with the West *and never had wanted war*. After reconsidering the American perception that the Soviet policy on nuclear disarmament was to cheat he said the record showed otherwise. When required by treaties to remove or dismantle missile launchers, bombers and submarines Russia actually did so, whereas the clearest violations of the SALT treaties were committed by the United States; instead of dismantling their nuclear missile silos the Americans simply hid them (McNamara, 1987).

As Secretary of State for Defense McNamara himself must have known that at the time, indeed it seems very probable that he himself issued the order to hide the weapons — presumably while telling himself 'it's not *me*, it's *them*.' In a documentary, *The Fog of War*, broadcast by one of the BBC's television stations at 10 pm on Sunday May 15 2005, McNamara expressed doubts about his political role in the Vietnam war and made a poignant comment on his own delusions:

> We ... didn't understand the Vietnamese. They saw us as colonialists, we saw them as Cold War thugs ... This was a Cold War activity ... We were wrong ... It carried such heavy costs ... *we see what we want to believe — belief and seeing are both often wrong* ... We should not exploit our status as the strongest nation. No-one, but no-one, supported us in the Vietnam war ... human beings need to think again about war (my italics).

No doubt some of the more warlike associates and successors of Curtis Le May and Robert McNamara will have concluded that those two men were not deluded in the past but have become deluded since.

Although McNamara changed his mind about war he retained an unthinking version of amoralism which he expressed as follows in the BBC broadcast:

> What law says we can't kill civilians? ... What is morally appropriate in war? Agent Orange — was it a crime? Do we have a law to make that illegal? Yes, I knew it was being used ...

Religion and philosophy

Buddhism teaching on war is simpler and clearer than that of main stream Christianity though it too has been ignored by rulers (and even by monks).

Christian attitudes to war have varied and remain equivocal but perhaps one day human beings, including the ones who rule over the others, will try to learn from the recent teachings of Catholic philosophers, from Buddhist advice on delusion and greed, and from Quaker suggestions about how to avert war.

It is fairly clear that some of the philosophical non-believers do not have, or rather cannot have, any clear knock-down arguments against all-out suicidal war. The authors Ayer, Mackie and Blackburn, when speaking as philosophers and not chatting at the dinner table, have said nothing important or convincing on the topic of warfare, at least not as far as I am aware. Russell of course had a lot to say about war but since he was a utilitarian he could never reach a settled opinion, he kept measuring one piece of elastic against another and getting different answers.

Non-believers could learn from the arguments of realist philosophers. They could also learn from teachings of religious pacifists without necessarily buying the whole supernatural package. In any case it is not the philosophers' atheism which causes their impotence but their theories, their anti-realisms and quasi-realisms and error theories and the egregious and ever-popular 'Boo-Hurrah'.

Although most people are not directly influenced by philosophy various philosophical theories, especially those concerned with ethical matters, do trickle down to journalists and military men and politicians and the general public. That being so it is important that philosophy teachers think again about logical positivism, subjectivism and 'quasi-realism' because these isms are varieties of amoralism and amoralism is false. It is also a way of thinking that cannot conceivably help mankind to abolish war or to reduce the savagery of modern warfare.

John L. Allen Jr., the Vatican correspondent for the (American) *National Catholic Reporter*, says Pope Benedict XVI, who was elected in April 2005, will be 'very political'. Some of Benedict's opinions are reminiscent of the attitudes of the Emperor Asoka. Long before he became Pope he had publicly expressed his opposition to the first gulf war. When the second President Bush initiated a pre-emptive strike against Iraq he sarcastically remarked that the concept of pre-emptive war does not appear in the *Catechism of the Catholic Church* (Allen, 2005). Asked in 2002 whether the Iraq war could be justified he replied:

> In this situation certainly not ... There is the United Nations. It is the authority that should make the decisive choice. The choice

must be made by the community of peoples ... (Allen, 2005, p. 193).

When Baghdad fell in 2003 Pope Benedict said that opposing the war had been the right thing to do and still was the right thing to do.

It is up to ordinary people to convince politicians that modern methods of waging war have become a threat to innocents everywhere and perhaps even to the continuing existence of the human race. It is up to ordinary people to convince their rulers that any other view of the matter is delusional. Those who live in countries where freedom of speech is permitted and valued surely have a special responsibility in this matter.

Appendix i

Civilian and other Caualties of Wars in SE Asia, Afghanistan and the Middle East (since 1964)

War in SE Asia 1964–74

In South Vietnam

Civilians killed: 1,435,000
Communist fighters killed: 932,863 (Pentagon figures)
War cripples: 362,000
Widows: 1,000,000
Driven from villages by American bombing: 10,000,000

In North Vietnam:

Civilians killed: 65,000
Industrial installations destroyed: All
Schools destroyed: 3,000
Hospitals destroyed: 350

The material above is taken from *Vietnam: Trial and Triumph* by R.S. Chavan. Dr Chavan, whose 1950s Canadian PhD had the title 'Nationalism in Asia', was posted to Hanoi in the 1960s — he doesn't give the exact date — as Head of India's Mission there.

Russian Invasion of Afghanistan 1979–89

Civilians and Afghan soldiers killed: about one million.

Source: Svetlana Alexeivitch (1992).

Current War in Iraq

The various estimates range from 25,000 to 100,000 Iraqis plus over 200 US soldiers.

Sources: news reports.

Appendix ii
Senator Joseph McCarthy

Joseph McCarthy (1909–1957), a Republican, has been aptly described as 'a politician and inquisitor'. In 1950 he asserted that there was a large number of Communists lurking in America's State Department and as a result many people working in the public services lost their jobs. He and his aides also accused various public figures of being Communists or 'soft on communism'; they too lost their jobs. The victims included ordinary members of the Democratic Party of America, people working in Hollywood (especially script-writers), academics and academic establishments and finally President Truman himself. Truman described the inquisitor as 'a pathological character assassin'.

There is little doubt that McCarthy's campaigns encouraged groupthink and fear of thoughtcrime.

McCarthy was discredited in 1954 not long after he agreed to conduct his enquiries in front of television and newsreel cameras. Though not the main cause of his downfall his appearances in the visual media probably made a contribution to that result. His manner was uncouth and he did not look like the heroic patriot some viewers might have been expecting. He was no matinée idol and an hour or two after shaving his chin darkened, a sinister signal to viewers accustomed to the conventions of Hollywood films.

Sources

Alexievich, Svetlana: *Zinky Boys; Soviet Views from a Forgotten War,* translated by J. and R. Whitby, London 1992, publisher anonymous.
Allen, John L: *The Rise of Benedict XVI,* Penguin, London 2005.
Anon: *The Song of Roland,* translated by C.K. Scott-Moncrieff, Ann Arbor 1959—especially LXXXIX, CXIX, CXXVI.
Anscombe, G.E.M: 'Mr Truman`s Degree' and 'War and Murder', in her *Collected Papers III,* Blackwell, Oxford 1981.
Anscombe: 'Modern Moral Philosophy', *Collected Papers III.*
Anscombe: 'On Brute Facts' *Collected Papers III.*
Aquinas: *Summa Theologica,* Blackfriars and Eyre and Spottiswoode, London 1966: vols 38 and 47, 2a2e, Q. 64, Q. 188.
Aristotle: *Politics,* in *The Complete Works of Aristotle vol. 2,* the Revised Oxford Translation edited by Jonathan Barnes, Princeton 1984.
Augustine: *On the Sermon on the Mount,* Library of the Nicene and Post-Nicene Fathers vol. vi, Grand Rapids USA 1887.
Augustine: *Contra Faustum* from *vol. v* of *The Works of St. Augustine,* Edinburgh 1870.
Ayer, A.J.: *Language Truth and Logic* (many editions: first published 1936).
Ayer: *Logical Positivism,* in the *Library of Philosophical Movements* (edited by Paul Edwards), Free Press, Glencoe USA 1959.
Bell, George, Bishop of Chichester: *Hansard (Lords) 1943-4,* 9/2/1944.
Betser, Moshe, with Rosenberg, Robert: *Secret Soldier,* Simon and Schuster, London 1996.
Bilton, Michael and Sim, Kevin: *Four Hours in My Lai,* Viking Penguin, London and New York 1992.
Blackburn, Simon: *Essays in Quasi-Realism,* Oxford Univerity Press 1984.
Blackburn: *Being Good,* Oxford University Press 2001.
Blixen Karen, *Out of Africa,* Century, London 1989.
Bourne, Peter: *Castro,* Macmillan, London 1986.
Brock, Peter: *Pacifism in Europe to 1914,* Princeton 1972.
Brock: *Twentieth Century Pacifism,* van Nostrand Reinhold, New York 1970.
Chatterjee, Margaret: *Gandhi and the Challenge of Religious Diversity,* Promilla and Co. Publishers, New Delhi and Chicago 2005.
Churchill, Winston: *The Second World War, vol. iv: The Hinge of Fate* Cassell and Co., London 1949.
Clausewitz, Carl von: *On War* (translated by Michael Howard and Peter Paret), Everyman Library, London 1993.
Coady, C.A.J.: 'The morality of terrorism' *Philosophy 60,* January 1985.

Collins, John: *Faith under Fire* : Leslie Frewin Ltd., London 1966.

Constitution of the United States of America (Article IV, section 2 and Article VIII) For sale by the Superintendent of Documents, U.S. Government Printing Office, Washington 25, D.C., 1961.

Council of Trent: *Canons and Decrees* (the Sixth Session), edited and translated by James Watermouth, Dolman, London 1858.

Cowdrey, H.E.J: 'Bishop Ermenfried of Sion and the Penitential Ordinance following the Battle of Hastings', *Journal of Ecclesiastical History 20,* 1969. 2.

Cox, Sebastian – see Harris.

Day, Dorothy: *The Long Loneliness*, Harper & Row, New York 1952.

Denyer, Nicholas: 'Just War', in R.P.L. Teichmann (ed.) *Logic, Cause and Action, Essays in Honour of G.E.M. Anscombe,* Cambridge University Press 2000.

Dershowitz, Alan: *Why Terrorism Works,* Yale University Press 2002.

Douglas, David C., (ed.) *English Historical Documents IV*, Cambridge University Press 1969, p. 849.

Dostoievsy, Fyodor: *The Brothers Karamazov* (translated by Constance Garnett), William Heinemann, London 1949.

Eisenhower, Dwight: *The White House Years 1953-1956*, Heinemann, London 1963.

Eisenhower: *Waging Peace 1956-1961* -Doubleday, NY 1965.

Elon, Menachem (ed.): *Principles of Jewish Law,* Jerusalem 1975, item on Criminal Law.

Finley, Moses: *The World of Odysseus:* Chatto and Windus, London 1956.

Finnis, John, with Boyle, Joseph and Grisez, Germain: *Nuclear Deterrence, Morality and Realism,* Clarendon Press, Oxford, 1987.

Foot, M.R.D.: *SOE/The Special Operations Executive*, Pimlico, London 1999.

Foot, Philippa: *Natural Goodness*, Oxford University Press 2001.

Foner, Philip S: *A History of Cuba* (two volumes), International Publishers Co. Inc., New York 1962 and 1963.

Flannery, Austin (ed.): *Vatican Council II*, Dublin 1974.

Freud, S: *Civilisation, War and Death* (edited by John Rickman) Hogarth Press, London 1953.

Geyer, Georgie Ann: *Guerilla Prince*, Little Brown, Boston, 1991.

Gjelsvik, Tore: *Norwegian Resistance 1940-1945* (translated by T.K. Derry), C. Hurst and Company, London 1979.

Glover, Jonathan: *Humanity: A Moral History of the Twentieth Century*, Jonathan Cape, London 1999.

Gowing, Margaret: *Independence and Deterrence: Britain and Atomic Energy*: Macmillan, London 1974.

Grotius, Hugo: *The Law of War and Peace* (translated by FW Kelsey), Oxford 1825.

Hall, J.W. 'William Joyce' in *Famous Trials 4,* ed. James Hodge, Penguin Books, Harmondsworth 1954.

Harcourt, Edward, 'Quasi-Realism and Ethical Appearances', *Mind*, April 2005.

Harford, Barbara, and Hopkins, Sarah: *Greenham Common: Women at the Wire*, Women's Press, London 1984.

Harris, Arthur (1): *Despatch on War Operations*: Frank Cass, London 1995; with Preface and Introduction by Sebastian Cox.

Harris, Arthur (2): *Bomber Offensive*, Greenhill, London, 1995.

Harway, Peter: *An Introduction to Buddhist Ethics*, Cambridge University Press 2000.

Herodotus: *Histories* (translated by Aubrey de Selincourt and revised by John Marincola) Penguin Books, London 2003.

Hirst, M.E.: *Quakers in Peace and War*, The Swarthmore Press, London 1923.

Hobbes, Thomas: *Leviathan*, Penguin Books, London 1968 especially chapters 14 and 15

Holy Bible (King James): *Isaiah*.

Homer: *The Iliad* (translated by Alexander Pope), Penguin Books, London 1996.

Hume, David: *A Treatise of Human Nature*, Part III, Chapter 1, section i reprinted from the original edition, Clarendon Press, Oxford 1968.

Huxley, Aldous: *Ape and Essence*, Chatto and Windus, London 1949.

Hyde, Montgomery: *The Trial of Roger Casement,* Penguin Books, Harmondsworth 1964.

John XXIII: *Peace on Earth,* translated from his 1963 Easter encyclical letter *Pacem in Terris* and distributed by Vatican Polyglot Press, Paul Hamlyn, London 1963-4.

Kant, Immanuel, *Critique of Practical Reason* (translated by Thomas K. Abbott), Longman Green and Co., London—no date.

Kaplan, Fred: *The Wizards of Armageddon*, Simon and Schuster, New York 1983.

Keenan, Brian: *An Evil Cradling*, London, Hutchinson 1991.

Kelly, J.N.P: *The Oxford Dictionary of Popes,* Oxford University Press 1986.

Kennan, George F.: *The Nuclear Delusion*, Hamish Hamilton, London 1983.

Kenny, Anthony J.P. : *A Path From Rome*, Oxford University Press 1986.

Lenin, V.I.: *Imperialism: The Highest Stage of Capitalism*, Pluto Press, London 1996, in English, with an Introduction by Norman Lewis and James Malone. The original edition appeared in 1916.

Lifton, R.J. : *Home from the War*, New York 1985.

MacIntyre, Alasdair: *After Virtue*, Duckworth, London, 1985.

MacIntyre: *Dependent Rational Animals*, Duckworth, London 1999.

Mackie, John: *Ethics: Inventing Right and Wrong*, Penguin Books, Harmondsworth 1977.

McNamara, Robert: *Blundering into Disaster*, Bloomsbury, London 1987.

Mill, J.S. : *Utilitarianism* (many editions): first published in 1863.

Monk, Ray: *Bertrand Russell* (vol. 2), Jonathan Cape, London 1996-2000.

New Catholic Encyclopedia (vol. 14), Washington DC 1967.

Nietzsche, Friedrich: *Beyond Good and Evil* (translated by R.J. Hollingdale), Penguin Classics, Harmondsworth 1962.

Origen: *Contra Celsum* (trans. Henry Chadwick), C.U.P., 1953, p. 509.

Orr, E.W.: *Quakers in Peace and War 1920-1967*, W.J. Offord and Son Ltd, Eastbourne, Sussex 1974.

Orwell, George: *Nineteen Eighty-Four*, Martin Secker and Warburg, London 1949.

Orwell: *Collected Essays, Journalism and Letters of George Orwell 1944-1950* (vol. IV), Martin Secker and Warburg, London 1968.

Phillpson, Coleman: *International law and custom in ancient Greece and Rome,* Macmillan, London 1911.

Plato *Republic* (translated by Robin Waterfield), Oxford University Press 1993.

Plato, *Euthyphro,* in *The Last Days of Socrates,* translated by Hugh Tredennick, Penguin Books, Harmondsworth, 1980.

Prior, Arthur: 'The Autonomy of Ethics' in *The Australasian Journal of Philosophy vol. 38 (3),* 1960.

Rhodes, Richard: *The Making of the Atomic Bomb,* Penguin Books, London 1988.

Roberts, Adam, and Guelff, Richard (eds): *Documents on the Laws of War,* Clarendon Press, Oxford 1982.

Rorabaugh, W.J.: *Berkeley at War,* Oxford University Press, New York 1989.

Russell, Bertrand: *Autobiography* (vol. III), George Allen and Unwin, London 1969.

Russell, F.H.: *The Just War in the Middle Ages,* Cambridge 1975.

Seaborg, Glenn T.: *Kennedy, Khrushchev and the Test Ban Treaty,* UCLA Press Berkeley, Los Angeles and London 1981.

Singer, Peter: *Animal Liberation,* Jonathan Cape, London 1976.

Skilly, John: *English Historical Docments IV,* p. 865, 869.

Smith, Philip: 'Integrational Pacifism' in Strub and Bleist, 2006.

Solzhenitsyn, Alexander: *The Gulag Archipelago I* (translator anonymous), Great Britain 1974.

Strub, F.D. and Bleist, B. (eds): *Pacifism: History, Ideas,Theory,* Haupt Verlag, Bern/Stuttgart/Wien, 2006.

Tertullian: *On Idolatry,* in *Ante-Nicene Christian Library,* chapter XIX, Edinburgh 1869.

Truman, Harry S: *The Year of Decisions,* Doubleday, Garden City New York 1955.

Vitorio, Francisco: *De Indis et de jure belli relectiones,* edited by E. Nys and translated by J.P. Bate, Washington 1917.

Vonnegut, Kurt: *Slaughterhouse Five,* Vintage Books, London 1991.

Von Wright, G.H. : *The Varieties of Goodness,* Routlege Kegan Paul, London 1963.

Waite, Terry: *Taken on Trust,* Hodder and Stoughton, London 1991.

Weale, Adrian: *Patriot Traitors,* Part ii, on John Amery, Viking Penguin, London 2001

Wittgenstein, Ludwig: *Lectures and Conversations on Aesthetics, Psycholgy and Religious Belief* (edited by Cyril Barrett), Blackwell, Oxford 1966.

Yoder, John: *Nevertheless,* Pennsylvania, 1971.

Websites:

www.fcnl.org/ (the [American] Friends' Committee on National Legislation website) — accessed on several dates during 2004 and 2005.

http//www.answers.com/topic/mustard-gas — 13/12/05

http//www.answers.com/topic/napalm — 13/12/05

http//www.historyhome.co.uk (for the *Bill of Rights* of 1689).
Ralph Schoenman's disquisitions—accessed *via* Google in July 2005 and December 2005. He has several websites.
www.SOAW.org. (School of Americas Watch website)—accessed on October 11 2004.

Television:

BBC broadcast, 10 pm May 15 2005; talk by Robert McNamara

Daily newspapers (various dates):

The Daily Telegraph, London
Figaro, Paris
The Guardian, London
The Independent, London
The International Herald Tribune, British edition
The New York Times.

Weekly journals (various dates):

The Spectator, London
The Week, London

Other:

The Catholic Worker, New York (various dates):
The Lancet, Britain

Index

Agammemnon, 19
Akhmatova, Anna, 86
Alexander the Great, 26
Alexander VI, Pope, 99
Allende, Salvador, 97
Amery, John, 211
Amin, Idi, 112f
Andrew, Duke of York, 13
Anscombe, G.E.M., 31f, 49, 227, 239
Anselm, 33
Aquinas, 24
Aristotle, 241
Asoka, Emperor, 155f, 213, 238, 246
Attlee, Clement, 55, 77, 184, 188
Augustine, 23, 33, 164
Ayer, A.J., 230, 234, 239, 246

Baader (Andreas) and Meinhhof (Ulricke), 111, 122
Battista, Fulgencio, 142f, 146
Bell, Bishop George, 56f
Bell-Burnell, Jocelyn, 237
Bergraev, Bishop, 132
Benedict XVI, Pope, 246
Bentham, Jeremy, 104f, 227
Betser, Moshe, 112
Bevin, Ernest, 185
Blackburn, Simon, 232f, 239, 241, 246
Blair, Tony, 87
Blixen, Karen
Bloch, Dora, 113
Bohr, Niels, 70
Bonaparte, Marie, 14
Bourgeois, Fr. Roy, S.J., 225
Braun, Werner von, 53, 69f
Brezhnev, Leonid, 84
Buddha, *see* Gotama

Bullock, Alan, 32
Bush, G.W., 33, 44, 71, 102f, 116, 246
Byrnes, James, 77

Calley, Lieutenant, 64, 234
Carter, Jimmy, 82, 113, 208
Carnap, Rudolf, 230
Casement, Roger, 211
Castro, Fidel, 115f, 121, 139f
Castro, Raul, 145, 147
Chamberlain, Neville, 53
Chibas, Edward, 143
Chomsky, Noam, 94
Churchill, Winston, 55, 58, 77, 85
Clausewitz, Carl von, 6-8, 17, 42, 47, 85, 108, 143, 148f
Coady, A.J.P., 94
Collins, Rev. John, 56, 106, 181f, 192f, 243
Columbus, Christopher, 140
Cripps, Sir Stafford, 182f
Cromwell, Oliver, 27, 173
Crowley, Aleister, 235
Curie, Marie (and family), 73

Day, Dorothy and Maurin, Peter, 223
De Gaulle, Charles, 128, 205f
D'Estaing, Giscard, 77
De Klerk, F.W., 215
Dershowitz, Alan, 91f ,100f, 112, 228
Doenitz, Admiral Karl, 137
Don John of Austria, 221
Dostoievsky, Fyodor, 241
Dulles, John Foster, 189, 202f
Duvalier, 'Papa Doc', 29, 224
Dunant, Henri, 41f
Dzerzhinsky, Felix, 217

Index

Eaton, Cyrus (of Pugwash), 189
Edward III, 166
Eisenhower, General Dwight, 59, 78, 83, 147, 184, 189, 201-3
Einstein, Albert, 11, 188, 202
Elizabeth I, 148, 212, 243
Elizabeth II, 13
Ermenfried, 164

Fermi, Enrico, 74
Fieser, Louis, 68
Finnis, John et al., 31, 37f, 79f, 82f, 86
Fonda, actress Jane, 40
Foot, M.R.D., 32, 125f
Foot, Philippa, 32, 106, 231, 241f
Fox, George, 166
Franco, General Francisco, 68, 121, 123
Franklin, Benjamin, 67
Freud, Sigmund, 11f, 65, 234
Furtwangler, Wilhelm, 182

Gaddafi, Colonel Muammar, 111, 117
Gaitskill, Hugh, 191
Gandhi, M.K., 153, 157f, 168, 170
Gautama, 153f
Geach, Peter, 33
George III, 27
George, Saint, 42
Ghosananda, 159
Glover, Jonathan, 1f, 60, 107f, 136
Goebbels, Josef, 53, 64
Gollancz, Victor, 183
Gorbachev, Mikhail, 75, 84f
Goss, Arthur, 187
Greenglass, David, see Rosenberg
Gregory XIII, Pope, 243
Gromyko, President Andrei, 207
Grotius, Hugo, 26
Guevara, Ernesto ('Che'), 139f, 193
Guthrie, Frederick, 68

Haakon VII, King of Norway, 128, 131
Hahn, Otto, 73, 202, 230
Hammarskjold, Dag, 202
Harold, King, 164
Harriman, Averell, 207-8

Harris, Arthur, 17, 39, 53f, 58, 68, 182, 229
Hastings, Max, 103
Haukeland, Knut, 136
Heisenberg, Werner, 70
Heseltine, Michael, 196
Hess, Dame Myra, 182f
Heydrich, Reinhard, 127, 133, 228
Himmler, Heinrich, 132
Hitler, Adolf, 6, 27, 39, 45, 53, 55f, 64, 70, 85, 107, 121, 125, 131, 137, 183, 187, 192, 212f
Hobbes, Thomas, 28, 232
Ho Chi-Minh (ne Nguyen That Thanh), 121f, 176
Hogg, Quintin (Lord Hailsham), 207
Hollenbach, Fr. David, 38
Hoover, President Herbert, 142
Hume, David, 231, 239
Huxley, Aldous, 10-12

Innocent IV, Pope, 99

Jefferson, President Thomas, 141
Jenco, Fr. Lawrence, 119
Jinnah, Governor-General M., 158
John, Augustus (painter), 191
John XIII, Pope, 36f, 243
John Paul II, Pope, 143, 147f, 243
Johnson, President L.B., 176-8, 202, 244
Joliot-Curie, see Curie
Joyce, William, 212

Keenan, Brian, 115f
Kennan, George, 79f, 201
Kennedy, J. F., 37, 78, 97, 148, 181, 191, 200-8, 234, 238, 244
Kennedy, Robert, 97, 207
Kenny, journalist Andrew, 139, 214, 228
Kenny, Anthony, 31, 34-8
Khomeini, Ayatollah Ruhollah, 113-114
Khrushchev, Nikita, 37, 82, 84, 147, 189, 200f, 203-5, 207, 238
Kissinger, Henry, 83, 208
Knox, Ronald, 31
Kosygin, Andrei, 193

The Philosophy of War and Peace

Lang, Archbishop Cosmo, 56f
Laval, Pierre, 129
Lawrence, T.E., 125
Le May, General Curtis, 17, 204, 208, 234, 244f
Lenin, V.I., 8, 86, 217
Leo IV, Pope, 165
Leonardo da Vinci, 67
Levi, Primo, 107
Lommel and Steinkopf, 68
Lucius III, Pope, 99

Mackie, J.L., 230f, 246
Macmillan, Harold, 185f, 203, 205, 207

Malenkov, Georgiy, 84
Mandela, Nelson, 215
Mao Tse Tung, 188 , 234
Marti, Jose, 140
Marx, Karl, 8, 234
Maximilian, Saint, 163
Mary I, 212
McArthur, General Douglas, 184
McCarthy, John, 115f
McCarthy, Senator Joseph, 74, 188, 199, 216, 250
MacIntyre, Alasdair, 1, 241
McKinley, President William, 8, 86, 141
McNamara, Robert, 78f, 202f, 238, 244f
Mathews, journalist Herbert, 144
Meadlo, P., 65
Menuhin, Yehudi, 183, 243
Miles, General Nelson, 142
Mill, J.S., 227
Montgomery, Field Marshal Bernard, 55, 85
Monroe, Marilyn, 97
Morgan, J.P., 26
Moro, Aldo, 111
Morrison, Philip, 74
Mosaddeq, Mohammed, 113
Mussolini, Benito, 39, 68, 121, 125, 133f, 186

Napoleon I, 5, 7
Naopleon III, 42, 72
Neave, Airey, 116

Nehru, Prime Minister Jarwaharwal, 202
Netanyahu, Yonni, 112
Newton, Isaac, 237
Neurath, Otto, 230
Nietzsche, Friedrich, 15, 70, 227, 234, 241
Nixon, Richard, 64, 82, 147, 208 , 244

Odo, Bishop, 24
Oppenheimer, Robert, 73
Origen, 163
Orwell, George, 9f, 26, 92, 156, 212, 214, 244

Pacelli, *see* Pius XII.
Pahlevi, Shah of Persia, 113f
Paul IV, Pope, 99
Pauling, Linus, 202, 206, 238
Penney, William, 71
Percival, Spencer, 96
Petain, General Philippe, 129
Pinochet, Augusto, 97, 224
Pius XII, Pope, 167, 186 , 202, 243
Polk, President James, 141
Polkinghorne, Professor Sir John, 237
Pol Pot, 159 , 176f
Portal, Viscount Charles, 126
Powers, Gary, 203
Prior, A.N., 240f

Quisling, Vidkun, 131f, 216

Rabin, Itzak, 111
Read, Herbert (poet), 191
Reagan, President Ronald, 116
Redgrave, Vanessa (actress), 191
Richard III, 166
Romero, Archbishop Oscar, 224f
Roosevelt, President F.D., 57f, 70, 77, 142
Rosenberg, Julius and Ethel, 75
Rotblat, Julius, 73f
Rowntree, Joshua, 174
Rumsfield, Donald, 44, 102f
Runcie, Archbishop Robert, 117
Rusk, Dean, 219
Russell, Bertrand, 74, 171, 187f, 191f , 246

Saddam Hussein, 33, 107, 114
Sakharov, Andrei, 75, 86, 238
Sanchez, General Ricardo, 102
Savanorola, 99
Schweitzer, Albert, 202
Schoenman, Ralph, 189, 191f
Scholl, Fr. James, 38
Sheehan, Mrs Cindy, 226
Simons, Menno, 166
Simpson, Varnardo, 65, 234
Soames, Christopher, 87
Solzhenitsyn, Alexander, 48, 86, 217
Stalin, Josef, 58, 82, 84-6, 96, 188, 121, 213, 217, 234
Stassen, Howard, 201
Strauss, Richard, 70

Taylor, President Zachary, 141
Teller, Edward, 70, 202
Tertullian, 163
Thatcher, Margaret, 85, 114, 116
Tito, Marshal (*ne* Joseph Broz), 119
Tostado, Alfonso, 29
Truman, President Harry, 32, 39, 58f, 78, 80f, 184, 188, 215, 229, 234
T'Souvas, Robert, 65

Urban II, Pope, 165
Urban VI, Pope, 166
Urrutia, Judge, 145

Valdes, Peter, 165
Van Allen, James, 206
Vitorio, 24f, 36

Waite, Terry, 117f
Walensa, Lech, 216
Washington, President George, 140
Weir, Rev. Ben, 117
Weldon, T.D., 182
Wilberforce, William, 166
Wilhemina, Queen of the Netherlands, 128
William I, 164
Wilson, President Woodrow, 9, 207
Wittgenstein, Ludwig, 1, 15
Woolf, Lord justice, 69

Xerxes, 19, 26, 56